Life in the 1960s: The True Story

Steven Mandeli

Copyright © 2019 Steven Mandeli

All rights reserved.

ISBN: 9781072971214

Nothing But the Truth

Life in the 1960s: The True Story

DEDICATION

For My Parents
For making me who I am, may they rest in eternal peace

For My Brother and Sister
For sharing my experiences with me

For My "New Family"
My wife, my girls, my granddaughter
For being with me now

"We went downstairs to grandma and grandpa. We gave grandpa cigarettes and a card."
- Diary, Father's Day 1969

TABLE OF CONTENTS

FOREWORD vii
1 HISTORY, CULTURE AND COUNTER-CULTURE 1
2 REEL ENTERTAINMENT 27
3 CLASSIC TV BEFORE IT WAS CLASSIC 35
4 MUSIC AND STYLE 67
5 DEALING WITH ANCIENT TECHNOLOGY 87
6 ANCIENT MEDICINE 101
7 SAFETY 113
8 WHAT WE DID WITH OURSELVES 121
9 SURVIVING PAROCHIAL SCHOOL 141
10 LIFE IN THE NAKED CITY 149
11 OUR VIEW OF THE FUTURE 175
NOTES 183
ABOUT THE AUTHOR 188

FOREWORD

This book has two objectives. First, it is intended for people who lived through the 1960s in America. For those people it is hopefully an enjoyable reminiscence of that time period. I would want them to think throughout the book, "Hey, I remember that!" or "Yeah, that sounds familiar" or "What the hell is the author talking about?"—well, not really the last one. Second, it is for people who were born any time after the sixties and find the time to actually *read*, within their busy schedules of posting the latest pictures of their kids or animals on Facebook, making progress on their favorite MMO/MMORPG or some other cyberspace activity—yes, I know, that is somewhat limiting. For those people, even though they know something about the sixties from occasional *Gilligan's Island* reruns or YouTube gems of that time, I hope to give a more comprehensive knowledge of that important decade (while having fun with it).

But what's *is* so important about the 1960s? Is it more important than any other decade? I think it is, but I may be prejudiced. The sixties covered my childhood—when they started, I was only two-and-a-half and when 1970 rolled along I was just short of being a teenager. Sure, I liked other decades (loved the big-hair eighties) but this is the decade I grew up in, so I witnessed it with the eyes of innocence. And on the surface, it *was* a more innocent time, though digging deeper I realize that was an illusion.

The sixties were unique, a decade of intense change. There was a *huge* difference between 1960 and 1969—differences in attitudes, acceptance, fashion, music and the arts, almost every category of life. It is a decade rich in important historical events and important makers of history. It is the decade of America's most unpopular war; the decade where we lost the President, his brother, and arguably the most famous civil rights leader in history, all to assassins' bullets; it is the decade when people landed on the moon; and it is the decade where two major powers very nearly engaged in nuclear war. How are those for special?

This book is a book by a man separated now from the sixties a half-century, with reminiscences based on that of a boy, and for some time in the late 60s his diary as well. Should be interesting, right? I hope you enjoy the journey as much as I have.

Steve Mandeli
September 2019

1 HISTORY, CULTURE AND COUNTER-CULTURE

Like everything else, there was good and bad in the 60s. Where people are involved, it can be no other way. Some things were better, I think, and others were worse—much worse.

AMONG THE GOOD STUFF…

In my humble opinion, people were more honest and I know for my case my parents instilled a strong sense of morality into us. For example, if we were to hit a baseball into a window, we were expected (and did) notify the owner of what we did and promise to make compensation. We would also tell our parents. I imagine not everybody did this then and not everybody tries "to get away with it" now, but overall this was generally true. Part of the reason, believe it or not, was television. We were actually "taught" by the TV shows at that time to be honest, law-abiding citizens. Modern TV doesn't bother as much about teaching morality, and indeed often shows us the opposite (e.g., *Breaking Bad*). In the 60s, even the silliest sitcoms like *The Munsters* boiled down to morality plays. Compare *Father Knows Best* (1954-1960) to *Married with Children* (1987-1997) and most modern sitcoms and you will see this difference to an extreme. I can't believe what I see on TV at times that kids would watch it—one single episode of a show from 8 PM to 9 PM on a major network, that was *directed to kids* and adults alike in its target audience, showed sexual sadomasochism, a severed human head, a cut-up body and a bloody shoot-out. You never saw that on sixties TV.

Sixties TV can be characterized as less sophisticated and less intelligent than modern TV. But you could put a kid in front of a TV in the sixties and not worry about what they would see. In other words, parental discretion was neither advised nor required.

People talked to each other a lot, on the fly. And it obviously wasn't through texting. Personal communication was much more common than today. We had a lot of friends, and we looked out for each other. Yeah, there were jerks—there always was and will always be—but the majority of people, even in the big cities, cared more for each other, or so it seemed.

We were safer from criminal acts. Crime existed, of course, and the legendary crime bosses did have people killed, sometimes right in the open. But kids were safe to spend elongated periods of time away from their parents. Home was safe, and so was school. The gangs back then were a joke compared to now. Back then a gang member might have a switchblade on them, instead of guns (see *Rebel Without a Cause* or *West Side Story*). There were no reports of shootings in school or practically anywhere else. Innocents weren't killed by stray bullets during gang fights. Kids and young adults didn't get their hands on assault rifles. There were fights, but they invariably ended with just bloody noses. Kidnappings were almost unknown, and we didn't hear about horrible sexual abuse, torture and killings of children who were taken. As for sex abuse itself, this has always existed, but I never heard of anything creepier than a man in my neighborhood ("Ed") who had young girls sit on his lap and kiss him on the cheek for candy—which is creepy enough for me.

Of course, terrorism in this country was non-existent. In fact, though terrorist acts occurred before 9/11, including against the twin towers (the 1991 attack), one can consider the Age of Terrorism in America to not begin until the 21st century. It is then that terror truly struck the hearts of Americans and affected our lives greatly. It is hard to accept that not that very long ago we could quite easily board a plane to anywhere, and not see marines with AK-47's in places like Penn Station, NY. Perhaps we were naive, but we thought no-one would dare attack our mainland as it was on 9/11. We did have the Cold War to worry about, but the only way that affected my life was having to undergo occasional air raid drills in school which us kids didn't take very seriously anyway.

As the sixties grew, so did pornography. Pornography has always existed. But in the 60s it was limited to X-rated movie theatres, peep shows and strip clubs you could keep your kids away from. Now it is in the *home*—courtesy of the internet, DVDs, and even TVs and smartphones. Kids have easy access to it. They couldn't get into places of ill repute in the sixties, at least not easily. Of course, where there is a Will there is a way, and when it comes to sex there is a lot of Will—so kids could sneak into blue theatres and also get their hands on pornography (generally tame pornography by today's standards), but all of that was harder to get to than turning on a computer or looking at a phone.

Expletives were spoken, but it sure wasn't on TV or in music. Even very little was heard in movies, before the MPAA ratings system. The first time I heard "goddamn" in the movies was in 1968, during the climax of the original *Planet of the Apes* movie. That movie also showed men's behinds from far away—which to me was quite literally shocking! Unfortunately, *where* verbal obscenity existed was in the streets and even at home. People cussed fine then, though you wouldn't know it from watching a 60s TV show (but people didn't go to the bathroom in those either), and the cussing included racial epithets. But now there is cussing on TV and very much in movies, and racial epithets are in many songs, though now it is claimed they are "OK" for some to say and don't mean the same thing.

We didn't need as much money because there was less *stuff* to get. Seriously. Back then you got a TV—one TV. Now you need more than one. And you need Cable. You need a DVD/Blu-Ray player. And it's nice to have a 7.1 sound system or at least a "sound bar" to go with that TV. Kids "require" a game system. And what about the money we spend on PCs and other items that didn't exist back then? With PCs, of course, you need internet. And, a sound system for PCs is nice. Some of these items I just mentioned are recurring costs—Cable, internet, and let's not forget cell phone fees. As you know these are a lot of money. For this reason, we need two sources of income in the family. This is not a problem for most, as many married couples want to both work and follow careers instead of following kids around. And they like their *stuff* (see George Carlin's routine on *stuff* on YouTube). But I'm old-fashioned and tend to think kids are better having a mom (or dad) around instead of at work. It's unfair to say one parent can't follow a career but even if one does want to stay home with the kids it is often not an option because we simply need to have more money to spend on *things*.

Speaking of families, they were stronger. Marriages lasted, and the number of kids born out of wedlock (a term that seems oddly unfamiliar in this age) was much less than today. Divorce was not common, except for the rich and famous. Of course, not all of this is "good." Women, for example, felt trapped in horrible marriages by their religious vows, even in marriages filled with violence.

The history of "bad" stuff in the 60s could fill volumes. But let's take a "light" look at that to get a better feel for the decade and how it affected us...

SEGREGATION, RACISM, PROTESTS

Segregation is a term usually attributed to the South. But I grew up in the North, specifically in the New York City county of Queens (the same county, and just several miles from where President Trump was born), and I can "assure" you that segregation was alive and well where I was, and to a greater granularity than you might think. We didn't have "coloreds only" bathrooms and drinking fountains and we didn't force African-Americans to sit in the back of buses, but we were good at segregating minorities from the rest of us.

Queens, NY, I am proud to say, is now "the most ethnically diverse urban area in the entire world, representing over 100 nations and speaking 138 different languages" (longisland.com). In fact, it is recorded in the Guinness Book of World records as the most diverse place on Earth. The population is nearly equally distributed at ¼ each for Whites (non-Hispanic), Hispanic of any race, African-American and Asian.

This was not the Queens, NY I grew up in, in the 60s. The census.gov figures show that in 1960 Queens was 91.5% white, 8.1% Black, 0.4% Asian, and 0.1% "Other." Hispanic ethnicity was not recorded. In 1970 Queens was 85.3% white, 13.0% Black, 1.1% Asian, and 0.5% "Other." Again, Hispanic ethnicity was not recorded, though that would change in the next census, and for 1980 it is reported that 23.5% of the population was Hispanic, of all races, close to the current figure.

This shift could hardly be greater! President Trump and I grew up in a lily-white county, where "diversity" was pretty much nil. In fact, the only blacks in my neighborhood lived in the nearby City Projects. In my Catholic grammar school, I never had a Black or Asian in my class; the closest to a Hispanic was a boy from Cuba.

As one would imagine, such lack of diversity breeds distrust and misunderstanding. I knew nothing about non-whites and learned practically nothing about them. In fact, only in the late 60s did we get a "special voluntary assignment" in school to write about a black hero, an assignment few accepted and the few that did (including me) got ostracized for it.

Fortunately for me, who as a child thought my hand would turn black if I shook a black hand (an old stupid urban myth), I went to a diverse High School where there were Blacks, Hispanics and Asians.

But I mentioned greater granularity. There was racism among white nationalities. They generally got along, but there were issues. My neighborhood was mostly Italian and Irish. If you were German, as I was, that wasn't quite accepted, and I would get ostracized from time to time. The usual idiocy would be kids saluting me when they found I was German and saying, "Heil Hitler." Since I had an Italian-sounding last name, I actually lied many times that I was Italian.

According to my father back then, city parks were segregated, and I don't mean just racially—there were German sections, Italian sections, etc. This sounds hard for me to believe now, but why would he make such a claim?

There were of course those nasty epithets for racial groups and nationalities that were used often in the 60s, but I don't want to repeat them here because I don't want to revitalize them. A lot of people have forgotten most of them, and that's fine with me.

Obviously, racism kept people from opportunities in the 60s—opportunities for housing, jobs, and education. Some overcame big obstacles by perseverance and working very, very hard. It hurts when I see people ignore opportunities that are now provided to them, as in the past people fought for them so strongly.

"Jim Crow" laws enacted after the Civil War in the former Confederate States of America continued into the 1960s, in fact until the Civil Rights Act of 1964 and Voting Rights Act of 1965 were enacted. Before these two important but grossly delayed Acts, racial segregation was enforced by state and local laws in those former Confederate states. Though the Fourteenth Amendment to the

US Constitution, adopted in 1868, provided "equal protection of the laws," to all citizens, now including African-Americans, it allowed the segregation between whites and non-whites for services, facilities (including rest rooms and drinking fountains), public accommodations, restaurants, housing, medical care, education, employment, and transportation. The "equality" of all these for whites and blacks was a farce; facilities for African-Americans were consistently inferior and underfunded compared to those available to European Americans; sometimes they did not exist at all. Though the non-Confederate states did not enact Jim Crow laws, their spirit was nevertheless alive and discrimination was practiced privately.

A major non-violent protest against segregation, inspired by Dr. Martin Luther King, happened in Greensboro, NC on February 1, 1960. Four black students sat at a "whites only" lunch counter in a Woolworth's Department Store and were refused service when ordering cups of coffee. They did not leave until the store closed. On the next day more than 20 black students joined the "sit-in." On the third day there were 60. The fourth day saw more than 300. The protest spread to other stores and other Southern cities. Eventually, over 70,000 people took part. By July 25 that Woolworth's began to serve all at the "white" counter, and by 1965 all Woolworths were desegregated.

Dr. Martin Luther King, leader of a Civil Rights Movement characterized by nonviolent civil disobedience, led the famous March on Washington for Jobs and Freedom on August 28, 1963. It is the time and place of his "I have a Dream" speech. Estimates of the number of participants vary from 200,000 to 300,000, 20 to 25 percent non-black. After the march its speakers traveled to the White House for a brief discussion of proposed civil rights legislation with President Kennedy. The march was considered a "triumph of managed protest."

Sadly, just a few weeks after the March, an act of white supremacist terrorism occurred at the African-American 16th Street Baptist Church in Birmingham, Alabama, on Sunday, September 15, 1963, when four members of the Ku Klux Klan planted at least 15 sticks of dynamite attached to a timing device beneath the front steps of the church. The explosion killed four young girls (aged 11-14) and injured 22 others. No-one was prosecuted at the time. Finally, 14 years later, in 1977 Robert Chambliss was tried and convicted of the first-degree murder of one of the victims, 11-year-old Carol Denise McNair. Thomas Blanton and Bobby Cherry were each convicted of four counts of murder and sentenced to life imprisonment in 2001 and 2002 respectively. The fourth man died in 1994 and was never charged.

The Civil Rights Act of 1964, the passage of which is said to have been helped both by the March on Washington and the tragedy at the Baptist Church, finally outlawed discrimination based on race, color, religion, sex or national origin, for the entire US. It enforced "the constitutional right to vote," "the constitutional rights in public facilities and public education," and promised "to prevent discrimination in federally assisted programs." It specified,

"All persons shall be entitled to the full and equal enjoyment of the goods, services, facilities, and privileges, advantages, and accommodations of any place of public accommodation…without discrimination or segregation on the ground of race, color, religion, or national origin." It also specified equal opportunity for employment. The Voting Rights Act of 1965 prohibited states from imposing any "voting qualification or prerequisite to voting, or standard, practice, or procedure … to deny or abridge the right of any citizen of the United States to vote on account of race or color."

The above Acts did not immediately solve all racist and segregationist activities of course. But they were a beginning, and grew stronger as the years went on.

The Civil Rights Act of 1968, approved only one week after the assassination of Martin Luther King in April, provided for equal housing opportunities regardless of race, religion, or national origin and made it a federal crime to "by force or by threat of force, injure, intimidate, or interfere with anyone … by reason of their race, color, religion, or national origin." Title VII of this act is known as the Fair Housing Act.

Thus, the 60s saw considerable advancement in Civil Rights for all, at least on paper. Dr. King kept the violence from getting out of hand, but could not help any longer after his demise. Fortunately, as time passed clear heads prevailed, and in general we now have a peaceful relationship between races that the 60s never saw. We hear of constant incidents in the News that indicate there is still much distrust between groups, especially police and African-Americans. I find those stories very disturbing, considering how far we have come, and at such a high cost. Racism still exists, by and against people of all colors and beliefs. But we are much, much closer to Martin Luther King's dream than we ever were in the 60s.

SEXUAL INEQUALITY

Sexual inequality was rampant in the 60s, but the 60s were a decade of change that saw many women fight for their rights. The National Organization of Women (NOW) was founded in 1966 by Betty Friedan. Its charter included the following: "…the time has come for a new movement toward true equality for all women in America, and toward a fully equal partnership of the sexes…The purpose of NOW is to take action to bring women into full participation in the mainstream of American society now, exercising all the privileges and responsibilities thereof in truly equal partnership with men."

The 1966 petition summarized how bad the situation was then: "Although 46.4% of all American women between the ages of 18 and 65 now work outside the home, the overwhelming majority—75%—are in routine clerical, sales, or factory jobs, or they are household workers, cleaning women, hospital attendants. About two-thirds of Negro women workers are in the lowest paid service occupations. Working women are becoming increasingly—not less—concentrated on the bottom of the job ladder. As a consequence, full-time women workers today earn on the average only 60% of what men earn, and that wage gap has been increasing over the past twenty-five years in every major industry group." In addition, "women earn only one in three of the B.A.'s and M.A's granted, and one in ten of the Ph.D.'s…Women comprise less than 1% of federal judges; less than 4% of all lawyers; 7% of doctors."

Some women in the 60s, like my mom, accepted the role of housewife and the job of child-rearing. But the point is, the alternatives were limited for those who did not accept that lifestyle.

My mom was very busy as a housewife and caretaker of us kids, and should have been paid well for it, in my opinion. It is true that the job of housewife and mother is pretty much a thankless one, a mixture of hard work and tedium, from dawn to dusk. My mother made the best of it, and took pride in the appearance of her house and children. She preferred it over the occasional paying jobs that she had to work from time to time, such as a housecleaner for a private house and a lunch server at a high school. But at times we needed the extra money, to my mom and dad's chagrin. My dad was ashamed that his wife had to work at times, and this was always considered a secret that we kids were allowed to share with no-ne—not even our teachers and other school officials.

Girls were taught the same things in school as us, but it was made clear that their duty in life was to be a wife and mother. One class that separated the boys from the girls was shop for boys and sewing for girls. Nowadays it would be perfectly acceptable to offer both (though sewing is no longer generally considered a required skill, nor shop as well, albeit still useful), if both were open to both sexes, but in the 60s no-one would consider crossing over into the opposite "gender-specific" class.

Homosexuality simply had no place in the 60s, not in the U.S., and certainly not in Catholic school. It was never mentioned by teachers, as if it didn't exist. Certainly no-one would admit to being one, for fear of intense ostracizing. In fact, when brought up in the street it was always with a negative connotation. I remember someone teasing me about what homosexuality was, I would guess around 1970 (didn't hear that word in the 60s, as far as I can remember), and saying it was something other than what it was.

Homosexuality wasn't shown on TV at all, in any direct manner or form. But sexuality in general was heavily censored (for example, no open-mouthed kisses). There wasn't much of a place for that either.

In the 60s homosexual acts were actually forbidden by law in most states. State and federal employers were often protected from hiring homosexuals by laws in the state and federal level. Homosexuals were not allowed to join the military. Private employers as well could get away with turning applicants away simply by reason of their sexuality.

For someone who experienced a time when homosexuality was forbidden, it appears to me there are a surprising number of gays and lesbians now. But in the 60s the percentages must have been the same—it was just all "in the closet," as it was a social pariah, possibly illegal, and an excuse for discrimination for opportunities described above. Now there are many openly gay and lesbian couples, including in my wife's and my family—something you never heard of then. The philosophy was simple in the 60s—if you put your head in the sand, any "problem" would go away.

THE CUBAN MISSILE CRISIS, OR: "WHERE WERE YOU IN '62?"

The question above was posed in the advertising of the nostalgic early George Lucas film, *American Graffiti* (1973). His characters were having interesting "coming of age" adventures in 62, in Modesto, California; I was having interesting "coming of childhood" adventures in Queens, NY, including starting Kindergarten and unfortunately spending some time in the hospital. In Washington, DC, President John F. Kennedy was making the most important decisions of his life to avert the United States from engaging in nuclear war with the Soviet Union.

The official story from the State Department (history.state.gov) admits that the Cuban Missile Crises of October 1962 was "the moment when the two superpowers came closest to nuclear conflict."

It also, a bit incredibly, acknowledges "calculations and miscalculations as well as direct and secret communications and miscommunications between the two sides."

When Fidel Castro took over Cuba in 1959 we found ourselves in the uncomfortable position of having a Communist regime right in our backyard—less than 100 miles away, in fact. During the last full year of the Eisenhower administration in 1960, the US planned for a clandestine invasion of Cuba, which would have the CIA aid rebels to overthrow Castro. When Kennedy became president, he inherited these plans and decided to go with them just three months into his term, in April 61. The results, at the Bay of Pigs, were a dismal failure, and the US was exposed in its attempt. To deter any future attempt, Soviet premier Nikita Khrushchev made a secret agreement with Castro to place Soviet nuclear missiles in Cuba. Construction of missile sites began in late summer, along with a general Soviet arms buildup. The US discovered this in routine surveillance flights.

Kennedy was given a full set of options by his staff, from stern warnings to bombing the sites and taking over Cuba while we were there. He decided on something in-between—a naval "quarantine" (not a "blockade," which implied a state of war existed). He informed Khrushchev that the US would not allow offensive weapons to be delivered to Cuba and that the USSR had to dismantle the bases and return the offensive weapons it had already provided Cuba.

Two days later Khrushchev defiantly responded to Kennedy that his "quarantine" was indeed a "blockade" and thus an act of aggression and that Soviet ships bound for Cuba would be ordered to proceed. Fortunately, his ships either turned back from the quarantine line or were stopped by US ships that searched them and found no weapons and let them continue to Cuba. But the Soviets did not dismantle the missile sites; in fact, they were nearing operational readiness. At this point Kennedy was ready to attack Cuba, but left diplomacy as an option.

Surprisingly, even at this point diplomacy became a viable option again. A Soviet agent approached an ABC reporter with the offer that the Soviets would dismantle the missile sites if the US promised not to invade Cuba. The reporter passed the offer down to the White House, which wasn't quite sure of its validity. Then Khrushchev sent Kennedy a long, emotional letter making the same offer, to avoid "doom[ing] the world to the catastrophe of nuclear war." The next day Khrushchev sent another message, this time insisting that the proposed resolution would have to include the US dismantling its missile sites (constructed in 1961) in Turkey—something Kennedy didn't even know existed *until the first day of the Crisis*, the construction of which some think *was the real Soviet motive of putting missiles in Cuba.*

Kennedy decided to ignore the second message and responded to the first, guaranteeing that the US would not attack Cuba if the Cuban missiles were removed. Meanwhile, JFK's brother, RFK, acting as attorney general of the US, met secretly with the Soviet ambassador, promising that the US missiles in Turkey would be removed within five months of the Cuban missile removal but that this agreement could not be part of any public resolution of the crisis; in fact, the deal would be abrogated if disclosed. Only a handful of administration officials knew of this "trade," and did not include Vice-President Johnson. Indeed, this deal was kept secret until the late 80s.

All agreements in place now, on October 28 Khrushchev issued a public statement that Soviet missiles would be dismantled and removed from Cuba. The naval quarantine continued until the Soviets agreed to remove their bombers from Cuba and, on November 20 the US ended its quarantine. The already-outmoded US missiles were removed from Turkey in April 1963. But H-bombs have been supplied to Turkey since, and continue to exist at a base there.

A BRIEF HISTORY OF A LONG WAR

The Vietnam "War" was never officially declared a War by the U.S. (we stopped doing that after WWII) but this "conflict," as it was called, had pretty disturbing stats for American servicemen:

- 58,148 were killed (average age 23).
- 75,000 were severely disabled.
- 23,214 were 100% disabled.
- 5,283 lost limbs.
- 1,081 sustained multiple amputations.

- Of those killed, 61% were younger than 21.
- 11,465 of those killed were younger than 20 years old.
- As of January 15, 2004, there are 1,875 still unaccounted for.

One-third of the men who served in Vietnam were conscripted, "drafted," forced into service. These "men" were 18 years of age and above. Some were married. It is important to note that at this time everyone had to be 21 to earn the right to vote.

It is also important to note that as many as 2 million *civilians* in North and South Vietnam died in the war and some 1.1 million North Vietnamese and Viet Cong fighters died.

America got involved in this already raging conflict to keep South Vietnam from being overcome by the Viet Cong from North Vietnam, who were communist. Thus, we were fighting the spread of communism. During this time of the Cold War the most powerful communist nations of China and the U.S.S.R. fought for control of third-world countries that the free nations of the world wanted on their side. Countries like Vietnam acted like a proxy for the hostile opposing superpowers to expand power and influence without direct hostilities against each other, made impossible by nuclear weapons and the threat of mutual annihilation. It was hoped by each side that a domino effect, started by Vietnam, would spread to other countries in Southeast Asia, which would considerably strengthen that side. It was feared by the U.S. and our allies that the fates of all Southeast Asian countries were closely linked and that a communist success in one must necessarily lead to the fatal weakening of the others. In 1961 newly-elected President John F. Kennedy and some of his close advisers subscribed to this domino theory, and in fact saw Vietnam as an "opportunity" to test the U.S.'s ability to fight communist subversion in third world countries. A successful effort in Vietnam—in Kennedy's words, "the cornerstone of the free world in Southeast Asia"—would provide to both allies and adversaries evidence of U.S. determination to meet the challenge of communist expansion in the Third World. As time passed, Kennedy wanted a victory for the U.S. in Vietnam even more, as embarrassments like the construction of the Berlin Wall and the failed Bay of Pigs invasion in Cuba threatened to tarnish his presidency.

Still, Kennedy was not that quick to send American troops into battle in Vietnam, even though reports indicated that the communists were winning. Kennedy wanted to provide "vigorous aid and guidance." This did include non-combat U.S. military personnel in Vietnam, which rose from less than 800 throughout the 1950s to about 9,000 by the middle of 1962. But the effort was characterized as "a legacy of indecision, half-measures, and gradually increasing involvement," which was passed on to President Johnson after Kennedy died from an assassin's bullet in November 1963, at which point Vietnam had 16,000 U.S. troops.

Johnson wasn't as interested as Kennedy in the Cold War; he was focused on getting bills passed for his "Great Society" of social programs. But he also saw the importance in not letting South Vietnam fall to the communists. Thus, a year after Kennedy's death the number of non-combat troops was increased to 23,000.

Attacks on U.S. ships in the Gulf of Tonkin in August 1964 caused Johnson to order retaliatory air strikes against North Vietnamese naval bases, and he requested congressional support for a broad resolution authorizing him to take whatever action he deemed necessary. He got it. By July 1965, Johnson now in his second term, took the final steps that would commit the United States to full-scale war in Vietnam: he authorized the dispatch of 100,000 troops immediately and an additional 100,000 in 1966. By the end of 1966, the United States had dropped more bombs on North Vietnam than it had dropped on Japan during World War II and more than it had dropped during the entire Korean War. Yet the bombing seemed to have little impact on the communists' ability to carry on the war.

On the Vietnamese New Year (known as "Tet") on January 31, 1968, while approximately 50,000 U.S. and South Vietnamese troops were occupied in defending or supporting Demilitarized Zone (DMZ) bases, the communists launched an offensive throughout South Vietnam. They attacked 36 of 44 provincial capitals, 64 district capitals, five of the six major cities, and more than two dozen airfields and bases. Aside from casualties, this "Tet Offensive" was a disaster for the War as seen by the American public. Those who had still believed we were doing well lost confidence, in the War and President Johnson. When it was reported in March that General Westmoreland had requested 206,000 additional troops for Vietnam, people at home saw the situation as dire.

Johnson re-evaluated the War and was persuaded by his new Secretary of Defense, Clark Clifford, that the current number of U.S. troops in Vietnam (about 550,000) should constitute an upper limit and that Johnson should make a dramatic gesture for peace. In a nationally televised speech on March 31, Johnson announced that he was "taking the first step to de-escalate the conflict" by halting the bombing of North Vietnam (except in the areas near the DMZ) and that the U.S. was prepared to send representatives to any forum to seek a negotiated end to the war. He followed this surprising declaration with news that he did not intend to seek reelection that year.

The communists announced they were prepared to talk (to the U.S., not the South Vietnamese), but initial discussions went nowhere. I remember from that time that it took weeks to decide on the *shape of the conference table*. After Johnson's speech, the fighting became the fiercest in the war. In the eight weeks following that speech, 3,700 Americans were killed in Vietnam and 18,000 wounded. Johnson announced the cessation of bombing on October 31, 1968. The bombing halt achieved no breakthrough but rather brought on a period of prolonged bickering between the United States and its South Vietnamese ally about the terms and procedures to govern the talks. By the time

South Vietnam joined the talks, Richard M. Nixon had been elected president.

Nixon and his adviser on foreign affairs, Henry Kissinger (1923-   ), recognized that the U.S. could not win a military victory in Vietnam but insisted that the war could be ended "honorably," with an outcome that would afford South Vietnam a reasonable chance of survival. He planned to achieve this through bringing pressure to bear from the Soviets and China, both of whom were eager to improve their relations with the United States, and through the threat of massive force against North Vietnam. He provided better weapons and training to the South Vietnamese so they could fight the ground war without us, a policy known as "Vietnamization." In June 1969 Nixon announced the withdrawal of 25,000 U.S. troops from Vietnam. In September he announced further troop withdrawals, and by March 1970 he was announcing the phased withdrawal of 150,000 troops over the next year.

On January 27, 1973, the Agreement on Ending the War and Restoring Peace in Vietnam was signed by representatives of the South Vietnamese communist forces, North Vietnam, South Vietnam, and the United States. A cease-fire would go into effect the following morning throughout North and South Vietnam, and within 60 days all U.S. forces would be withdrawn, all U.S. bases dismantled, and all Prisoners of War (POWs) released. On March 29, 1973, the last U.S. military unit left Vietnam. The peace between North and South Vietnam was an uneasy one, and fighting soon continued. The Viet Cong won. On April 30, 1976 what remained of the South Vietnamese government surrendered unconditionally. The remaining Americans escaped in a series of frantic air- and sealifts with Vietnamese friends and coworkers, a sight splashed on the news over and over and heartbreaking (I saw people holding on to overburdened helicopters and falling to the ground). A military government was instituted, and on July 2, 1976, the country was officially united as the Socialist Republic of Vietnam.

Vietnam was left impoverished, but in 1986 the government initiated a series of economic and political reforms which began Vietnam's path towards integration into the world economy. By 2000, it had established diplomatic relations with all nations. Since 2000, Vietnam's economic growth rate has been among the highest in the world, and, in 2011, it had the highest Global Growth Generators Index among 11 major economies. It joined the World Trade Organization in 2007.

Vietnam has become a major tourist destination since the 1990s, assisted by significant state and private investment, particularly in coastal regions. About 3.77 million international tourists visited Vietnam in 2009 alone. Happyland, a 2.2-billion-dollar project inspired by Disneyland and supported by Michael Jackson's father Joe, is well under construction in Southern Vietnam, though it is experiencing delays. It includes a theme park that costs $600 million, a 3.7 km boardwalk, a shopping center, 3-5 star hotels, water parks, studios, indoor and outdoor theaters, restaurants, a floating market, and other facilities. I cannot help but think of such a project as a disgrace to the memory of the men who died there.

THE DRAFT

The Vietnam War was not a popular war in the United States, especially for those that were of conscription age. The U.S. had already had a "draft" system in place since 1940, and all young men between the ages of 18 and 26 had to "register" for Selective Service. This system was in place since 1940 not only to conscript men in WWII and the Korean Conflict, but also ensure coverage during peacetime in the Cold War.

Part of the reason of the draft was to "scare" young men into volunteering for Military Service, for if they volunteered they were given preferential placement or less dangerous postings. One general estimated that for every man drafted, three or four more were scared into volunteering. It can be argued that up to 60 percent of those who served throughout the Vietnam War did so directly or indirectly because of the draft. Since approximately 1/3 of all U.S. soldiers in Vietnam were conscripted, then simple math indicates that about 30% of volunteers were influenced by the draft, many probably "scared," as was hoped by the military. This is in line with defense recruiting reports showing that 34% of the volunteers in 1964 and up to 50% in 1970 indicated they joined to avoid placement uncertainty via the draft. The draft itself encompassed almost one-third of all eligible men during the period of 1965–69.

"Deferments" provided an incentive for men to follow pursuits considered useful to the State, while keeping them from being drafted. This helped push men into educational, occupational, and family choices (as in getting married and having children) they might not otherwise have pursued. The marriage deferment, with or without children, was ended by Johnson on August 26, 1965, just a month after he committed the United States to full-scale war in Vietnam. College deferments thus became very popular during Vietnam as most men of conscription age wanted to go to college anyway, as my brother, who kept out of the draft just by attending college as he had planned (though a computer glitch temporarily stripped him of his deferment). Unfortunately, some young men also joined college simply as a means to avoid the draft and thus there was a glut of college students who didn't meet up to academic standards. Back then, colleges were a lot cheaper than now, and in fact any college in the City University of New York system was *free*. When you finished college and lost your deferment, you then had the option to join the military as commissioned officers. So, going to college was a win-win. In 1968, educational deferments were dropped for first year graduate students. Those further along in their graduate study could continue to receive a deferment. So, my brother, who would graduate in 1973, knew he was open for the draft then. According to my diary, my brother had registered at the draft board on November 7, 1969, eight days before his 18th birthday.

However, things got worse for my brother and many others as deferments were overridden by a lottery system based on your year of birth and what number you got in the lottery—the one lottery you didn't want to win! On December 1, 1969, this lottery was held to establish a draft priority for all those born between 1944 and 1950. It was quite simple—birthdays were randomly assigned numbers and the higher number you had the better chance you had of not being drafted. In fact, if it was high enough, you didn't have to worry about being drafted at all. If you had a low number, your chances were obviously high. As many as 100,000 draft eligible young men ("draft dodgers") fled the U.S., mostly to Canada. On Sept. 16, 1974, President Gerald R. Ford granted them amnesty and they could return home.

President Nixon campaigned in 1968 that he would end the draft. He didn't—at least not right away. Another lottery was held in 1971, to include men born in 1951—the year my brother was born. I sat with him nervously as the numbers came up on TV. In fact, we were watching Eyewitness News on ABC, and what they did was inexcusable—they showed films of rigorous military training in the background as the numbers came up. It was awful. Then, almost at the end, my brother's birthday came up—he was #362. He asked me if I was sure that I saw the same number on the TV. I was, and from the point my brother did not have to be worried about being drafted ever again.

Another lottery was held in 1972, for men born in 1952. They were the last to be possibly conscripted. On February 2, 1972, a drawing was held to determine draft priority numbers for men born in 1953, but in early 1973 it was announced by Secretary of Defense Melvin Laird that no further draft orders would be issued. In March 1973, 1974, and 1975, the Selective Service assigned draft priority numbers for all men born in 1954, 1955, and 1956, respectively, in case the draft was extended, but it never was.

In 1980 President Jimmy Carter re-instated the requirement that young men register with the Selective Service System, including anyone (citizen or non-citizen) born on or after January 1, 1960. It is interesting to note that I was born in 1957, one of the few years (1957-1959) that men could be born in and did not have to register. I never had to register and don't have a draft card.

It is also interesting to note that non-citizens could have been drafted. In fact, my father, quite new to the United States and well before he became a citizen, was called in for a physical for the Korean Conflict in 1952. Fortunately, as previously noted, the Selective Service took into account then that he was a married man, and with a baby son—my brother. He was not called into service.

THE PROTESTS

Protests against the War began mostly on college campuses, as members of the leftist organization Students for a Democratic Society (SDS) began organizing "teach-ins" to express their opposition to the way in which it was being conducted. The first "teach-in" against the war was held in the University of

Michigan in March 1965 and was attended by about 3,500 people. It consisted of debates, lectures, movies, and musical events aimed at protesting the war. Aided by good media coverage, this first "teach-in" went on to inspire 35 more on college campuses within the next week. By the end of 1965, there had been teach-ins at 120 campuses. Hundreds more followed, until the end of the war. The largest Vietnam teach-in was held on May 21–22, 1965 at U.C. Berkeley. The event was organized by the newly-formed Vietnam Day Committee (VDC), an organizing group founded by ex-grad student Jerry Rubin (1938-1994) and others. Over the course of 36 hours, an estimated 30,000 people attended the event.

On November 27, 1965 there was a major anti-war demonstration in Washington, D.C. It was very successful, attracting 25,000 anti-war protesters and receiving substantial press coverage. This resulted in greatly increased national prominence for SDS, becoming the leading student group against the war on most U.S. campuses. Nationally, the SDS used the draft as an important issue for students, and over the rest of the 65-66 academic year began to attack university complicity in it, as the universities had begun to supply students' class rankings, used to determine who was to be drafted. The University of Chicago's administration building was taken over in a three-day sit-in in May 1966. Rank protests and sit-ins spread to many other universities.

On October 21, 1967, one of the most prominent anti-war demonstrations took place, as some 100,000 protesters gathered at the Lincoln Memorial; around 30,000 of them continued in a march on the Pentagon later that night. After a brutal confrontation with the soldiers and U.S. Marshals protecting the building, hundreds of demonstrators were arrested.

One of the ugliest protests was near the 1968 Democratic National Convention in Chicago, which was held from August 26 to August 29. The Youth International Party was one of the major groups in the organization of the protests there. It was run by Jerry Rubin and Abbie Hoffman (1936-1989, suicide), its members known as "Yippies," a play on words with "Hippie." The Yippies were a highly theatrical, anti-authoritarian and anarchist group. They decided to take a radical approach to the Democratic National Convention. Before the Convention, they wrote articles, published fliers, made speeches and held rallies and demonstrations, to announce that they were coming to Chicago. Threats were made that nails would be thrown from overpasses to block roads; cars would be used to block intersections, main streets, police stations and National Guard armories; LSD would be dumped in the city's water supply and the Convention would be stormed. None of these things fortunately came into fruition, but Chicago of course prepared for trouble. Besides the standard gun and billy club, Chicago Police Department officers were issued mace and riot helmets. Large numbers of police were put on standby. Police officials and Chicago Mayor Richard J. Daley (1902-1976) had worked with the National Guard to put them in place at their armories so the Chicago Police Department could request and receive assistance from them quickly.

About 10,000 demonstrators showed up. Violence broke out over a misunderstanding in nearby Lincoln Park, where the protestors had amassed for a concert, and scuffles occurred between protestors and police. No-one was killed, but roughly 500 people were treated in the streets suffering from minor injuries and the effects of tear gas. Inside the convention hall itself, tensions were so high and security so tough that reporter Dan Rather (1931-   ) of CBS News was roughed up.

On October 15, 1969, there was the "Moratorium to End the War in Vietnam." It was a massive demonstration and teach-in that occurred throughout the US. I recorded the event three days after it happened in my diary, with the following admittedly naive statement that was based on the hype I remember at the time about it:

> Johnny had no school today [Queens College] because of the Moratorium, a conference used for peace in the world and to stop the Vietnam [War]. But I know now it was a failure.

Demonstrations, as already noted, lasted until the end of the war. It should also be noted, however, that campus protesting was an irritant to students who wanted to just attend class. Such was the case for my brother, who complained of windows in class having to be closed on warm days because of the loud protesting outside. Sometimes classes were cancelled. Former Fox newsman Bill O'Reilly complained in his best-selling memoir *A Bold Fresh Piece of Humanity* that some demonstrating student tried to keep him from entering a building where he had a class. O'Reilly picked him up and threw him to the ground.

ASSASINATIONS

The 60s unfortunately were a decade of assassinations right here in the homeland.

As every school child knows (or should know), President John F. Kennedy was assassinated in Dallas, Texas, on November 22, 1963. What many are *not* sure of is who was responsible. Of course, the standard accepted story is that he was assassinated by Lee Harvey Oswald (notice most killers have three names?), for his own reasons, acting alone. But even this accepted story gets weird, as Oswald was assassinated himself, just two days later, *while in police custody*, by nightclub owner Jack Ruby (originally named Jack Rubenstein). Jack Ruby was a shady character, with ties both to the police and the Mafia. He provided free liquor, prostitutes and favors to cops and others. Ruby was convicted of the murder of Oswald and sentenced to death. Ruby's conviction was later appealed, and he was granted a new trial. However, on January 3, 1967, as the date for his new trial was being set, Ruby became ill in his prison cell and died of a pulmonary embolism from lung cancer (he also had brain and liver cancer). So, just over 3 years after killing Oswald, Jack Ruby was "silenced."

And that's just the "official" story, "blessed" by the Warren Commission, the official body that was assigned to investigate the Kennedy assassination.

It is reported that Ruby had made many interesting statements in prison. They indicate that he wasn't exactly a fan of Kennedy, didn't vote for him, and didn't go to see his motorcade in which he was assassinated. He also held no bitterness against Kennedy's assassin, Oswald, this according to actual Warren Commission testimony made by a Mr. Knight, who quoted Ruby as saying Oswald was "a good-looking guy."

A year after his conviction, in March 1965, Ruby conducted a brief televised news conference in which he stated: "Everything pertaining to what's happening has never come to the surface. The world will never know the true facts of what occurred, my motives. The people who had so much to gain, and had such an ulterior motive for putting me in the position I'm in, will never let the true facts come above board to the world." He was asked by a reporter, "Are these people in very high positions?" He responded, "Yes."

But it gets even stranger. Dallas Deputy Sheriff Al Maddox claimed: "Ruby told me, he said, 'Well, they injected me for a cold.' He said it was cancer cells...[Then] one day when I started to leave, Ruby shook hands with me and I could feel a piece of paper in his palm... [In this note] he said it was a conspiracy...And that was the last letter I ever got from him." Not long before Ruby died, according to an article in the *London Sunday Times*, he told psychiatrist Werner Teuter that the assassination was "an act of overthrowing the government" and that he knew "who had President Kennedy killed." He added that he was framed to kill Oswald.

Many people associated with the assassination, not just Oswald and Ruby, mysteriously died. In his book *Crossfire*, Jim Marrs gave accounts of several people who said they were intimidated by FBI agents or anonymous individuals into altering or suppressing what they knew about the assassination; later Marrs presented a list of 103 people he believed died "convenient deaths" under suspicious circumstances. *New York Times* best-selling author and attorney Vincent Bugliosi, who wrote *Helter Skelter*, the account of the Manson killings (to be visited later), for which he was prosecutor, described the death of journalist Dorothy Kilgallen—who had said she was granted a private interview with Jack Ruby—as "perhaps the most prominent mysterious death" cited by assassination researchers. Dorothy Kilgallen was known by most, including myself, as a regular panelist on the game show *What's My Line?*, where she was the best on the panel in guessing occupations of regular people, and, blindfolded, identifying celebrities, just by asking questions while they disguised their voices. On November 8, 1965, Kilgallen was found dead in her Manhattan townhouse. Her death was determined to be caused by a fatal combination of alcohol and barbiturates. She had appeared just hours before on *What's My Line?* On the following Sunday night's live telecast of the show, on November 14, the shocked host, John Daly, acknowledged the death and that he had been in contact with Kilgallen's family, who agreed that the show should go on, so soon after her death. She was quickly replaced on the panel with Kitty Carlisle.

There are many more theories, including that Vice President Johnson was involved in the assassination, or the CIA, or Fidel Castro, or the Soviet Security agency KGB, or the Mafia, but there are enough books and websites that document that. One thing I believe is that the Mafia felt betrayed by Kennedy—for good reason. John Kennedy's father, Joseph Kennedy, was a powerful man with many connections who reportedly got the Unions to vote for his son via Mafia help from Sam Giancana (using Frank Sinatra as the messenger, which his daughter Tina attests to). In turn, Kennedy won the election and appointed his brother, Robert F. Kennedy, as Attorney General. As Attorney General, Robert Kennedy pursued a relentless crusade against organized crime and the Mafia; convictions against organized crime figures rose by 800 percent during his term. One can certainly understand the Mafia feeling betrayed.

Robert Kennedy was assassinated in 1968 (see below) and Giancana in 1975.

John F. Kennedy was a popular president, and even to this day the only President to be successfully killed by an assassin since William McKinley in the beginning of the 20th century. He was the first Roman Catholic President, and only Roman Catholic President up to this time. As such, in addition to his being Irish, he was extremely popular in my neighborhood, almost worshipped. My neighborhood took it hard. Amazingly, with a good memory of things long past, I don't personally remember his assassination. I have known other people my age who never forgot. One theory I have for this is that I was only 6 years old at the time, and adults at home and school "protected" me from this tragedy.

Malcolm X (born Malcolm Little) was a controversial African-American Muslim minister and human rights activist of the early 60s. He first did not share the "dream" of Martin Luther King that blacks and whites could live together in peace. Instead, he painted whites as "devils" and only saw freedom for his people if living separately from whites. He considered the black race superior to the white race and that the white race would some day meet its demise. These were the teachings of The Nation of Islam that he embraced.

During 1962 and 1963, events caused Malcolm X to reassess his relationship with the Nation of Islam, and particularly its leader, Elijah Muhammad. On March 8, 1964, Malcolm X publicly announced his break from the Nation of Islam. He wanted to begin his own black nationalist movement that would work with other civil rights leaders, something Elijah Muhammad had not allowed him to do.

On a pilgrimage to Mecca in April 1964, Malcom X witnessed Muslims of "all colors, from blue-eyed blonds to black-skinned Africans," interacting as equals. He recognized Islam as a way for racial problems to be overcome—whites and blacks did not have to separate. He still did not embrace the nonviolent policies of MLK, saying that blacks had to do all they could to defend themselves—including violence.

The Nation of Islam was unhappy with Malcolm X's new teachings and planned to assassinate him. He saw it coming, but bravely ignored threats. On February 21, 1965, while appearing to make an address in a Manhattan ballroom, a man shot him in the chest with an automatic shotgun and two men shot him with semi-automatic handguns. He was pronounced dead shortly after arriving at Columbia Presbyterian Hospital, one of NYC's best, riddled with 21 gunshot wounds.

His three murderers, all members of the Nation of Islam, were arrested, convicted and sentenced to life in prison.

Dr. Martin Luther King was assassinated on April 4, 1968. He was killed by a fugitive from the Missouri State Penitentiary, James Earl Ray, a white man, who was arrested two months later in London. Country-wide riots in 110 cities followed King's assassination.

In all honesty, though King was loved by many whites because of his nonviolent stance, whites were very frightened after his death at the hands of a white man, for the retaliation that could ensue. Though his killing was a great tragedy, I remember this fear overpowering sadness at that time. But my home town of NYC was not greatly affected. Rioting was limited to Harlem and Brooklyn, and there was looting and businesses set on fire; it could have been much worse.

The heaviest impacts were in Washington, DC, Chicago and Baltimore. The occupation of Washington by 20,000 rioters against 3,100 police and 13,600 federal troops was said to be the largest of any American city since the Civil War. Some 1,200 buildings were burned, including over 900 stores. This affected Washington's inner-city economy for *decades*, until a bit after the turn of the century. Chicago, where 10,600 police with 6,700 national guard troops were engaged with the rioters, ended up with 11 people dead and 500 injured; over 200 buildings were damaged. Baltimore had 5,000 paratroopers, combat engineers and artillerymen to combat the rioters, and 6 people ended up dead, 700 injured; more than 1,000 businesses were either looted or burned, many of which never reopened.

Just two months after Martin Luther King's assassination, NY Senator Robert F. Kennedy, brother of John F. Kennedy, was assassinated, on June 5, 1968, while on the campaign trail for president, in Los Angeles. He was the leading candidate for the Democratic nomination. His assassin was Sirhan Sirhan, a Palestinian with Jordanian citizenship. Kennedy was shot three times, once in the head and twice in the back. This deed was clearly televised; the media played the footage many times over. I remember Kennedy finishing his speech, the audience applauding, hearing the shots, and the camera focusing on his head as he lie on the floor, blood pooling out of it. He actually survived for

26 hours.

Sirhan Sirhan was wrestled to the ground by audience members, some of them famous, like football legend Rosey Grier and journalists George Plimpton and Pete Hamill. He was disarmed. Five other people were shot but all recovered.

Despite Sirhan's admission of guilt, recorded in a confession made while in police custody on June 9, a lengthy trial followed. The court judge did not accept his confession and denied his request to withdraw his not guilty plea so that he could plead guilty.

It was not clear why Sirhan committed the murder. He would ramble about the Jewish-Arab conflict in the Middle East and claimed he had premeditation of the act since the creation of the state of Israel. He faulted Kennedy for his support of Israel. His Defense claimed he had diminished capacity. In either event, he was sentenced to death, three years later commuted to life in prison. At the time of this writing he remains in prison, aged 75. He claims to have no memory of the assassination, confession or trial. He has a parole hearing every 5 years. His last, his 15th, in 2016 was denied and he'll be up again in 2021.

TO THE MOON, ALICE! TO THE MOON!

The perhaps arcane reference above is a tip of the hat to *The Honeymooners* (1955-56), and Jackie Gleason's repeated threat to his wife Alice when she pissed him off. Of course, threatening a wife is in bad taste, but Gleason never actually hit his TV wife and always in fact showed great affection towards her; in fact, she always got the better of *him*.

I thought it proper to title this section with something relatively humorous as this chapter probably makes the 60s seem awfully dark and dreary. One of the most uplifting endeavors of humanity happened throughout the 60s—the challenge to land a human on the Moon before the end of the decade.

The promise was made by President Kennedy in a speech held before a joint session of Congress on May 25, 1961. In Section IX of that speech, addressing Space, he said:

> I believe that this nation should commit itself to achieving the goal, before this decade is out, of landing a man on the moon and returning him safely to the Earth. No single space project in this period will be more impressive to mankind, or more important for the long-range exploration of space; and none will be so difficult or expensive to accomplish.

He addressed the difficulty of achieving this goal in an address given more than a year later at Rice University (Houston), on September 12, 1962):

> We choose to go to the moon. We choose to go to the moon

in this decade and do the other things, not because they are easy, but because they are hard, because that goal will serve to organize and measure the best of our energies and skills, because that challenge is one that we are willing to accept, one we are unwilling to postpone, and one which we intend to win, and the others, too.

And thus NASA was allocated the funds to make this dream happen. We had some catching up to do—the Russians had achieved a number of firsts, like the first artificial satellite, *Sputnik 1*, put in orbit (October 4, 1957), and the first human in space, Yuri Gagarin, launched on April 12, 1961. The US took nearly four months after Russia to get their first satellite, *Explorer 1*, successfully launched, on January 1, 1958. But our first astronaut, Alan Shepherd, got in space just a few weeks after the Russians—on May 5, 1961. It should be noted that Shepherd was the first man to be launched in space and return in his launch vehicle; Gagarin parachuted out of his on re-entry.

I was too young to appreciate the single-man Mercury missions of 61-63 and most of the two-man Gemini missions of 65-66, but I followed the three-man Apollo missions closely, recording them in my diary and cutting out articles about them from newspapers and collecting them (yes, I still have them). On a day (July 17, 1969) that Apollo 11 "speeded 25,000 m.p.h. toward the moon," I also noted in my diary that I had "all articles of space in a folder in my dresser starting from before Apollo 6 to the present." I always enjoyed the fact that my life started almost as the Space Age did, less than two months before it began with the launching of *Sputnik 1*.

My first diary entry concerning the Apollo missions was on December 21, 1968, and was quite succinct: "In the morning, Apollo 8 was starting its journey to the Moon. It is going to orbit the Moon." I didn't actually record its successful orbits of the Moon, but History (per nasa.gov) certainly does. About 69 hours into the mission, "NASA's three astronauts became the first humans to see the moon's far side." Ten orbits of the Moon later they started their journey home.

On March 1, 1969, I reported that the three Apollo 9 astronauts who were supposed to liftoff on that day had to have their liftoff postponed because they had colds. Nasa.gov does not report this, but is in agreement with my diary that liftoff did not occur until two days later, on March 3, 1969. These astronauts did not head toward the Moon, but instead tested the Grumman (my future workplace, 1987-94) Lunar Module in Earth orbit. I recorded that we watched the Apollo 9 splashdown on TV live, in school, on March 13, 1969, "a few minutes before 12:00 [EST]." Nasa.gov records the landing time to be 12:01 PM EST. Pretty close!

On May 22, 1969, I proudly reported the following:

Last night we made history. We saw the first color film of the

> moon (we saw it via Apollo 10, which at this exact time I'm writing should be 50,000 feet above the surface of the moon).

The Apollo 10 mission encompassed all aspects of an actual crewed lunar landing, except the landing itself. It was the first flight of a complete, crewed Apollo spacecraft to operate around the moon. Objectives included a scheduled eight-hour lunar orbit of the separated lunar module (LM), and descent to about nine miles [47,520 ft.] off the moon's surface before ascending for rendezvous and docking with the command and service module.

Well, that "50,000 feet" I recorded seems pretty accurate. "All mission objectives were achieved," Nasa.gov reports. We watched this mission splashdown while in school as well. I noted on that day, May 26, 1969, that "I don't know when it came down, but it was supposed to come down at 12:54." I apparently investigated this back then, for on May 27 I noted that according to the *NY Daily News* it was 12:53; according to the *NY Times* it was 12:50. Nasa.gov records the time as 12:52:23 PM—just about the *Daily News* figure, and just about when it was "supposed to" land.

The pinnacle of course for Apollo was the Apollo 11 mission, the first to land men on the Moon. On July 16, 1969 I recorded watching its liftoff:

> At 9:32 AM we watched on television <u>live</u> the liftoff of Apollo 11, which will bring three astronauts, Armstrong (who will make the first steps on the Moon), Aldrin (who will follow Armstrong), and Collins (who'll be orbiting the moon in the command module) to the moon…at the time I'm writing, the Apollo spacecraft (lunar, service and command modules) have been hours out of Earth orbit and is heading toward the moon.

I recorded frequently on the progress of Apollo 11. Already noted above when I recorded about my newspaper clips collection of space articles, on the following day (July 17, 1969) Apollo 11 "speeded 25,000 m.p.h. toward the moon." On July 19 I reported that "A few minutes before 2:00, Apollo went into moon orbit." Then, finally, I proudly (and perhaps a bit defiantly) reported:

> At 4:15 we witnessed an historic moment—man landing on the moon. Why historic? There are 100,000,000 reasons why.

I'm just guessing here that my "reasons" statement was perhaps in defiance to the naysayers at the time, who said things like "Yeah, it's historic, but they should have instead spent all that money here for people on Earth."

On July 21 I recorded, perhaps too "historically":

> Last night, somewhere after the 10th hour, me, Johnny [my 3-year-old sister had been put to bed], mommy, and daddy witnessed an historic moment—man's first steps on the moon. Me and Johnny watched the most of all—exactly half of the walk: 1 hour, 20 minutes (whole walk: 2 hours, 40 minutes)...Today is the first day of a holiday—moon day.

I got the "moon day" thing from some guy on TV who would prove out wrong, but I agree it should have been made a holiday. In either event, I will never forget that night. My family and families around the world sat around their TVs trying to see in a grainy transmission astronaut Neil Armstrong climb down the ladder of the Lunar Module to the moon's surface. I had waited throughout the 60s for this moment, and it was finally about to happen—just days before my 12th birthday. When it happened, there were cheers around the Earth. My father, who used to shake all our hands every new year, shook our hands for this fantastic event.

Why did my brother and me not see the whole walk? We had to go to bed!

On July 24, I reported that near 1:00 PM we watched the splashdown live.

I should mention that for people like my mom the first Moon landing may have been exciting, but it could become the cause of the End. She and others would claim after the landing that whenever something bad happened that it was because we put people on the Moon. I don't get the connection, but I think they were afraid that God had thought we had just gone too far.

[Also, my mother was frightened of the year 2000. She said that the "old people" had claimed the world would end by then. Well, it didn't, of course—it was supposed to end in 2012!]

That wasn't the end of Apollo for the 60s. Not only did we meet President Kennedy's goal of a man on the Moon before the end of the 60s (in fact, we sent two at once), we did it all again before the decade was out—with Apollo 12.

Again a bit too "historically" I reported on November 20, 1969:

> Early in the morning (at the twelfth and eighth hours) the 3rd and 4th men to walk on the moon walked on the moon. It was the Apollo 12 mission.

Quite succinct, but to the point. I didn't follow this mission as closely as Apollo 11, but I did record the splashdown on November 24:

> Later, while doing homework, I watched the splashdown of Apollo 12, which occurred at 3:48 PM...The Apollo astronauts—Conrad, Gordon, Bean—returned to Earth safely, days after exploring the Moon. Their capsule landed upside down, but are now safe on the carrier *Hornet*.

Nasa.gov does not mention the capsule landing upside down, but perhaps it isn't important (cover-up, cover-up!). It mentions a splashdown time 10 minutes later than my figure, but these things seem kind of vague anyway.

The Apollo missions of course carried on to the 70s, with the ill-fated Apollo 13 and successful Apollos 14-17. I followed them all, closely.

Sadly, after Apollo 17 near the end of 72, no-one has returned to the moon, in close to a half-century. We didn't even return with an unmanned spacecraft until the failed Japanese probe *Hagoromo* in 1990 and then the successful NASA/DoD *Clementine* spacecraft in 1994 and *Lunar Prospector* in 1998. In fact, I was frustrated before the *Clementine* mapping mission in the attempt to find good lunar photos that we were investigating at the time at Northrup Grumman to use to test an algorithm my manager and I developed to identify lunar features, that could have been used by the *Lunar Prospector*. Alas, our software algorithm was not used for the *Prospector* anyway, though we received a patent for it, and I enjoyed working on anything related to space exploration. I had missed working at Grumman during the "LM" days of the 60s, which my older associates at Northrup Grumman spoke of so fondly (and had great stories of working with the astronauts).

Fortunately, NASA's eyes are again looking to the Moon for manned exploration, as well as commercial endeavors and endeavors by Russia, Europe (ESA), China, Japan and India. We'll be back.

Now there are naysayers who say we never went, despite pictures taken recently by unmanned spacecraft of the stuff we left there. To add insult to injury, their claims are seemingly given credence (at least to them) by the fact that original Apollo 11 videotapes have mysteriously gone missing.

THE COUNTER-CULTURE

The counterculture of the 1960s refers to an anti-establishment cultural phenomenon that developed first in the United Kingdom and the United States and then spread throughout much of the Western world between the early 1960s and the mid-1970s, with London, New York City, and San Francisco being hotbeds of early countercultural activity. The Vietnam War had a lot to do with creating this, but there were other factors as well, including civil rights movements for minorities and women and experimentation with psychoactive drugs. Hippies were an example of a liberal counterculture of the 60s. Hippies created their own communities, style, music, open sexual practices, and used drugs such as marijuana, LSD, and psychedelic mushrooms to explore altered states of consciousness. I remember their popular phrase well: "tune in and drop out."

For the "rest of us" the counterculture just seemed bizarre and a bit scary. Perhaps a validation of this, my diary records that my sister went out on Halloween 1969 as a "hippie." When seeing them in trips to Manhattan, I stayed far away from them; they looked sloppy and dirty, just like many city bums.

In January 1967, the "Human Be-In" in Golden Gate Park in San Francisco popularized hippie culture, leading to the "Summer of Love." 20,000 hippies attended. In March 10,000 hippies came together in Manhattan for the Central Park Be-In. The Monterey Pop Festival from June 16 to June 18 introduced the rock music of the counterculture to a wide audience and marked the start of the Summer of Love. Scott McKenzie's rendition of John Phillips' song, "San Francisco," became a hit in the United States and Europe. The lyrics, "If you're going to San Francisco, be sure to wear some flowers in your hair," inspired thousands of young people from all over the world to travel to San Francisco, sometimes wearing flowers in their hair and distributing flowers to passersby, earning them the name, "Flower Children." It is estimated that around 100,000 people traveled to San Francisco in the summer of 1967. The center of the Hippie culture was Haight-Ashbury, the district surrounding the intersection of the two streets.

On July 7, *Time* magazine featured a cover story entitled, "The Hippies: The Philosophy of a Subculture." The article described the guidelines of the hippie code: "Do your own thing, wherever you have to do it and whenever you want. Drop out. Leave society as you have known it. Leave it utterly. Blow the mind of every straight person you can reach. Turn them on, if not to drugs, then to beauty, love, honesty, fun."

Alas (to some) there was soon disillusionment among the hippies. In August 1969 hippie Charles Manson (1934-2017) and his "family" of hippie followers killed late-term pregnant actress Sharon Tate and two others for no logical reason. In December 1969, about 300,000 hippies and the like attended a rock festival in Altamont, California, about 30 miles east of San Francisco. The *Hells Angels* motorcycle club provided security (you heard that right). 18-year-old Meredith Hunter was stabbed and killed during The Rolling Stones' performance after he brandished a gun and waved it toward the stage. Some of the hippie supporters left them behind. By the end of 1967, many of the hippies and musicians who had initiated the Summer of Love moved on. Beatle George Harrison, a hero among the hippies, had once visited Haight-Ashbury and found it to be just a haven for dropouts, inspiring him to give up LSD. Haight-Ashbury could not accommodate the influx of crowds (mostly naive youngsters) with no place to live. Many took to living on the street, panhandling and drug-dealing. There were problems with malnourishment, disease, and drug addiction. Crime and violence skyrocketed. None of these trends reflected what the hippies had envisioned, basically peace and love.

Much of the counterculture, though, led to good things that were assimilated into normal culture. Many social issues were addressed, such as segregation, poverty and pollution. Constitutional rights, especially freedom of speech and freedom of assembly, were put to the test. There were Movements for Civil Rights, Feminism, Gay Liberation, Free Speech, and Environmentalism, as well as Movements against Nuclear Energy and, of course, the Vietnam War. Modern culture is defined by much of what the counterculture Movements of the 60s accomplished.

Life in the 1960s: The True Story

2 REEL ENTERTAINMENT

The 60s was a great time for Entertainment in movies and TV, during which were created many classics that we still enjoy today. It was also a time of great change for both of those mediums. The 60s generally were portrayed as innocent in media in the early part of the decade and more "radical" in the latter part of the decade, as the sexual revolution and drug counterculture came upon the scene.

The larger change was in the movies. Since the 30s, in response to outcries about homosexuals and supposed perversions and nudity in some films, movies had to strictly follow the guidelines of something called the "Motion Picture Production Code," or "Hayes Code." This code allowed no profanity of any kind, even using normally acceptable words such as "God," "Jesus," or "Christ," used in a profane manner. "Hell" and "Damn" were even forbidden, though if there was a good reason to use such a word it might be allowed, such as Clark Gable's famous "Frankly, Scarlett, I don't give a damn" at the end of *Gone with the Wind* in 1939, which shocked audiences at the time and prompted complaints. Nudity was not allowed, though could be implied, such as in a fairly long scene that takes place in a nudist colony in the second Pink Panther movie, *A Shot in the Dark* (1964), starring a delicious Elke Sommer. Sex was hinted at, especially in the early James Bond movies, but never, ever shown, which gave rise to silly scenes of phallic nature to imply the sex act—like rushing water. [Refer to *Monty Python* and the *Police Squad* movies to watch hilarious examples of this.] Sexual "perversion" was a forbidden topic, with "perversion" defined by the moral attitudes of the period—which in the 60s would include homosexual acts. Illegal drugs were forbidden as well, though somehow the breakthrough movie *The Man with the Golden Arm* made it to the silver screen in 1955, with an excellent performance by Frank Sinatra as a heroin addict.

One of the Code's taboos I find laughable: "Willful offense to any nation, race or creed." Apparently the "race" part only included the white race. Blacks were portrayed in both live-action movies (see below), movie shorts (*The Little Rascals*) and cartoons (see *Scrub Me Mama with a Boogie Beat* from 1941 on YouTube) in a very derogatory manner. Certainly period pieces that exhibited slavery were offensive to blacks, portraying them as "happy" slaves, such as in *Gone with the Wind* and the banned Disney movie *Song of the South* (1946). As for Asians, cartoons from the WWII period portrayed them in very stereotypical fashion and in the case of the Japanese as evil-looking caricatures.

Movie censorship made a great turn in the 60s. The Production Code was stretched, for example, to allow bare breasts to be seen in the holocaust film *The Pawnbroker* (1964). In 1966 *Who's Afraid of Virginia Wolf* was filmed with explicit language. The MPAA negotiated the language; the word "screw" was removed, but other language remained, including the phrase "hump the hostess."

The Code was abandoned in the late 60s. The MPAA developed a rating system under which film restrictions would lessen. The MPAA film rating system went into effect on November 1, 1968, with four ratings: G for general audiences, M for mature content (which would soon become "PG"), R for restricted (under 17 not admitted without an adult), and X for sexually explicit content (much later to become NC-17).

The first X-rated movies, which would be considered either R or NC-17 now, were movies like *Midnight Cowboy* (1969), *Last of the Mobile Hot Shots (*1970), *Beyond the Valley of the Dolls* (1970), *Myra Breckinridge* (1970), *A Clockwork Orange* (1971), *Fritz the Cat* (first X-rated cartoon, 1972) and *Last Tango in Paris* (1972). Some of these are classics, like *Midnight Cowboy* and Kubrick's masterpiece *A Clockwork Orange*. Others were garbage, and should have never been made. *Myra Breckinridge*, which I had the displeasure to see decades after it was released, has been cited one of the worst films ever made. If you like seeing a middle-aged Brando nude, check out *Last Tango in Paris*. *Fritz the Cat* was for years a college-crowd cult classic—I saw it in college, in fact.

AT THE MOVIES

The first movie I was *supposed to* see was *Have Rocket, Will Travel* (1959), starring The Three Stooges. At that time The Three Stooges were popular with kids via their 1930's/1940's film shorts being syndicated on TV. In NYC, they appeared on WPIX-TV, channel 11, hosted by "Officer" Joe Bolton (1910-86), who padded the time to fit to a half-hour by just talking to us kids about whatever came to his mind. He was dressed as a policeman, and would authentically twirl his baton.

I was two years old when this movie premiered, and the coming attractions on TV for it *frightened me*. Yes, the Stooges were a comedy team, but they were violent in their comedy, and in the commercials for the movie one of the Stooges was forced to wear a helmet with electrodes on it and he appeared to be electrocuted by it. This wasn't even a tad "funny" to me, and being at that tender age I was having difficulty separating fantasy on TV and movies from reality. My family (Mom, Dad, and my 8-year-old brother at that time) wanted to all go see the movie at the local theatre, especially since *Joe Bolton himself* was making an appearance at the theatre. [This was a time when personal appearances at movie theatres were not unusual.]

But I chickened out, refusing to go. My father was understanding about this, and proposed that he stay home with me while my mom and brother went to see the movie. He said we would have our own "movie" at home, and made some popcorn to watch TV with. Thus was created a sweet early memory of me and my dad. Years later I saw that movie on TV and it was pretty awful.

The first movie that I actually saw in a theatre was *Dinosaurus!* (1960). Yep, a year after the kid who refused to see a Three Stooges movie because it looked scary was taken to a dinosaur movie. Keep in mind that back then nothing on TV appeared too scary, as it was in black-and-white, on a small screen, and with inferior sound. The theaters of that day were large and only played one movie at a time. The screen was huge and most movies were in color, and dinosaur sounds reverberated well in the cavernous theater. I was *horrified*. My memory of at the age of three seeing that movie is clear—I curled up in my seat and held my hands to my ears. Mercifully, my mother finally took me outside, where we sat the movie out.

I saw *Dinosaurus!* years later on TV, and it wasn't very good, despite having a memorable (and silly) scene where a man fights a Tyrannosaurs (who was brought back to life along with a Brontosaurus and caveman after it was dug up, thawed, and re-energized by lightning) with a mechanical digger. *New York Times* reviewer Howard Thompson said of this film, "If ever there was a tired, synthetic, plodding sample of movie junk, it's this 'epic' about two prehistoric animals hauled from an underwater deep-freeze by some island engineers."

I didn't trust my parents anymore after *Dinosaurus*, so at an early age I was afraid to go to the movies. Of course, they did bring me to more, including *another monster movie*, in 1961—*Mothra*. Mothra, though, was just one of many Japanese monster movies, and a silly one at that, including two 12-inch Japanese girls (probably someone's fantasy) and a giant egg that hatches into an enormous caterpillar and then builds a cocoon that hatches into a huge moth. I didn't find it that scary; I remember actually watching it.

In 1966 I actually *wanted* to see a dinosaur movie, and saw it with my mom—*One Million Years BC*, starring the voluptuous Raquel Welch (though then, at the age of nine, I only liked the dinosaurs).

During some Christmases in the early 60s, we would go to Radio City Music Hall to see the Christmas show, which continues to occur in NYC to this day. Back then, after the Christmas show they also showed a movie—usually a cheap one. In 1963 at Radio City I saw the romantic comedy and thriller *Charade*, starring Cary Grant and Audrey Hepburn. At the age of 6 then, the movie was totally incomprehensible to me and I would later learn it was quite adult and complex. From its first viewing I only remember two scenes, because they shocked me—one, in the beginning, with a dead man thrown off a train at night, and another, in which James Coburn holds a lit match in Miss Hepburn's face while she is trapped by him in a phone booth.

In 1964 at Radio City after the Christmas show we saw another romantic comedy starring Cary Grant, this time set in WWII, called *Father Goose*, in which Mr. Grant was set up this time with Leslie Caron. This was a simple, silly yet inoffensive movie, albeit boring to me, with a pleasant theme song ("Pass Me By").

I saw other movies with my parents, including Disney's *The Absent-Minded Professor* (1961) and *That Darn Cat!* (1965). But in the latter half of the 60s I mostly saw movies with my brother.

One of the first movies I saw with my brother alone was *Batman and Robin* (1949). No, you didn't read that date wrong. That movie was re-released in 1966 to capitalize on the Batman craze created by the Batman TV series that premiered in that same year. It was one of the very few movies I saw in black-and-white in a theatre. To call it low-budget would be an understatement. There was no batmobile—just a regular car, which they used to change into costume. To state that I "saw" it is also an understatement. I forgot my glasses, and only saw blurry black and white images. Well, didn't miss much.

[OK, to avoid any e-mail on the above (though I would actually welcome any), let me explain that some claim seeing this movie and the first *Batman* movie (1943) as well, before the 1966 series aired, even back in late 1965, and that they were packaged as "An Evening with Batman." I have concluded that indeed there was a limited release as such of both movies at that time, but a further claim that the movies sparked the 1966 series is in conflict with the history of the formation of that series. As for either 40s Batman movie, they are available on YouTube for your enjoyment, but beware that *Batman* was made during WWII and exudes an anti-Japanese prejudice throughout. The master villain was a Caucasian made up to look Japanese (though not as stereotypical as Mickey Rooney in *Breakfast at Tiffany's*), and he was an agent for the Japanese government. The movie includes a "Cave of Horrors" of Japanese atrocities through the ages, and at one point, over footage of a vacated "Little Tokyo" business area supposedly in Gotham City, a narrator proudly proclaims that "since a wise government rounded up the shifty-eyed Japs, it has become virtually a ghost street…"]

Later in 1966 a new Batman movie premiered, based on the TV show. I wanted to see it, but no-one would go with me. My brother said it was "too silly." In retrospect, it was.

1968 was *the* year at the movies for my brother and me. It is the year that two of our favorite movies of all time premiered—the original *Planet of the Apes* and *2001: A Space Odyssey*. Those movies were *awesome*. The first was exciting and the second was nothing short of a religious experience for me. *Planet of the Apes* was a perfect movie for an 11-year-old boy. It was sci-fi, it was action, it was everything. The ending where Taylor finds he was on Earth all along was totally unexpected and mind-bending. [As an adult I visited the stretch of Malibu beach where it was filmed and was awed; I even tried to recreate Charlton Heston's scene where he pounds the wet sand and screams, "Damn you all to Hell!"] *2001* was scary at first, with the spooky music playing as the man-apes discover and touch the Monolith, but when it cut to the space scenes with the *Blue Danube* in the background it was probably the most beautiful thing I had ever experienced at that point. I went home so exhilarated about the future, and believed it would be exactly as Kubrick portrayed.

CLASSIC 60s MOVIES I DIDN'T SEE IN THE THEATRE

There were many classic 60s movies I didn't see. I was supposed to see *The Sound of Music* (1965) on a class trip, but this eight-year-old still had a problem with going to the movies after *Dinosaurus!*, and seeing anything without my parents made me nervous—even something as innocuous as *The Sound of Music* (which, I understand, makes me sound actually *traumatized* by that silly first movie). My parents did see that movie without us kids (I really didn't want to see it anyway, nor did my brother) because it was filmed in Austria, the country where my mother grew up. They would also see some movies without us kids that they determined inappropriate, like the second James Bond movie, *Goldfinger*, also in 1965, considered risqué by them for my tender age of 8. James Bond movies started in 1962 with *Dr. No* and continued throughout the 60s and into the present day.

I shall yield my opinion to Ranker.com, which collects ranking data from a tremendous amount of people on the internet, to list the best movies of the 60s, including ones I never saw in a theater but did see on TV either in the 60s or 70s. Number 1 in 1960 was *Pyscho*, the Hitchcock classic. No. 2 was *Spartacus*, the classic gladiator movie starring Kirk Douglas (who is still with us, at 102 years of age!). No. 3 was *The Magnificent Seven*, which was a truly "magnificent" Western, based on the Japanese film *The Seven Samurai* and remade quite magnificently in 2016. I am surprised but pleased to see on the list as No. 5 *The Time Machine*, one of my favorite sci-fi movies of all time, based on the H. G. Wells classic; I fondly remember when this film first appeared on TV, in the mid-60s.

Moving along to 1961, the No. 1 ranked movie was the film adaptation of *West Side Story*, which I found OK on TV but my friends and I were disappointed that when the two gangs were about to "have it out," they ended up just dancing. *Breakfast at Tiffany's* is in the No. 3 slot, which behooves me, as I never did really "get it" and Mickey Rooney's aforementioned performance is so over the top. *Judgment at Nuremberg*, about the famous trial of Nazi war criminals, is at the No. 5 spot, and was indeed a fine film; it is probably the only film with William Shatner in it where he is not overacting.

1962 has two movies at the top which are top classic movies that I have seen but not enjoyed as much as I "should" have. At the No. 1 spot is *To Kill a Mockingbird*, surely a fine movie concerning racism but not focused enough on that subject as I would have hoped. At No. 3 is *Lawrence of Arabia*, which maybe had to be seen in the theatre to be truly appreciated as it was filmed in "Super Panavision 70," a *very* widescreen format. I found Peter O'Toole's performance quirky as most of his are, though the character he portrayed, T. E. Lawrence, was admittedly a quirky, though interesting, man. The movie ran over 220 minutes in theatres (3 hours, 40 min.) and on TV with commercials it was very loooong.

I am in agreement with the masses on top pictures of 1963. No. 1 is *The Birds*, another great Hitchcock film that scared the heck out of me when I first saw it (another movie I clearly remember seeing the first time on TV). I never looked at birds the same again, just like people became wary of taking a shower after *Psycho*. No. 2 is a "great" movie—*The Great Escape*. I'm sorry I never saw that in a theatre. This WWII epic was based on a true story of men planning and executing an escape from a German military concentration camp. *The Pink Panther* was rated No. 4, the first appearance of Peter Sellers as the ridiculous Inspector Cousteau. Though this film was centered on actor David Niven as "The Phantom," out to steal the largest diamond in the world, the "Pink Panther," this movie led to five other Clouseau movies starring Peter Sellers, and more without him, most recently two movies (in 2006 and 2009) starring Steve Martin as Clouseau. There were many other fine movies from 1963, but I must move on…

I am in *total agreement* with the No. 1 pick from 1964, Stanley Kubrick's *Dr. Strangelove or: How I Learned to Stop Worrying and Love the Bomb*. This is must-see stuff. I first saw it on late-night TV and have watched it many times since. The classic "spaghetti-western" (so-called because they were produced and directed by Italians and filmed in Europe) *A Fistful of Dollars* is ranked at No. 2. It was Clint Eastwood's first leading role and led to two other movies. Though released in 64 in Italy, it was not released in the US until 67. The No. 3 and No. 4 spots are given to two classic musicals, *My Fair Lady* and *Mary Poppins*, respectively. No. 5 was *Goldfinger*. The "serious" version of *Strangelove*, with a similar (unplanned nuclear attack) but grim story and no connection to Kubrick, was 64's *Fail Safe*. I must mention my favorite Beatles movie (and the only one I really liked) in the No. 10 spot, *A Hard Day's Night*. This, their first, is one hell of a funny movie, and has good tunes. I note that *Father Goose*, which I mentioned that I saw at Radio City, is ranked at No. 25 for 1964, and the classic *The Pawnbroker* is No. 45. C'mon, people!

Topping the list at No. 1 in 1965 is *The Sound of Music*, which is actually a really nice movie it turns out, though cornier than an episode of *The Brady Bunch*. It was my mom's favorite movie. No. 2 is the sequel to *A Fistful of Dollars*, called *For a Few Dollars More,* though it also wasn't released until 1967. At No. 3 was *Doctor Zhivago*, about a romance during the Russian Civil War. It had a powerful cast, a great score (including "Lara's Theme"), and was of great length, over 3 hours. Critics actually weren't thrilled with the movie at first, saying it trivialized history with a soppy romance, but as time has gone by it has become more appreciated. James Bond's *Thunderball* is at No. 5. A movie I did see that year, *That Darn Cat!*, amazingly is ranked No. 7.

The third movie in the *Fistful of Dollars* trilogy, *The Good, the Bad, and the Ugly*, is listed as No. 1 in 1966. Like its predecessors, it was not released in the US until 1967. This is probably the most mythic of the three, and is not only considered one of the best *westerns* of all time, but one of the best *movies* of all time. No. 2 was *Who's Afraid of Virginia Woolf?* And to my surprise the sci-fi thriller about people in a miniature sub who try to save a man's life from inside his body, *Fantastic Voyage*, is No. 5. I am also surprised, pleasantly again, to see that one of my favorite sci-fi movies, *Fahrenheit 451*, is ranked at No. 8. Another excellent movie is rated highly at No. 10, though you probably never heard of it. It is called *Seconds*, and stars Rock Hudson as a man given a second chance in life by a mysterious society. *Batman*, alas, only rated a 17. And *One Million Years B.C.* is all the way down at 82!

The No. 1 ranked movie in 1967 is *Bonnie and Clyde*, starring Faye Dunaway and Warren Beatty as the infamous gangsters of the early 30s. Personally, I found the film entertaining but not very special, however in the context of 1967 it was considered a landmark film because of its open portrayal of sexuality and violence. No. 2 is the classic *In the Heat of the Night*, starring Sidney Poitier and Rod Steiger, a murder mystery with a black detective (Poitier) forced into working with a racist white detective (Steiger). This movie spawned two sequels (in 1970 and 1971), and a long-running TV series from 1988 to 1995, starring Carroll O'Conner and Howard E. Rollins, Jr. The original 1967 movie, though, is historic for the unprecedented scene of Poitier, a black man, being slapped by a white man, and slapping him back. 1967 was a good year for Poitier, also starring in the No. 8 film, *Guess Who's coming to Dinner*, about a white liberal family's forward-thinking beliefs being tested by the decision of their daughter to marry a black man. This film also starred the celebrated duo of Katherine Hepburn and Spencer Tracy, Tracy literally dying when the film, his last, was made. Poitier was also in the No. 9 film, *To Sir, with Love*, about a black teacher in the London slums.

No. 3 in 1967 was *The Graduate*, a highly successful classic (I remember it playing in theatres for years) starring a young Dustin Hoffman, Anne Bancroft and Katherine Ross in a comedy-drama that pokes fun at The Establishment. The movie had a "hip" soundtrack by Simon and Garfunkel, including the No. 1 song, "Mrs. Robinson." At the No. 4 spot was the classic WWII movie, *The Dirty Dozen*, starring a strong cast as military prisoners chosen by Lee Marvin to undergo a seemingly impossible mission in order to earn their freedom. In 1967 there was also the classic movie *Cool Hand Luke*, rated at No. 6, about the harsh life in a Florida prison camp. It contains one of the most classic lines in movies: "What we have here is a failure to communicate." There were many more notable movies in 1967, including *In Cold Blood* (No. 10), the James Bond *comedy Casino Royale* (No. 11), and the "serious" James Bonk flick, *You Only Live Twice* (No. 12).

As mentioned previously, 1968 was a great year for me *in* the theatre. *2001: A Space Odyssey* is ranked at No. 1 and *Planet of the Apes* is at No. 2. I couldn't agree more on these rankings. At No. 4 is *Rosemary's Baby*, whose trailers in the theatre spooked the heck out of me back then. It is a great classic horror film that relies on believable characters and a spooky storyline instead of blood and gore. But speaking of blood and gore, at No. 5 is the classic, original *Night of the Living Dead*, which started the whole modern flesh-eating zombie craze that continues to this day. In a lighter vein is the movie adaptation of the Neil Simon stage play of the same name, *The Odd Couple*, No. 8 on the list, which led to the highly successful TV show of the 70s and a disappointing but personally entertaining sequel, *The Odd Couple II*, of 1998, as well as the 2015-2017 TV series, and, not to forget, previous versions with the gender roles reversed (a 1985 play) and an African-American version (TV, 1982-83). For Disney fans, *The Love Bug* was rated at No. 10, premiering Herbie, the anthropomorphic VW "Beetle" who would appear in numerous sequels, including *Herbie: Fully Loaded* in 2005 with Lindsay Lohan. At No. 13 is, in my opinion, one of the funniest movies of all time, Mel Brook's *The Producers*, which in 2001 became a Broadway play and after that a movie again (2005)—though nothing as great as the original. 1968 had many more classics.

I am very pleased to see *Midnight Cowboy* at the No. 1 spot for 1969. Though I have never seen this movie in a theatre, I have seen it many times. Like *The Graduate*, this movie was available in theatres for a very long time. It has everything—comedy, pathos, tragedy, satire, sex, perversion—everything that we experience in real life. It also has a realistic, gritty portrayal of a declining NYC. It is definitely a must-see. Nos. 2 through 5 are classic entertainment: *Butch Cassidy and the Sundance Kid* (Paul Newman and Robert Redford), a non-conventional Western that takes place at the end of the 19th century; *Easy Rider*, the classic biker movie starring Peter Fonda, Dennis Hopper and Jack Nicholson; *The Wild Bunch*, another non-conventional Western, this one with a sharp edge, also set later than most, in 1913; and *True Grit*, a more conventional, classic John Wayne Western. There was quite a mix of themes in 1969 movies, as Hollywood experimented with the counter-culture of the time, bringing us more adult themes, such as wife-swapping in *Bob & Carol & Ted & Alice* (No. 7); desperation and cruelty in *They Shoot Horses, Don't They?* (No. 8); a lying lover and a suicide attempt in *Cactus Flower* (No. 11); class conflicts and premarital sex in *Goodbye, Columbus* (No. 32); and love and sex with homoerotic undertones in *Women in Love* (No. 41). But we also had the Woody Allen screwball comedy *Take the Money and Run* (No. 9) and even musicals—*Goodbye, Mr. Chips* (No. 12; rather dear to me as we used music from it in my grammar school graduation) and *Hello, Dolly!* (No. 23).

Life in the 1960s: The True Story

3 CLASSIC TV BEFORE IT WAS CLASSIC

To me, the 60s were the ultimate classic period of television. To support this claim, consider the many 60s shows that continue to be aired this day, a half-century later, *with some that have been aired since the 60s in syndication continuously during that time* (*Star Trek*, *I Dream of Jeannie*, and *Gilligan's Island* just to name a few). Many of classic 60s shows have been re-invented into modern movies, and *Star Trek* alone has spawned at current count 13 movies and 5 more TV series. But more on *Star Trek* later.

Television didn't change as much in the 60s as movies did; it remained constrained throughout the decade by network censors. There were changes in programming, but not in what you could or not could see on TV.

Profanity was forbidden throughout the decade, for example. On the *Dean Martin Show*, in a skit that had Dom Deluise play the devil, he didn't say he was from Hell—he was from heck. On *Star Trek*, however, in the episode *City on the Edge of Forever*, first aired on April 6, 1967, William Shatner does say in his role of Captain Kirk, in the final line of the episode, "Let's get the Hell out of here." So apparently "Hell" could not be joked about, but in the right context it could be used.

As in the old MPAA Code, one could not use words like "God" as a profanity, and I don't mean appended to the word, "damn." In the TV airing of the 1967 film *The Producers*, Gene Wilder's "God" got bleeped when he exclaimed "Oh my God!" in the movie's beginning. Words were bleeped all the time on the late-night *Tonight with Johnny Carson*, and I would guess most of the time the expletives bleeped were pretty lightweight. In fact, Johnny Carson once quipped, "I wish sometime people knew what we bleep out, because it's probably not as bad as what they think we bleep out." He was absolutely correct.

The first time "son of a bitch" was uttered on network television was not until September 23, 1974, when Bea Arthur said it to her TV husband when she found out he faked a heart attack to cover up his cheating, on *Maude*. There was much hoopla about this, even before the episode aired, as it was revealed beforehand that she would say that word. I wasn't even a regular viewer of *Maude*, but I made sure I watched this episode to witness history. It was the last line of the episode, and it was amazing. I remember my father asking at the time "they can say that?" Yep, they could.

Of course, expletives would sometimes leak out on live or taped live TV (TV taped but not edited before airing). In an episode of Groucho Marx's game show *You Bet Your Life*, which originally aired in the 50s, and I saw for the first time in syndication in the 70s, I heard a contestant who flubbed a question start to say "Oh, Shit," and catch himself before completing the sentence. Ball games could be listened to closely in the 60s and you could hear fans cuss. But *intentionally broadcast* cussing was not allowed.

Nudity certainly had no place on TV in the 60s, and producers went to incredible lengths to scintillate the audience with as much exposed female flesh as possible without showing any "naughty bits" (a phrase I borrow from *Monty Python*). Naughty bits included more than just the obvious—it included too much cleavage, ass cheeks, nipple impressions, and navels.

Many know the famous story of Barbara Eden's forbidden navel in her show, *I Dream of Jeannie* (though she was allowed to display great boobage). But recently Dawn Wells, Mary Ann of *Gilligan's Island*, revealed that similarly she was not allowed to show her navel either. In fact, her costuming was under great scrutiny, to show as much flesh as possible, while covering any ass cheekage and being very careful with boobage. She has said that the Network was very meticulous about that.

Sex was only hinted at. The most risqué sitcom in the 60s I remember was *Bewitched*. Darrin often hinted about going to bed was his wife, from the first episode, but we never got close to seeing them "do it." On *I Dream of Jeannie* Major Nelson and Jeannie didn't share a bed until they got married, though technically they were the first unmarried couple living in the same house, albeit Jeannie in her bottle. Captain Kirk of *Star Trek* was reputed to be a lady's man, but it was only hinted a couple of times that he got laid, in typical 60s fashion. In the episode "Bread and Circuses" (1967), he was smooching at night with a Roman slave girl on a bed, and the camera panned over to a lamp over the bed, and then dissolved to that lamp in daytime with its flame extinguished. He is then shown in bed, fully clothed, sleeping alone. In the episode "Wink of an Eye" (1968), sex is hinted at by Kirk sitting up in his bed, just pulling up the last of his boot (at the time *how much* he could pull it up had been discussed at some length with the Network). His implied sex partner, fully clothed, brushed her hair using his bedroom mirror.

As many have noted, most couples in 60s TV shows slept in separate beds, though there were exceptions. For example, "Ozzie" and Harriet (Nelson), in their eponymous comedy, slept together because they were married in real life. In *The Munsters* Herman and Lily slept together I guess because they were not human anyway. In *The Flintstones* Fred and Wilma slept together because they were just cartoon drawings. But at the end of the decade, in 1969, *The Brady Bunch* debuted, and two real, unmarried actors, Florence Henderson and Robert Reed, actually slept together in a single bed. This is a bit ironic, though, considering Robert Reed was gay in real life.

The Caucasian race was well-represented on TV in the 60s, but not other races. For the most part, you didn't see non-whites much and when you did, they were stereotypes. There was progress, however, in this decade and towards its end this situation changed much, though most of the entertainment industry was still very white at the decade's close. In the mid- to latter-part of the 60s, it was fashionable to have an African-American "token" in a show's cast. Sometimes they had to make special allowances for them—like Greg Morris in *Mission: Impossible*. In that show the Impossible Mission Force team would travel to a lot of international "white" places, so a black would stick out. So in every episode Mr. Morris, conveniently being an electronics and communications expert, would mostly stay in the background, working behind walls, in plumbing, in sewers, wherever, installing some gadget that the team needed to use at the right time. Another example of this is the "Kinch" character portrayed by Ivan Dixon in *Hogan's Heroes*. It was even admitted at times that Kinch just couldn't get away with impersonating German solders well. So, he spent most of his time in the barracks and the escape tunnel. He was also an electronics and communications expert, away from sight like Mr. Morris, working the radio and telegraph and fooling the stupid Nazis with his German-sounding voices. Almost to prove my point that he was a "token," when he left the show, Ivan Dixon was replaced with another black actor, playing a different person but doing the same things.

Star Trek was a show that was praised for its international cast, and it had a black *woman* who was on the Bridge of the ship and was an officer. A story of legend in *Star Trek* is that when Whoopi Goldberg saw this on TV she ran to her mother very excited about it and became a *Star Trek* fan on the spot, years later working herself into the cast of *Star Trek: The Next Generation*. The woman in the original *Star Trek* was the multi-talented Nichelle Nichols, who was the show's communications officer and electronics expert. Yep, even on *Star Trek* the black person had the same expertise as on the aforementioned shows, but at least she was out in the open, and could be found singing (and very well at that) in the Rec Room, beaming down to planets, and in general having a big presence on the show; occasionally she was granted some meaty and interesting things to do, even taking part in saving the day in some episodes.

In fact, Nichelle Nicholls and William Shatner shared the first interracial kiss on television, in late 1968—though it wasn't much of a kiss and they were forced to do it by sadistic aliens with telekinesis. And the Network (NBC) not only allowed it, but didn't get much flack about it. This was a far cry from just months earlier, in that same year and network, when singer Petula Clark smiled and briefly *touched* Harry Belafonte's arm on her Special program, which "prompted complaints from Doyle Lott, the advertising manager of the show's sponsor, Plymouth Motors. Lott wanted to retape the segment, but Clark, who had ownership of the Special, told NBC that the performance would be shown intact, or she would not allow the special to be aired at all." Lott was fired for this and the Special did very well in the ratings.

A color barrier was broken through when the secret agent series *I Spy* premiered in 1965 and co-starred a black man—Bill Cosby. *I Spy*, which also starred Robert Culp, was a successful show, and ran until 1968. The first series to star an African-American woman in a non-stereotypical role was *Julia*, which premiered in September 1968, starring beautiful singer and actress Diahann Carroll. It was also successful, running until 1971. The first successful variety show starring an African American was the *Flip Wilson Show*, which just missed the 60s, premiering in September 1970 and running until 1974. In its first two seasons it was actually the second-highest rated show and it won two Emmys.

The problem with the above shows is that they were meant to appeal to a white audience, so they didn't explore issues that were important to blacks. The fact that they starred blacks was almost incidental—the characters could just as well have been white (as unique and entertaining these power-stars were). In Diahann Carroll's own words, in 1968, "At the moment we're presenting the white Negro. And he has very little Negroness." The good news is that these shows did introduce more black actors to the television audience.

I feel that Asians got the shortest end of the stick in the 60s, and continue to this day; they just don't have enough presence on TV and in movies. In the 60s we did have the cool character of Kato, played by the incredible martial arts master Bruce Lee, in *The Green Hornet*, which premiered in 1966 but only lasted one season. We also had Mr. Sulu in *Star Trek*, who was far from a stereotype. But we also had the character of Hop Sing in *Bonanza* (1959-1973), played by the American-born actor Victor Sen Yung, who though he spoke perfect English, spoke in a very stereotypical thick accent on the series, and had the stereotypical job as a cook. Of course, that show was based in the 19th century (and not the 23rd as Sulu lived in), so perhaps we can forgive some of that. Also, though Hop Sing was treated a little harshly in the first episode (with Lorne Greene chasing him to make supper), the character was allowed to develop and became more like family than servant. There were even episodes that displayed the racism against Chinese then and the *Bonanza* Cartwright family defended their cook and his race.

At least there were Asian-Americans playing Asian roles in the above, because earlier TV and movies many times starred white actors in Asian roles (including John Wayne absurdly cast as Genghis Khan in 1956's *The Conqueror*). Even in the 70s, in the show *Kung-Fu* (1972-1975), the half-Asian character Caine was portrayed by three actors (for three different ages) who were all completely non-Asian.

In 1969 *The Smothers Brothers Comedy Hour*, a successful comedy/variety show with strong ratings since its premier in 1967, was suddenly taken off the air permanently because network executives thought it had become too politically inappropriate for TV. Though the network, CBS, and their censors had watched closely for some time for material they considered offensive, the show was cancelled abruptly on April 4, 1969, before the end of its second season. What incensed CBS so much was a comedy bit in the last show (which it never aired) wherein guest comedian David Steinberg performed a "sermon" routine similar to one he had performed on a 1968 episode which had prompted hundreds to write angry letters to CBS. In his second "sermon" routine Steinberg, referring to the story of Jonah being swallowed by a whale, said that Gentiles claimed in the New Testament that they "literally grabbed the Jews by the Old Testament" to throw into the whale, which was actually a guppy. This single joke, alluding softly to testicles when saying "Old Testament," was what made CBS yank the plug. Tommy Smothers later admitted that he had Steinberg do another sermon because CBS *didn't* want him too. But he was surprised at his show's sudden demise, and his brother Dick and he sued CBS for breach of contract, which they won after four years of litigation, being awarded over $4 million 2016 USD. Their cancelled show won an Emmy the year it was cancelled for Outstanding Writing Achievement in Comedy, Variety or Music. By the way, the unaired episode can be presently enjoyed on YouTube.

KID'S TELEVISION

As a small child, I watched a lot of old stuff on TV (i.e., syndicated from *before* the sixties), though I just accepted them as current. This included a lot of old cartoons, from the 40s and 50s, some of which still appear on TV, like *Looney Tunes* (with Bugs Bunny, etc.) and *Tom and Jerry*. Some even went back earlier (the 30s), like *Popeye*, which, like *The Three Stooges*, was introduced on a local station, WPIX-11, by a live host to pad out the half-hour. The host was "Cap'n Jack McCarthy," in reality announcer John McCarthy (1914-96), who, dressed in a Naval Uniform aboard a tiny set of some simple ship, would kill time by telling unscripted stories and ringing the ship's bell. In his "spare time," he hosted the NYC St. Patrick's Day Parade, for 41 years.

But even Popeye, from the 30s, was not the oldest cartoon I watched on television. There were some that dated back to the 20s—yep, silent cartoons. They weren't completely "silent," of course, as there was background music.

Old TV programs would appear on 60s Saturday morning TV, like *My Friend Flicka* (1956-57), about a boy and his horse, based on the 1943 movie starring Roddy McDowell as the boy, later to become the ape Cornelius in *Planet of the Apes*.

One of my favorite old TV shows that played endlessly in syndication in the 60s, every day in the afternoon, was *Adventures of Superman* (1952-58). This was a live-action series, serious at times and campy at others. As noted earlier, I couldn't tell the old stuff from the new stuff then, and one day my brother pointed out that the cars on Superman were old, and that the show was from the 50s. I had really had no clue.

Of course, there was new children's programming in the early 60s, though not as much as today, and certainly very low-budget and unsophisticated by today's standards. For really young kids, like me, there was *Romper Room*, which incredibly ran on TV in one form or another from 1953 to 1994. This show was nationalized but large markets like NYC had their own versions. The show just consisted of a "teacher" and a class of little kids who did basically uninteresting things for a half-hour—at least to adults. I enjoyed watching the kids "drive" cardboard "cars" that they would hold around them, and I wanted one. The teacher would claim she could "see" kids in the home audience—how creepy is that? She did this using something that looked like a tennis racket that had some whirling thing on it you couldn't see through and then she'd make a switch to the same device but with now just a wide hole in the middle (think of a tennis racket without strings) that she looked through. She'd then say she could see a variety of kids, which she referred to by first name. I swear, when she said she saw Steven I really thought she saw *me*.

Another favorite kid's show of mine was *Captain Kangaroo* (1955-84), the titular character played by Bob Keeshan (1927-2004), a fellow Long Islander (and family friend of a current work associate of mine). Bob had played the original Clarabelle the Clown previously, on the *Howdy Doody* Show (1947-60), which was before my time but had entertained my brother. There wasn't much exciting going on in this program either, but I and many kids like me found it entertaining. The "Captain" (I don't know why kid show hosts were mostly "captains" and "officers," and it was never clear to me what he was a "captain" of) was a nice old fellow with a gentle voice who intentionally wanted kids to feel a grandfatherly connection to him. Interestingly, he was too young to play a grandfather in my young days, so he wore makeup and a wig to look older, only to discard these as the show continued throughout the years and he really was old. His set was a fascinating place called the *Treasure House*, a perfect name. He had a dancing bear and an old coot named Mr. Green Jeans, as well as puppets that they interacted with. He would read stories and have interesting guests and characters. Basically, you didn't know what was going to happen in any given episode, and that was part of the charm. His theme song seemed so perfect for him, but I later found out he used an old song from the public domain, "Puffin' Billy," about a locomotive.

There were other low-budget local kid shows which I enjoyed. *Wonderama* (1955-86) was a NYC-based show which expanded to other markets, and was created and first hosted by Sandy Becker (1922-96), who later went on to his own kid show, and in the 60s starred Sonny Fox (1925-   ) and then Bob McAllister (1935-98). The show included music, cartoons, games, audience participation and even education. *Bozo the Clown* was another local show, becoming national in the 60s. Chuck McCann (1934-2018) hosted a local eponymous show in the 60s that featured singing puppets. During the 114-day NYC newspaper strike from late 1962 well into 1963, Chuck not only read the comic strips on TV (following in the footsteps of Mayor Fiorello LaGuardia, who had read them on the radio during a 17-day NYC newspaper strike in 1945), but he read them dressed up like the characters.

The 1960s saw the birth of "Saturday Morning Cartoons," a wonderful innovation that has been sadly lacking since the 1990s. From 8 AM to 12 Noon, every Saturday, we were graced with new (and some old) cartoons on our TV sets. I remember that the cartoon lineup for each year was advertised in two-page advertisements in comic books. We were treated with new adventures of familiar superheroes such as Superman and Spider-Man, as well as new superheroes such as *Space Ghost* and *The Herculoids*. There was also sillier fare, such as *George of the Jungle* and *Underdog*, nonetheless enjoyable. 1969 saw the beginning of the classic *Scooby-Doo* franchise, which continues to be fruitful to this day.

Wonderful, now classic, cartoons started on TV in the 60s. As a child, one of my favorites was *Felix the Cat*, the titular character having its origin back in the silent movies of the 20s but having been retooled for TV in 1958. The cartoon was simple fare, aimed at small kids like me in the early 60s. Felix was always hounded by an evil professor to get his hands on Felix's "magic bag of tricks," from which Felix would pull out anything he needed to save the day. Another favorite of mine was *Courageous Cat and Minute Mouse*, a cartoon which debuted in 1960 that was a parody of Batman, and created by the same man who created Batman—Bob Kane. The animation and sound were terrible, but the cartoons were interesting to young lads like me and short enough (at *five minutes* length) to possibly match our immature attention spans. The big gimmick in this one was a ray gun that could do anything that was required to save the day—like Felix's bag, and similar to Batman's Utility Belt. The tone of the show, though harmless for kids, was rather dark, like Batman was in the comics then, but of course nothing like the Batman movies and shows of today. Another great cartoon of the 60s was the *Rocky and Bullwinkle Show* (1959-64), which paired the implausible team of a flying squirrel and a moose against the evil Soviet spies Boris Badenov and Natasha Fatale (perfect villains for this Cold War era). This show actually consisted of two short Rocky and Bullwinkle segments, separated by cartoons such as Fractured Fairy Tales (humorous spins on familiar fairytales), Peabody's Improbable History (a time travelling dog and his boy—yes, that's right, and they got their own movie in 2014) and others. What made this show great for kids was that in a half-hour you saw two episodes of Rocky and Bullwinkle, other cartoons, and usually a Short—going for that short attention-span again. What made it great for adults was a slew of jokes aimed at adults that the kids would not understand—for example, in one episode, Bullwinkle stated that he graduated *Magna Cum* "Lousy" instead of *Magna Cum Laude*.

A cartoon of the 60s of special note was Hanna-Barbera's *The Flintstones* (1960-66), which most would recognize today because it spawned two movies much later (1994 and 2000). The Flintstones was the *first animated primetime American television series*. It involved elements of adult sitcoms of the time (actually it was so close to Jackie Gleason's *The Honeymooners* of the 50s that Jackie at one point wanted to sue) though it did not involve adult situations of course in this "innocent" time. This broke new road for television, paving the way for hits like *The Simpsons* and *Family Guy*. Set in 1,000,000 BC or thereabouts, the Flintstones endured the same trials and tribulations as live-action family sitcoms but with the additional humor of being set in that time. Though clearly they possessed a lifestyle like 20th century America, they lived in stone houses, sat on stone chairs, slept on stone beds, watched TVs made of stone, and utilized many household conveniences of the 60s, except they were realized using animals (an elephant shower and vacuum cleaner, a large-beaked bird record player and typewriter, etc.). Since *The Flintstones* played on prime time, they were sponsored by companies for adult products—including cigarettes. In fact, the Flintstones themselves were in a commercial for *Lucky Strikes*, the male leads Fred and Barney actually puffing away at the product (check out YouTube). Though *The Flintstones*' original run ended in 1966, it had later incarnations on TV, as well as the aforementioned movies.

Because of the success of The Flintstones, Hanna-Barbera quickly created other cartoons for prime-time. One was *The Jetsons* (1962-63), which was also displaced in time from the 60s, but this time in the future—sometimes stated to be the year 2000 in promotional ads. Though it only lasted a year in primetime, *The Jetsons* has lasted decades in syndication, with new episodes later produced, and yes, a movie (1990). My head always being in the future, that show fascinated me more. But a year *before The Jetsons*, Hanna-Barbera studios produced *Top Cat* (1961-62), which, if *The Flintstones* was a copy of *The Honeymooners*, was a copy of *The Phil Silvers Show*, with the "Top Cat" sounding like Phil Silvers in character as con-artist Sgt. Bilko. Other cartoons had short runs in primetime, including *Jonny Quest* (1964, one season) and *The Alvin Show* (1961-62), starring the singing stars Alvin and the Chipmunks and their human adoptive father Dave Seville. Alvin did much better in syndication and out of primetime, with further cartoons produced and even multiple movies. The Alvin cartoons originated out of "The Chipmunk Song (Christmas Don't Be Late)," which was a hit of Christmas 1958 and is in the collection of Christmas classics we hear every year.

Speaking of Christmas, endearing animated Christmas specials that have endured the test of time to this day started in the 60s. The first was *Mr. Magoo's Christmas Carol* (1962), a sweet yet faithful cartoon within a cartoon starring the absurdly myopic Mr. Magoo in a stage production of Dickens' overproduced classic, as Mr. Scrooge. Mr. Magoo was voiced by the great Jim Backus, who just a couple of years later would star as Millionaire Thurston Howell III in *Gilligan's Island*. This special spawned *The Famous Adventures of Mr. Magoo* in 1964.

Speaking of 1964, my favorite animated (via stop-motion) Christmas classic premiered in that year—*Rudolf the Red-Nosed Reindeer*. Besides its charming animation, characters, story and music, this show when first aired was a pleasant surprise to me, at age 7, at a time I was very upset. My father and brother had gone just about a block away to buy a Christmas Tree at a small vacant lot, and I had wanted to go with them, but it was determined that I was too young and would "be in the way." I remember being in tears about that. My mom saved the day by planting me in front of the TV and searching for something special for me to watch. That "something special" was *Rudolf the Red-Nosed Reindeer*, which kept me glued to the TV, alone, while my mother either made her famous Christmas butter cookies or wrapped some presents. My sorrow peeled away quickly as I became engrossed and entranced by the show. I had never seen or heard anything like it in my life. By the time it was over I was in a superb mood and my dad and brother arrived with a beautiful tree fresh with wonderful natural pine scent.

In 1965 the big buzz in the third-grade was about the upcoming *A Charlie Brown Christmas*. I didn't know much about Charlie Brown as his comic strip wasn't syndicated in the newspaper my parents bought. But my class obviously read his strip and were very excited about it, and I gave it a chance. I loved this innocent yet adult cartoon. It exposed the commercialization of Christmas at such an early time, and had an ending that was so satisfying. I still find it satisfying to this day, as its religious overtone, which would never be made in this PC day, is intact and now unfortunately unique.

In 1966 I not only received a little sister but yet another Christmas classic – *The Grinch Who Stole Christmas!* Like everyone else, I was familiar with Dr. Seuss' books, but this was the first time one of his stories were on TV, and it was great. It is such an endearing classic to me, and like other Christmas classics there are no limits to how many times I can watch it. It was made into a successful live-action movie in 2000 but for me it just didn't possess the charm of the original. As if that wasn't enough, it was remade in 2018 as a computer-animated film.

Frosty the Snowman premiered in 1969. I was 12 then, so it didn't seem to possess the charm of the earlier Christmas classics, but I have fond memories of watching it with my little sister, and later my daughters. I'm cheating a bit by mentioning the stop-motion *Santa Claus is Coming To Town*, because it didn't premiere until 1970, but I have to mention that classic for its charm and great story. At 13, I still enjoyed it. I must also add a new Christmas favorite, this one a movie, that I watch every year. It's *The Polar Express*, which didn't "arrive" until 2004, but to me is the most awesome Christmas presentation since the classics of the 60s.

"ADULT" TELEVISION – THE COMEDIES

"Adult" television in the 60s, though more directed toward adults, was generally very innocent and it was appropriate for children to watch any show. In fact, some "adult" prime-time fare was very juvenile in nature, and was obviously directed to children as well as adults. Almost anyone who has seen the popular *Gilligan's Island* can attest to that!

In the early sixties the more standard family comedies carried on from the 50s: *Father Knows Best* (1954-1960), *Leave it to Beaver* (1957-63), *The Adventures of Ozzie and Harriet* (1952-1966), and *The Donna Reed Show* (1958-1966), for example. These shows all had some charm and probably provided more warm feelings than belly laughs. The characters were likable, with good-natured kids and perfect parents, who always had time to solve their children's problems and seemed like they were always home. The fathers always wore suits and ties, even though air conditioning was usually not present, and the moms were dressed up as well; in the case of *Leave it to Beaver*, the mom, Barbara Billingsley (1915-2010), was always wearing pearls, even when cooking supper. The dads were always very fatherly and the moms motherly, though they were handsome and attractive leading men and ladies. My favorite, and first love, was Donna Reed (1921-86). I didn't care what was going on in her show—I was happy just to stare lovingly at her perfect features. Her teen-age TV daughter, Shelley Fabares (1944-), though cute and closer in age to me (as well as being the sweet-voiced singer of number-one song "Johnny Angel" in 1962), never took my fancy over her TV mom.

I must say that though these family sitcoms were heartwarming and nice to look at, they portrayed a vision of a perfect American family life which was unrealistic and made you feel that your real family was weird and dysfunctional. I would watch these shows thinking that they portrayed how life was supposed to be, wondering why mine wasn't that way. I assumed we were just different, and everyone else was like the families on TV. My mother was usually in a house dress and when my father came home he stripped down to his underwear on warm days to deal with the heat. He certainly didn't want to hear my problems during the week, especially after work, when he just wanted to cool down with a couple of beers and read the paper. He and mom weren't always planting pecks on their cheeks, but hey, at least they were *real*.

Also, as noted above, these sitcoms weren't really *funny*. I found the *Three Stooges* shorts from the 30s and 40s funnier. I found *The Abbot and Costello Show* (1952-54), in syndication in the 60s and well-beyond, the funniest of all. In that show, Bud Abbot (1897-1974) and Lou Costello (1906-59) brought to TV their best bits from their movies and burlesque acts, including one of the funniest bits of all time, "Who's on First?" about a baseball team with Who on first base, What on second, and I Don't Know on third. My brother and I found laugh-at-loud hilarity in situations like these:

Bud: Suppose you bore a hole in that wall…Lou: OK, I bore a hole in that wall. Bud: Why? Why did you bore a hole in that wall? People don't do these things, Lou!

Bud: Aren't you going to put mustard on that hot dog? Lou: No. Bud: But mustard *goes with* the hot dog. Lou: I don't like mustard. Bud: Oh, so you're going to put the mustard companies out of business…what about the kids of the mustard workers—you want them to starve?

A woman passes Lou in the street and pauses. She hits him with her bag, saying "How dare you remind me of someone I hate!"

And many more…

The 60s saw the birth of the fantasy comedies. Each show was more fantastic than the previous. *Mr. Ed* (1961-66) was about a talking horse, that only Alan Young (1919-2016) in the character of Wilbur Post could hear. His beautiful wife, the very scrumptious Connie Hines (1931-2009), always wondered why her husband spent so much time in the barn with Mr. Ed, the horse. I would have been back in the house with Connie. *My Mother the Car* (1965-66), considered by many to be one of the worst shows of all time, moved the incredibility meter much further up by having a 1928 Porter Stanhope touring car being the reincarnation of attorney David Crabtree's mother, Gladys. Of course, only son David (played by Jerry Van Dyke, Dick's less-successful brother) could hear her talk.

1964 brought about the birth of two TV classic macabre comedies, that though successful, only lasted two seasons each. CBS brought us *The Munsters*, a very juvenile affair with a family that consisted of Frankenstein's Monster as the dad, an odd, many-times-dead mom, a grandfather who was of the Dracula family, a son who would howl at the moon while in a stone coffin for a bed, and a pretty young woman (played by two different actresses in two seasons) who was considered the ugly, "black sheep" of the family. Oh, and there was a fire-breathing dragon that lived under the stairs called "Spot." *The Munsters* was greatly entertaining for kids and completely harmless, with the ghoulish cast behaving like they were a normal American family. It helped to have Fred Gwynne (1926-93) play the dad and Al Lewis (1923-2006) play the grandpa because they had previously played sweet policemen in the extremely juvenile *Car 54, Where are You?* (1961-63), actually filmed in the Bronx, and the first show that I did impressions for all that would listen, to the delight of my parents. Yvonne DeCarlo (1922-2007) played the mom, who, even under the pasty makeup, exuded her natural exotic beauty. The "pretty young woman" was played at first by the pretty girl-next-door type Beverly Owen (1937-2019), and then by the sexy Pat Priest (1936-   ), who became a girl of my dreams and others as well.

ABC was considered a third-class network then, behind CBS and NBC. As a result, they seemed to copy some of CBS's ideas. Their answer to *The Munsters* was *The Addams Family*, based on the cartoons of Charles Addams (1912-88). This was quite a different show, however. It was much more adult and macabre. While the Munsters sought to be the typical American family, the Addams family relished in its differences from the mainstream. They were inexplicably rich and the ultimate hedonists. Their hedonism went to strange lengths, including torture. This was perhaps the first show that hinted at S & M, an amazing feat at the time. The family patriarch, Gomez (John Astin), was a horn dog, turned on by his beautiful svelte wife (deliciously and perfectly named Morticia) just speaking a few words of French, at which he would kiss her arm up and down and want to depart to "the playroom," which had instruments of torture. Weird characters and situations were always afoot, and the cast included a giant, baritone, gravelly-voiced butler called Lurch as well as the sadist Uncle Fester (who could light bulbs in his mouth), a grandmother that looked like a witch, two weird kids and a disembodied hand known only as Thing, as well as a jabbering all-hair monstrosity called It. As a kid, I found it a fun show and their house was cool (I even bought the plastic model of it and built it). Gomez liked electric trains and so did I, except he blew them up. The S & M and sadism just went right over my head. The Addams family made it to the silver screen twice, in 1991 and 1993.

Another fantasy comedy of the 60s, though not well-known, was *It's About Time* (1966-67). This one wasn't particularly funny, but I liked its science-fiction premise, which involved two astronauts somehow passing through a time warp to prehistoric times. It had cave people in it and dinosaurs as well. It was created by *Gilligan Island* producer Sherwood Schwartz, whom despite the outlandish premise couldn't be turned down by the Network because of the success of *Gilligan's Island*. This show however, was not a success, and the premise was incredibly changed mid-season—the astronauts made it back to the present, bringing a few of their cave friends along. Thus, it became a classic "fish-out-of-water" vehicle, and a cheaper one at that, since it didn't require special sets and dinosaurs anymore. But the reversed premise failed as well.

Two incredibly successful fantasy comedies began in the sixties and lived for decades, to the present, in syndication around the world. One was ABC's *Bewitched* (1964-72). It starred the awesomely likable Elizabeth Montgomery (1933-95) as the Witch who preferred mortal life over flying and living in the clouds (which would have been OK with me) and immersed herself in the role of a mortal suburban housewife, married to a successful mortal advertising executive ("Darrin"), and later becoming a mother—twice, to kids who inherited her magical powers. Ms. Montgomery was beautiful, in both a wholesome and demure yet sultry way, and if it sounds like I was in love with her, so be it. She exuded charm as well, and could be funny too. Much of the success of the show can certainly be attributed to Ms. Montgomery, but there were many other great characters, mortal, witch and warlock, and the writing was superb. It possessed some of the corniness of regular sitcoms, but provided many belly-laughs as well. The witchcraft that was forbidden by the husband but constantly used in "special situations" anyway, would be the perfect trigger for all sorts of hilarity. The "meddlesome mother-in-law" (Agnes Moorhead), a common sitcom device for both marital tension and humor, was the ultimate pain-in-ass since she had magical powers. Another device, "wacky neighbors," was used, but in this case what made them wacky was that the wife would constantly witness the witchcraft next door and the husband would always miss it and just think that his wife was nuts.

Now *Bewitched* is also a period piece, as well; watch how in almost every episode the advertising execs and others drank liquor—when they got home, every party, in bars, and sometimes at work, truly "Mad Men." Like *It's About Time*, the show went through a major change midstream, but this time between seasons. Dick York (1928-92) played Darrin from the beginning, but had to quit in 1969 because of debilitating pain from a back injury. He was replaced by the not-so-similar-looking but aptly-first-named Dick Sargent (1930-94). The characters just all pretended that Darrin didn't change a bit. Only in the 60s! [Just noticed Liz and her two beaus were all cut down young, in the small period of 1992-1995. Hmm.]

The other incredibly successful fantasy comedy that began in the sixties and has been in syndication constantly on this planet since was NBC's *I Dream of Jeannie* (1965-70). This series was created and produced by Sidney Sheldon (1917-2007) in direct response to the success of ABC's *Bewitched*. The two shows admittedly were very different, though the catalyst for comic situations in one was a fictional magical character, a witch, and in the other a fictional magical character, a genie. The genie, of course, had to be female and stunning, and Sheldon had seen a genie movie called *The Brass Bottle* (1964), which starred Burl Ives (the Snowman from *Rudolf*) as the genie and Barbara Eden (1931-   ), among others. He took a liking to Barbara, and in *Jeannie* so did we all. Barbara Eden was, in my opinion, the sexiest woman on television at that time. We all dreamt of Jeannie, in many ways. Her harem costume was cute, even though the censors ordered her navel covered. [It literally stuck out at times, to our delight, and I recently saw a painstakingly collected collage of these incidents on YouTube]. Better yet, I thought, was in the later episodes when Jeannie would go out in the world wearing typical garb for the period—miniskirts and mini-dresses (which I also enjoyed on Elizabeth Montgomery as well then). It was then that I realized how great her legs were.

As noted earlier, *Jeannie* was ground-breaking at the time as it was the first show that had an unmarried woman living with an unmarried man—albeit in a bottle on a piece of furniture. Jeannie would later get married to her "master" Tony (Larry Hagman), but most sitcoms "jumped the shark" (got bad) when couples got married, and this show was no exception. Of course, the show wasn't all about Jeannie—she interplayed with a wonderful cast of funny characters, and the scripts were funny, more so I think than *Bewitched*; it was faster paced and more slapstick, complete with pratfalls, especially by Tony. Tony's best friend Roger (Bill Daily), though in character an astronaut who was a Captain and later a Major in the Army Corps of Engineers, played a buffoon, in great contrast to the serious Tony. And as *Bewitched* had nosy neighbors, one of which always saw the magic and another who didn't and thought she was nuts, *Jeannie* had Dr. Bellows, the Air Force Colonel and Psychiatrist who reported all sorts of weird goings-on to the General, who thought the Psychiatrist himself was crazy.

Even "mainstream" comedies in the sixties had fantastic elements, characters and situations. *Green Acres* (1965-71), for example, was based on the unlikely premise that a successful NY lawyer would leave his practice and penthouse behind and drag his wife to a dilapidated farm in the town of "Hooterville" (don't know how *that* got past the censors) to grow crops, which he consistently proved to the TV audience he was comically terrible at. The bizarre characters in this improbable sitcom included a constantly vacillating county agent ("This seed is perfect for your soil; well, not exactly *perfect*—in fact, it's not good at all…"), a seemingly mind-reading con-man (as soon as you said you needed something he'd be there in seconds with junk in his trunk that he thought would satisfy your need), and a pig that was treated like a human child by his pig farmer "family," who, incidentally, understood his pig sounds as English. In one particular surreal episode, moon rocks were shown talking to each other.

Another example is the very successful *The Beverly Hillbillies* (1962-71), about hillbillies finding oil on their land and paid millions for it, and then "moving on to Beverly…Hills, that is. Swimmin' pools. Movie Stars," right from their theme song. Their banker loved their money but not them, and somehow got them as neighbors. Another "fish out of water" series, the hillbillies were incredibly out of touch with modern society. Their source of wisdom was the young man Jethro, who was the only family member to graduate sixth grade—which took him many years to do. In one of Jethro's antics, he tried to build a spaceship to Venus, because he read in a comic book (defending himself by saying, "they wouldn't put it in a comic book if it weren't true!") that Venus was populated with beautiful girls and no men.

Then of course, there was *Gilligan's Island* (1964-67), familiar to us all, with the premise that a boat on a local tour in Hawaii was blown *way* off course to an unknown desert island, with everyone intact. Almost every episode gave new hope to the castaways of leaving the island, with Gilligan messing things up in the end. Somehow, they still always liked Gilligan and incredibly did not kill him. Also, they had a "professor" among them with six university degrees who could come up with a bunch of genius-level ideas but couldn't design a boat that would take them home. Somehow this implausible and silly show became so popular that it has been playing for decades to this day around the world.

Hogan's Heroes (1965-71) was a very funny show but it is incredible that it ever made it to TV. How a comedy could be made about American POWs in WWII is beyond me. I knew a person who saw American POWs incarcerated for real and a friend that had a dad in one and I know it was obviously a very horrible experience—they were frightened and so starved that they would sandwich dead bodies between them to get extra food.

But in the show the prisoners were lucky to be in Stalag 13, run by the inept Colonel Klink (Werner Klemperer, himself Jewish), with the "I know nothing" gentle rotund guard Sergeant Shultz (John Banner, also Jewish). This allowed Hogan and his heroes to create a Special Operations Unit that performed espionage and sabotage against the Nazis, support the Underground, and help Allied POWs from other camps and defectors to escape Germany. Even the Generals and Gestapo were idiots, so Hogan's missions, though not easy, were always successful. By the way, one of his "heroes" was Jewish actor Robert Clary, who in reality spent three years in concentration camps, including Buchenwald. He is alive at the time of this writing, aged 93. As for Hogan, played by Bob Crane, you might know he was a sex addict who was bludgeoned to death in 1978 with a camera tripod, probably by his creepy friend John Carpenter, whom he tried to separate from, but his guilt was never proven, and Carpenter died in 1998. The movie *Autofocus* (2002) recounts these events, though some doubt its accuracy.

SCI-FI/FANTASY TV

Some Sci-Fi TV frightened me in the early sixties. *The Outer Limits* (1963-65) was a hard-sci-fi anthology show, often featuring scientists developing interesting things in a laboratory, that usually ran amuck. The aliens that popped up often were actually silly looking, with fake rubber masks. The tone of the show was rather dark, so even the silly aliens would spook me. Quite honestly, I also did not find the show very interesting at that time. As an adult I began to appreciate some very fine episodes of the show, such as the two written by Science Fiction great Harlan Ellison (1934-2018), "Demon with a Glass Hand" and "Soldier," the latter of which had elements of *The Terminator* movie series, so much in fact that Ellison sued the Terminator producers over it and settled out of court. *The Outer Limits* was uneven in quality, though, with many mundane episodes separating the good ones. The series was rejuvenated in the 80s to decent success, and I enjoyed most of those episodes.

The Twilight Zone (1959-64), another anthology series, similarly frightened me, though now I can hardly see why. It was dark at times, but also light, and occasionally very sentimental. Quite honestly, I was just too young to "get" that show when it originally aired, though the surprise endings, some of which had to be explained to me then, were awesome. *The Twilight Zone* mixed sci-fi with fantasy and a touch of the supernatural, and I only liked the sci-fi episodes, which had spaceships and astronauts. What I didn't "get" then were the episodes about the human condition that connected with adults. Fortunately, *The Twilight Zone* went into syndication and never left, playing to the present, even in "marathons."

As I got older, I began to really appreciate the more "adult" episodes, and indeed learned to love them and watched them over and over again. I can now relate to Gig Young (1913-78) in the Episode "Walking Distance" (1959), where he played a 30-something ad executive tired of the rat-race and a life with no fun, no "merry-go-rounds." He drives out of NYC into the countryside, only to find himself in his home town—but 25 years previous. He meets himself as a kid and his parents as they were then, and finally gets accepted as their son from the future. He wants to stay, and enjoy another halcyon summer, but his father tells him that those summers come only one to a customer, and he can't interfere with his young self's happiness. His father offers him hope that maybe there are "merry-go-rounds" as well in his time, which he returns to. Another adult favorite of mine is "A Stop at Willoughby," where another NYC ad exec, this time played by James Daly (1918-78), is suffering constant pressure at work, where his boss tells him to "push, push, all the way." Things aren't better at home for him, as his wife, we find, likes the finer things in life and has always pushed him as well to be very successful, something which is not apparently in his very nature. He only finds solace in his long ride home in the train from NYC to Connecticut, where one day he dozes off and dreams of a non-existent stop called Willoughby, where it is eternally July 1888 and "a man can slow down to a walk and live his life full measure." After experiencing this dream twice, he decides to jump off the train the next time it stops there in his dream. He does just that, and everyone recognizes him and welcomes him to his paradise. In the next scene we find that he actually jumped off the train in the present, in-between stops, and died. He is hauled off in a hearse for the funeral parlor "Willoughby and Sons."

I now consider *The Twilight Zone* the best series ever on television. It was intelligent TV at its best, and its producer and writer of a majority of episodes was Rod Serling (1924-75), one of the best writers, TV or otherwise, of all time. The shows were consistently good, though there were of course clunkers, but the good-to-bad ratio has to be one of the highest TV ever had. It has stood the test of time, after 60 years. It was rejuvenated as a series from 1985-1989, with fine writing, acting and production values. It was again revived in 2002-03, though this time not very successfully; however, there were some good episodes. In 2019 it was revived yet again, but available only through streaming services. It was also made into a movie in 1983, but was not well-received and entered the annals of infamy as during production a helicopter stunt with explosions that occurred too close to the actors killed one adult (Vic Morrow, star of the 60s WWII series *Combat!*) and two child actors, which Morrow tried to save but got decapitated.

The "fun" and "light" Sci-Fi series of the 60s were produced by Irwin Allen, and I looked forward to them every week. The first was *Voyage to the Bottom of the Sea* (1964-68), based on the 1961 movie of the same name (whose cast included Barbara Eden and her husband, Michael Ansara), about a space-age nuclear submarine like no other. It took place about ten years in the "future," though only the sub and its gadgets were futuristic. Like most of Mr. Allen's productions it had a great premise and special effects, but stories got weaker as the series progressed, to the point of absurdity (aliens and monsters in the oceans, etc.).

Mr. Allen's next foray into sci-fi was *Lost in Space* (1965-68), which started out in a futuristic October 1997. This featured a family lost in the universe, trying to make their way back to Earth or at least to their original destination,

Alpha Centauri. The reason for their predicament was Dr. Smith, who was an intruder who constantly caused them problems, and, like Gilligan, should have been killed (the pilot, Don, did want to beat him up on occasion). This was a very entertaining show for me, even though the science was bad and the scripts got worse as time went on. The ship was neat and there were great production values. Unfortunately, Dr. Smith ended up hogging the show and by the third season we had an episode with talking carrots. Enough was enough.

Mr. Allen moved on to *The Time Tunnel* (1966-67), perhaps my favorite of his efforts. In this series two men, Tony and Doug, are lost in time after Tony walks into the Time-Tunnel, produced by an impossibly giant, expensive government project known as Project Tic-Toc, in an attempt to prove it worked so government funding would not be discontinued. Well, he proved he could go back in time but also that he couldn't be retrieved. Doug tried to save him, but only got lost together with him. Every week, the home base at Tic-Toc, in 1968, two years in the future from the TV present, tried to bring the boys back but only succeeded in moving them to another time, usually in the past. Amazingly, they almost always ended up in the middle of an historic event, whether it be the 1941 attack on Pearl Harbor, sinking of the Titanic, battle at Little Big Horn, or whatever incident that *Irwin Allen had footage of from movies*. The movie footage was intercut with the new footage actually well, and the show worked. The show was known for its historical accuracy, and my brother was even told to watch it for history class. In one episode, Tony and Doug were sent into the biblical city of Jericho by Joshua and I verified *in the Bible* that indeed two men were sent into that city by Joshua. Of course, nothing is perfect, and a friend of mine showed me years later that some conquistador-type guy actually lit a torch *with a Zippo lighter*. Unfortunately, the stories got silly, and always seemed to introduce aliens in the past. Though the show did not have a "finale," in the last episode Tony and Doug are transported to the first place they were transported, the *Titanic* in 1912, and the same events begin happening again. Thus, they are stuck in an endless time-loop.

The last successful sci-fi TV series produced by Irwin Allen was *Land of the Giants* (1968-70). In this show, which I also found very entertaining, a sub-orbital aircraft in 1983 passes through a space-warp that delivers the crew and passengers to a planet of giant people—about 12 times taller than us. Their civilization is similar to ours in advancement, so you saw giant cars and other giant familiar objects. The special effects were good, very good, and there were some good stories to go along with them, but again things got very silly as the series progressed. It ended with "the little people" stuck on the world of giants.

And thus we come to *Star Trek* (1966-69). This was, in my opinion, the best Science Fiction show to grace TV. In fact, before I re-discovered *The Twilight Zone*, I considered this the best of television. I have already written of how much this show spawned, and it is amazing—for it was not a success during its first run.

I like to say that I was a fan of *Star Trek* before it was even aired, as I waited in anticipation of the show as its TV ads enticed me during the Summer of 66. In fact, I have personally told Walter Koenig, who played the character of Chekov in that series, of that fact. It just looked like a cool show, exactly up my alley, and my brother shared in the excitement.

After all the hype, *Star Trek* finally premiered on Thursday, September 8, 1966, on NBC. The first episode was "The Man Trap," basically about a shape-shifting "salt vampire" (yep) loose aboard a starship of 430 people. When it attacked them it changed into a hideous creature with suction cups that drew all the salt out of them—which killed them.

I found it slow, plodding and boring.

I gave up on this episode at some point and spent time with my mom in the kitchen. My brother seemed to enjoy it, but it just wasn't for me. I preferred the mindless, literally explosive action of *Lost in Space*. But that would change...

The episode "Arena" was first broadcast on January 19, 1967. I was glued to the TV set for this one. It had a lot of action and it had...the *Gorn*. The Gorn was a bipedal reptilian creature, intelligent, incredibly strong, and captain of his vessel. He couldn't speak English without a Universal Translator (though most aliens seemingly did) and his natural language sounded like a collection of hisses and grunts. And he was ugly as hell.

"Arena" was I believe the first episode that I saw without my brother, and it both frightened and fascinated me. The Gorn was one scary dude, and when he made his first appearance it was a close-up that literally made me jump from the TV set, which I would watch very closely without glasses then.

From that point forward I loved *Star Trek*. I watched it religiously, usually with my brother, and waited impatiently for every episode. By the second season I was a fanatic about the show, and would make drawings of characters and their technology in my own technical manual in a notebook.

Alas, *Star Trek* indeed was not a successful TV show. It's amazing, in fact, that it even made it on TV at all. Its creator, Gene Roddenberry (1921-91), showed it to the networks in the early 60s and got some interest but not a sale. CBS showed a lot of interest, asking him all sorts of questions about his concept, but then simply stated that they already had a sci-fi show—*Lost in Space*. But he finally got a pilot commissioned by NBC, and produced an episode called "The Cage." This was well-received, and indeed is a great episode of *Star Trek*, but was considered "too cerebral" for TV. He was actually commissioned to produce a *second* pilot, something unheard of at the time, but later occasionally practiced (I've heard some shows have had *three* pilots now). This one had an almost entirely new cast, the one we are now familiar with, and lots of action. NBC bought it.

The Production Company was Desilu, founded by Lucille Ball and her husband Desi Arnaz. Legend had it that Lucy liked the title and originally thought that it was about amateur TV Stars, like *Star Search* would be. She didn't understand the show, but stuck with it, even though the first season's ratings were less than astronomical. A second season was produced, and was excellent in my opinion, but again ratings were not good. In fact, it was slated to be cancelled. But a letter-writing campaign ensued that saved the show. It is of much disagreement of *exactly* how many letters NBC received, but it was enough for NBC to renew the show, and in fact they broadcasted a segment during one show that *Star Trek* would be renewed, and *please stop sending letters*.

This sounds like a happy ending, but though the show was renewed NBC lost interest in it and did things like reducing its budget and moving it to a horrible time-slot—10 PM on Fridays. Roddenberry lost interest in the show as well, and scripts that should have never been produced were. Some of the third season shows were not just silly but outright embarrassing and boring. That season caused the show to be cancelled. There was no finale, but the last words uttered in the last episode were "If only…"

The third season, though, was critical back then as it produced just enough episodes that the show could be syndicated. And syndicated it was; at one point it was estimated that *Star Trek* was being transmitted somewhere in the world at any given time. Fans like me watched and watched, and new fans arrived in the 70s. News that there would be a *Star Trek* movie teased me throughout the 70s, until finally, almost as that decade literally expired, on December 7, 1979, the first *Star Trek* movie finally premiered. Yes, I know where I was on that date. In the 80s there was speculation about a new network for Paramount that would air new episodes of *Star Trek* in syndication, and in 1987 that finally happened too, with the premiere of *Star Trek: The Next Generation*.

As for Desilu, they got their hit that made them money: *Mission Impossible* (1966-73). A highly successful TV show, it survives to this day not only in re-runs but movies.

Not sci-fi but surely fantasy in the 60s was *Batman* (1966-68). This show is often described as "campy" (which got worse each season) but was a lot of fun for all to watch. It took the country by storm, in a phenomenon that became known as *Bat-mania*, named after *Beatle-mania*. The show made good use of merchandising to make as much money as possible; some examples were costumes, bubble-gum cards, record albums, model kits, bat-ears, coloring books, board games, and *Hot Wheels* cars. I collected the cards (beautifully painted), built the Batmobile model (my brother built the Batman model) and had my parents buy The Batman Record (and later, even a Robin record).

Batman aired twice a week, on two contiguous days, during its first two seasons. Each episode was a half-hour, and the first episode always ended in a cliffhanger that would be resolved the next evening. *Batman* utilized well the "heroes in peril" spin in the cliffhanger, with an announcer (William Dozier, the producer of the program) warning us that the "dynamic duo" was indeed in trouble this time, and that we should "tune in tomorrow at the same bat-time, same bat-channel."

My brother was disappointed with the series because of its lack of seriousness. I didn't care at first but by the third season it had become just too bat-silly. It was also reduced to a single half-hour spot in the week. A new character, Batgirl, was introduced to pump things up a bit, and though the delectable Yvonne Craig (1937-2015) played her character well with the appropriate spunk in her tight spandex, it wasn't enough. *Batman* was like a big flame that just sputtered out.

The same year that *Batman* appeared, and on the same "bat-channel," brought to us by the same "bat-producers," was *The Green Hornet* (1966-67), based on a radio series from the 30s-50s and film serials from the 40s. In the 1966 incarnation, the Green Hornet was a newspaper publisher and owner and TV Station owner who would fight crime with his servant Kato, the one-and-only super martial arts expert Bruce Lee (1940-73). The Green Hornet, AKA Britt Reid, was played seriously by the handsome Van Williams (1934-2016), familiar to TV viewers from such shows as *Surfside 6* (1960-62). Two people knew the Green Hornet's identity, and were also regulars on the show: his Secretary Casey AKA Lenore Case, played deliciously by the awesomely attractive Wende Wagner (1941-1997) and the District Attorney, played by Walter Brooke (1914-1986). The Green Hornet lived with Kato in a cool apartment that had a wall with a fireplace that would rise up to allow the DA to enter, on a metal stairway. To exit his apartment as the Green Hornet, with Kato, the duo would enter a room that had Reid's car, Kato would push some buttons, and the car's wheels would be clamped to the floor and the floor would rotate 180 degrees to reveal their limo, the "Black Beauty," similarly clamped to the floor. The clamps would release and the duo would enter the car, a wall would rise to allow them to exit, and they would pass through a billboard that magically opened up. How cool is that!

All of the magic above, like similar "magic" in *Batman*, was actually only filmed once, and the same shots showed over and over again, in each episode. The Green Hornet wore a much simpler costume than Batman—a long green overcoat, green fedora, green gloves and a green mask, a white shirt and black tie under the overcoat. Kato simply wore a chauffeur's outfit and mask. The fight scenes were much better than in Batman, as Bruce Lee made incredible moves that looked like they could really hurt (or kill) people. The show was played seriously compared to the campy *Batman*, but not too seriously. The stories were quite far-fetched, including one that even included space invaders that fortunately for the credibility of the show were exposed as fakes. The Green Hornet, different from Batman, was considered a criminal and sought by the police; the way he infiltrated gangs was by demanding a part of their "cut."

Literal schoolyard banter at the time was who was better, the Green Hornet or Batman, and who would win in a fight. I took Batman's side. On an episode of *Batman* the two did go against each other but the result was disappointing. After fighting a villain together, they began fighting each other and the announcer declared it a standoff, though Burt Ward as Robin was no match certainly for Bruce Lee. Word was that Lee was annoyed at this "standoff" and

Ward was afraid of Lee. In either event, they just stopped fighting and the Green Hornet and Kato left the scene, presumably to go back to their show!

Because of Bruce Lee's fighting scenes and his later popularity (and mysterious death), Green Hornet clips would appear in movies in the 70s. In 2011 *The Green Hornet* got its feature film release, and made money, though, unlike the show, it was played for laughs.

WESTERNS

A popular genre in the 60s carried on from the 50s, the Western. 60s programming was full of them, of which the following were the most successful (i.e., lasted at least four seasons each):

Gunsmoke (1955-75) – America's longest-running prime time, live-action drama to this day, about lawman Matt Dillon (James Arness) trying to keep the streets of Dodge City, Kansas safe during settlement of the American West.

The Rifleman (1958-63) – A show about a rancher (Chuck Conners) and his son in 1870s and 1880s New Mexico Territory.

Rawhide (1959-66) – A show about 1860s cattle riders, including Clint Eastwood. Its theme can be heard in the 80s movie *The Blues Brothers*.

Bonanza (1959-73) – More on this below.

The Virginian (1962-71) – Television's first 90-minute Western, about a tough foreman of a ranch in late 19th century Wyoming and his top hand, played by Doug McClure. [In *The Simpsons*, the character of Troy McClure is based on a combination of Doug McClure and Troy Donahue, both actors very successful in their time but who had difficulty later regaining that success.]

Daniel Boone (1964-70) – Based on the famous pioneer, frontiersman and explorer (1734-1820), ably played by Fess Parker, who had previously played American hero Davy Crocket in segments of the *Walt Disney* show of the 50s. Back then he created a craze wherein young boys wore coonskin hats, which Mr. Parker also wore as Daniel Boone, though the craze did not occur again.

The Big Valley (1965-69) – Starring classic movie Star Barbara Stanwyck, as a widow of a wealthy California Rancher, whose four children included Linda Evans (Mrs. Carrington in the 1970s hit *Dynasty*) and Lee Majors (Steve Austin, the bionic man, in the 70s hit *The Six Million Dollar Man*).

The Wild Wild West (1965-69) – See below.

High Chaparral (1967-71) – Produced by the same people as *Bonanza*, a show about a rancher (Leif Ericsson) living in the Arizona Territory of the 1870s, with his brother and son, and, later a new wife, his first wife being killed in the first episode.

Bonanza was very special to me and my family. Watching *Bonanza* on Sunday nights at 9:00 PM on NBC was a tradition that we never broke. *Bonanza* wasn't a typical Western. It was more about family and familial love, justice and decency more than anything else, set in the "lawless" territory of Nevada "one hundred" years ago, mostly the 1860s (there were inconsistencies, but it was established in a few episodes that the series occurred 100 years prior to its airing). The area of Nevada the characters lived in was by Lake Tahoe, which was gorgeous, making *Bonanza* one of the most beautiful shows to watch. NBC filmed and broadcast all episodes in color, so as soon as you got a color TV you could enjoy the beautiful scenery (and NBC had the best color of the networks then). The incidental music was provided by David Rose, who loved pretty music, and created a theme for the ranch in the series, the Ponderosa (named after the Ponderosa Pine), that was one of the prettiest themes ever on television.

The show was about a rich but righteous man, Ben Cartwright, who had started out his adult life as a seaman in New England, and married his superior officer's daughter, of English descent. She died after giving birth to a son, Adam, and Ben decides to move West. On the way West, in a wagon train, he meets up and marries a Swedish woman, who gives birth to a strong son, Eric, also known as "Hoss." Unfortunately, she gets killed in a crossfire, and now Ben is left to finish his journey widowed again, with two sons. Sometime after establishing himself in the Ponderosa, Ben visits Louisiana and falls in love with a beautiful French Creole woman, in fact even dueling for her. She joins him in the Ponderosa and gives birth to a third son, Joe, but one day she gets thrown from her horse and dies.

Thus is the setup for Bonanza, the details actually established in separate episodes over the course of some years. Ben Cartwright is the widowed matriarch of three disparate sons of three disparate mothers. Adam is the logical one, subdued (in fact, almost sleepy as played by Pernell Roberts), Hoss is the huge, lumbering gentle giant with a heart of gold but the constitution of a horse, and Joe is the horny young one who likes to fight but of course also has a heart of gold.

The Ponderosa Ranch was a large piece of land to keep control of, said to be more than half a million acres, or nearly 100 square miles. Anything could happen on it, and did. It is said that Bonanza was about a biblical Jewish Patriarch and his sons, which makes sense as its creator David Dortort was Jewish, and he chose the name of the patriarch to be Benjamin and his first son Adam. As it turned out, the actor who played Ben Cartwright, Lorne Greene, was Jewish, as well as his "son" Joe, played by Michael Landon (AKA Eugene Orowitz). Certainly there is no doubt that the show espoused Judeo-Christian values. It also took on serious issues for its time, including racism (against Native Americans, Chinese, Jews and African Americans, for example), domestic violence and even substance abuse.

There was one special feature of *Bonanza*. Chevrolet was a major sponsor of the show, and every year when the new models came out we were treated to an extended commercial in the middle of the show that introduced the new cars. This was really a big treat for us. On some occasions, earlier in the series, the series regulars would get behind the wheels of the Chevies and drive them into the western town sets, a fascinating anachronism. This can be found on YouTube (BTW, Adam always got the Corvette, I think).

The Wild Wild West was also not your typical western. In fact, it was more a combination of James Bond and a western, with even science fiction elements as well. It was about secret service agents working for President Grant (1869-77). In addition to keeping the President safe, they also often fought against super villains with super plans. They travelled the country in their own fancy train, which included luxury accommodations as well as stables and laboratories. Unlike cowboys, they had at their access all sorts of spy-like gadgets that sometimes really seemed too advanced for their time; unfortunately, the villains had fancy anachronistic gadgets too. And, of course, there were always beautiful women. But the eye candy wasn't just for men. Robert Conrad, who played agent James West, always managed to wear tight pants that he nonetheless could mount horses with when jumping from the roof. The reality is, of course, that Robert Conrad constantly ripped his pants.

The show was really akin to James Bond as the Network had bought rights to Ian Fleming's first Bond novel, *Casino Royale*. I found the show also akin to *Star Trek*. The character of the captain in *Star Trek* was known as James T. Kirk; in *Wild Wild West*, Robert Conrad played James T. West. The show was produced by some of the same men as *Star Trek*. And many guest characters also guested on *Star Trek*.

I liked the show maybe in part for the reasons above, but it was also just entertaining. It was made into a theatrical movie in 1999 (Will Smith played James West) that did not do well, but personally I thought it was fine.

THE DRAMAS

Of course, the 60s had its share of contemporary dramas, thrillers and adventure shows. Among them, some were more "serious" than others. Shows like the aforementioned *Mission: Impossible* had to be taken with a grain of salt, while *The Man from U.N.C.L.E* (1964-68) had to be taken perhaps with a glass of beer. The Man (actually, "men"—two agents, one American and one Soviet, working together), from the United Network Command for Law and Enforcement, saved the world regularly from people and organizations that wanted to take it over. Like *The Wild Wild West*, except with more standard secret agents in contemporary surroundings, this was an answer to the James Bond films. In fact, Ian Fleming had something to do with the series, including naming of the Napoleon Solo character. In all honesty, *TMFU* wasn't much more over the top than Bond, but would never achieve Bond's class. While Bond ordered Martinis "shaken, not stirred," Solo would order a milkshake. Solo certainly did not bed women, as that was not allowed on TV. Unfortunately, as the series progressed, it became a parody of itself, intentionally, because of the popularity of *Batman*, and the ratings went down. That unwise decision killed it.

A more serious detective/adventure show of the 60s was *Mannix* (1967-1975). Another Desilu success, *Mannix* started out with an angle that related it to shows about agencies fighting crime. In the first season Joe Mannix worked for a large, high-tech Los Angeles detective agency called Intertect, which used computers to help solve crimes and track their agents. However, Joe didn't like computers or being tracked by his superiors and always ignored the agency's help and disconnected their tracking devices. He was their best agent, but a maverick. After the first season, he went out on his own (with only his secretary Peggy helping him, one of the first black women on TV in a leading role) and never went back to Intertect. Mannix was a macho show, played by the cool Mike Conners (1925-2017), who performed many amazing stunts by himself (often getting hurt). I assume he was tapped for the role based in part on his super-cool performance in *Tight Rope!* (1959-60), where he played a super-secret undercover man for the police (please see YouTube for free episodes!).

Now we are getting more serious. One of the best dramas of the 60s was *The Fugitive* (1963-67), which most know about because of the highly successful 1993 film starring Harrison Ford and Tommy Lee Jones. The TV "Fugitive" was played by David Janssen (1931-80), who ran from the law for four years until the last episode, where he spectacularly fought the "one-armed man" that had killed his wife, after he was finally found innocent of that crime. This last episode was the first in TV history that properly concluded a series. All previous series had been unceremoniously axed in mid-air. Part 2 of this two-part finale was *the most-watched television series episode up to that time.*

The "man on the move" concept of the Fugitive was copied by other shows. In *Run for Your Life* (1965-68) a man with a limited time to live travels the country to experience as much as he can. In *The Invaders* (1967-68) an architect accidentally learns of a secret alien invasion already underway and thereafter travels from place to place attempting to foil the aliens' plots and warn a skeptical populace of the danger. In *Then Came Bronson* (1969-70) a journalist, played by Michael Parks (1940-2017), spooked by the suicide of a journalist friend (played by Martin Sheen), drops out to see the country on his Harley. In *The Immortal* (1970-71) a man whose blood chemistry and resistance to almost all diseases (including old age) makes him both almost immortal and a target of several wealthy men who would basically use him as a personal blood bank, so he runs from them.

The most serious show I would watch with my family was *Dragnet* (1966-70). The title of the series actually changed every year—so there was *Dragnet: 1967*, *Dragnet: 1968*, *Dragnet: 1969* and *Dragnet: 1970*; each year in the title was the second year of that season (e.g., *Dragnet: 1968* was for the 1967-68 season). Being a sci-fi fan, I loved the title that started one year in the future. *Dragnet* identified itself with a year to distinguish it from the original *Dragnet* series, which ran from 1951-59.

Dragnet was a half-hour police drama whose scripts were based on real cases. In fact, an announcer (an uncredited George Fenneman, Groucho March's announcer on *You Bet Your Life*) at the beginning of every show would claim, "The story you are about to see is true. The names have been changed to protect the innocent." All versions of *Dragnet*, back to the 50s, starred Jack Webb (1920-82) as Detective Joe Friday. He always had a partner, who in the 60s was Harry Morgan, better known as Colonel Potter on M*A*S*H in the 70s and 80s. In a very serious show, it was Harry Morgan that provided the comic relief; this usually exhibited itself in a short segment in the beginning of every episode where Morgan's character, Detective Bill Gannon, would engage Webb's character, Friday, into a conversation about some nonsense—like how cutting out coupons saves you big money. Joe would invariably shake his head after asking questions of Gannon and his weekly obsession. Joe, of course, always got the best of him, gently proving his foolishness.

But the above was the only humorous part of this show. The show was so serious it worried me. Being in the 60s, a lot of episodes focused on drugs, which was a scary subject to me anyway. One of the most infamous shows was about a character named Blue Boy who dropped acid. He painted half his face blue, and the scene which made me recoil in horror from the TV set, much like the Gorn in *Star Trek*, was when Joe Friday first revealed the character, pulling Blue Boy's head out of a hole that he was kneeling next to. The garish blue makeup and spaced on expression on his face was frightening. That particular episode taught me about LSD, and for some reason I was afraid that someone would trick me into taking it. In fact, in general, what concerned me about drugs was that someone would force them upon me and I would have a horrible experience.

Another drug episode was one with an incredible but frightening ending. A baby's parents were so high on pot they forgot that they had put their baby in the bathtub and it drowned. The mother's scream upon the discovery of their dead child was unforgettable. Bill Gannon, a veteran detective, said that for the first time in his job he was going to throw up.

Not all drug episodes were as dramatic as the above. In fact, there was an episode that took place entirely in a single room with Joe, Bill, and an obvious Timothy Leary - like character. The whole episode was a debate about drugs, which of course the detectives won.

The seriousness of Jack Webb's character was of course prime for parody, as Dan Aykroyd played him for laughs, against a young Tom Hanks as his partner, in the *Dragnet* movie (1987). Harry Morgan appeared as the Captain of Detectives.

In the 60s and beyond, there was a major part of Television that doesn't exist on network (CBS, NBC, ABC) TV anymore, and has entirely moved to cable channels. This was the televising of movies. In the 60s the only way to see a movie again after it left the theatres was to wait for it to appear, usually quite a few years later, on television. So the movies that would appear on a network for a given season were a big selling point to watch that network. Since movies were more risqué in general than TV, they were often heavily edited. Movies on TV attracted a lot of viewers, and the networks got the idea in the 60s to create movies for TV. This didn't become commonplace, however, until the 70s, which had a glut of TV-movies, some of them good and many not-so-good.

THE BRITISH TV INVASION

Much has been said of the "British Invasion" in music in the 60s, but a similar "invasion" occurred on TV as well during that time.

Danger Man was shown in the United States as *Secret Agent* (1964-66). Its British theme song would be replaced by the famous Johnny Rivers hit, "Secret Agent Man." The show starred Patrick McGoohan who, though he was raised in Britain, was actually born in the United Sates, specifically Astoria, Queens, where I grew up. The show certainly had elements of James Bond, but was also quite different. It had gadgets, but they were simpler and more credible, my favorite being a simple, flat flip-up pair of binoculars that I had to have and made me feel ultra-cool. McGoohan was a religious man and as such did not romance his pretty female guest stars. It was a serious show, but family-friendly.

McGoohan would return to American TV right after *Secret Agent* as a former secret agent in the cult classic *The Prisoner* (1967-68). Though absolutely bewildering at times, I loved this show, probably because it had science fiction elements. At 17 episodes, it was more of a miniseries, though that form of TV did not exist until the 70s. The opening credits (with an awesome theme song accompanying them) espoused for each episode the premise: A secret agent resigns and is summarily kidnapped and brought to a strange resort-like "prison" where he is asked for "information," in particular the reason why he resigned. In each episode some clever scheme hatched up by "Number 2," who was someone different in nearly every episode and leads The Village, as the place is called, is used to find why the former agent resigned, only to fail. The attempts go as far as invading the Prisoner's dreams, making him think he escaped, and even actually letting him escape and returning him (actually, he flies back of his own volition, in a military jet, to prove to his superiors the place exists, but only to be ejected by his co-pilot and parachuting down).

The Prisoner was an intelligent, fascinating show but quirky. For example, the prisoners were kept in The Village by using large balloons (actual weather balloons) that acted like robots and could track a prisoner and retrieve him or smother them. The show's conclusion was much-anticipated—would the Prisoner finally escape? Well, he does, but not in a very spectacular way, and only after a bunch of strange stuff occurs in an underground lair. He, Number 2 and a strange young dude in a top hat are literally driven out of The Village in a large mobile cage by Number 2's dwarf man-servant through Wales, where The Village is revealed to be (though in an earlier episode it was established to be on an island, and in another Eastern Europe), all the way to London, where the Prisoner and the man-servant end up running from a policeman, into a bus, the young man thumbs a ride, and Number 2, all dressed up properly, enters Parliament. I still shake my head over this, and Mr. McGoohan, who penned this final episode himself, went into seclusion as he correctly surmised this just might not go over too well. Still, this is a great show and is suggested viewing for all. [*** Spoiler Alert ***] By the way, it is revealed that Number One is the Prisoner himself ("looking out for Number One" means looking out for yourself), though he was Number 6 in the series. It is speculated that The Prisoner is John Drake, the secret agent from *Secret Agent*, though Patrick McGoohan denied this. Interestingly, the *Secret Agent* theme clearly states, "they've given you a number, and taken away your name."

The Saint was a series that ran in the UK from 1962 to 1969 and first came to the US in 1966. The series starred Roger Moore, who had already appeared on some American television and would later play James Bond from 1973 to 1985, in 7 movies. *The Saint* almost always started with someone recognizing the Saint character, Simon Templar, and then a halo would appear above his head, which he usually craned his head upward to look at. The Saint was a good guy, helping out good people, but had no problem taking money from bad guys and keeping it—he liked a rich lifestyle. The stories were mystery, spy, or even fantasy, but usually entertaining.

The Avengers ran in Britain from 1961 to 1969. It starred Patrick Macnee throughout, and after the first season he was always paired with a beautiful but dangerous woman: Honor Blackman (1962-64), Diana Rigg (1965-68) and Linda Thorsen (1968-69). Honor Blackman would later star as the infamously-named Pussy Galore in the James Bond (*him* again) movie *Goldfinger* (1965). The show did not appear on American television, though, until the Diana Rigg years. I consider this "just in time."

Diana Rigg was so…sexy. She always wore tight (catsuit-tight) or short outfits and would lovingly twist and turn in them in fight scenes. She was a tease, yet also direct at times. One would quickly assume Macnee and Rigg were "doing it" throughout their time together, but this was never made obvious and Macnee seemed to enjoy just being teased. The show's credits sequence was amazing, with an incredible theme and a wonderfully choreographed sequence of nonsense that was nonetheless incredibly stylish and sexy. In one part, Rigg just appeared around a corner with a gun, and did something seemingly innocuous, but ever so lovingly—brushing her hair aside. In a great symbolic erotic moment, Macnee held up a bottle of champagne, and Rigg shot the cork out of it, the bubbly spewing forth like…well, you know.

It almost doesn't matter what *The Avengers* was about (it was "about" an hour LOL) as it contained so much style and sexiness and "hipness." In fact, I'd venture to say that it wasn't really a *great* show, but it was fun to watch. It was, of course, of the spy genre, but with science fiction (complete with mad scientists), humor, and fantasy elements. It never took itself seriously, and in fact was a parody of multiple genres and existing shows. It was just *fun*. It was a bit risqué for American television, and in fact, was aired in late time slots and five Diana Rigg – era episodes were simply too risqué for American TV, including an episode that was mostly S & M!

A VARIETY OF ENTERTAINMENT…

Variety Shows were in their heyday in the 60s. They provided comedy, singing, dancing, circus acts, almost anything you can think of.

The Ed Sullivan Show was broadcast on Sunday nights (8-9 PM) from NYC on CBS during the years 1948 to 1971. We never missed it (well, *practically* never), like many families. During that time period the show booked almost every famous act out there, and many infamous as well. Today, *Ed Sullivan* is mostly recognized as the show that introduced the Beatles to America, in three separate shows aired in February 1963—the beginning of the British music invasion. In the 50s he had Elvis appear three times, the last time only from the waist up because of his "obscene" swiveling hips.

Yes, a lot of greats were on Ed Sullivan. But Ed Sullivan himself had no talent at all. He would just introduce acts—poorly. Though he was on TV forever, he never looked comfortable. And he chose many poor acts for his show. For this he once told Jack Benny on air on his own show that he was paid $100K a year—though he misspoke at first and said he got paid $100 million a year. He couldn't even do a little "bit" with Jack Benny right (and if true, $100K a year for doing what he did back then was amazing).

Some of the minor "acts" on Ed Sullivan were as follows. I remember once he had a tightrope act where the rope was only *a few feet from the floor* and a man just ran over it from one side to another. On *multiple occasions* I watched the "dish-balancing" act where a man would spin about 6-8 dishes, each at the end of a stick, and keep them from falling—that was the whole act (the "Sabre Dance" would play in the background for excitement). There were many acts borrowed literally from a circus—including juggling and animal acts. On too many occasions, Ed would introduce "for the children" Topo Gigio, "the Italian mouse," a hand puppet that talked to him that was supposed to be intentionally funny (note I say *intentional*—my brother and I would always laugh at the effort).

The Dean Martin Show (1965-74) on NBC was generally more entertaining, and was more up for laughs. Crooner Dean Martin was about as mellow as a host could be, and indeed seemed drunk, as was his intention, though it was said the signature glass of whiskey he had in his hand during the intro of the show was apple juice. His jokes were corny but he played against very funny and talented guests. He sang sentimental songs hopelessly out of date but he sang them well. In 1968 Dean introduced The Goldiggers to the show—a dozen girls of varying beautiful characteristics with the voices of angels. At the end of the show Dean, ever-present cigarette in hand, once sang "Welcome to my

World" with the Goldiggers, and then segued to other songs with them. It was...nice.

ABC had *The Hollywood Palace* (1964-70), which had guest hosts and many stars of the time. The most significant act of the show was probably the introduction of the Rolling Stones to America in 1964, with guest host Dean Martin. Dean made it obvious that he didn't think too kindly of them, and asked sarcastically at the completion of their act "Aren't they great?" and rolled his eyes, to which the audience howled; he pleaded when going to commercial for the home audience to return, saying "You wouldn't leave me here alone with the Rolling Stones, would ya?" ("The Rolling Stones, Hollywood Palace 1964," YouTube). However, more important to me was an episode in 1966, when Adam West (1928-2017) appeared as Batman. In fact, they showed footage of him driving to the theatre in his Batmobile, and running on stage to join guest host Milton Berle. After some banter with Berle, he went backstage to change into his civvies, to which Berle quipped, "Well I know it's going to take him awhile to change and meanwhile I have about a few hundred jokes to tell," and a second later Adam West appeared again, this time in a Tux ("Adam West on Hollywood Palace," YouTube).

A new kind of variety show, *Rowan and Martin's Laugh-In*, or *Laugh-In* for short, ran from 1968 to 1973. The show actually was first seen in September 1967 as a one-time special and was so successful it was brought back as a weekly series in January 1968. This variety show broke the format of traditional ones. For one thing, it was "hip." There were psychedelics in the background, a lot of dancing girls in mini skirts and bikinis (with tattoos), and high levels of innuendo. The jokes on the surface were just plain silly, and that's all there was for some, but others mixed in satire, social and political commentary and the aforementioned innuendo. As a youngster in the years it aired, *Laugh-In* just appeared very silly to me, but upon watching some episodes as an adult I realized the heavily-veiled adult humor. For example, things forbidden from TV then, like homosexuality, were alluded to, including one of the members of the comedy troop that acted like a gay stereotype. Made-up words like "bippy" replaced naughty ones. The show's writers, were fresh, including a very young Lorne Michaels, who later created *Saturday Night Live* and has produced most of that show since, to the present. At times, the show was direct in its social and political commentary, having a popular segment where they would award "The Flying Fickle Finger of Fate Award" to a politician or government agency who had, in their opinion, said or done something dumb. Words and phrases used in the show were added to the lexicon of the time, like the aforementioned "bippy" (never identified as to what part of the body it actually was), the phrase "look *that* up in your Funk and Wagnalls!" mentioned earlier (also used by Johnny Carson) and "Sock it to me!" Republican presidential candidate Richard M. Nixon used that last phrase, expressed as a question, when he appeared on the show when running for president in September 1968—an apparent bid to look "hip." Later Nixon would claim that cameo appearance had won him the election, and his Democratic opponent, Hubert Humphrey, who had denied an offer to appear on the show, later said that declining the appearance may have *cost* him the election.

In addition to variety shows, there were music shows. To say they were corny, though, would be an understatement. One was the hugely successful *Lawrence Welk Show* (aired nationally on ABC from 1955-1971). The rhythmless big-band music Welk conducted was old, as was a lot of the Geritol-drinking audience, but people my parents' age liked it as well. Lawrence Welk was born and raised in North Dakota, but in a German community, which gave him a permanent German accent. He would make humorous mistakes reading from cue cards, like reading "World War II" literally as "World War eye eye." He also introduced "Take the 'A' Train" as "Take a train." The music was very white bread, and they were not afraid to play a polka. I liked the show to some degree because they had a bubble machine always going, keeping in line with their "champagne music" motif.

A less successful music show but popular at the time was *Sing Along with Mitch* (1961-64), starring band leader Mitch Miller and his all-male chorus. It was truly a "sing-along" show, as the song's lyrics appeared at the bottom of the TV screen. Mitch appeared as an odd man, with a goatee (and bald head) that was definitely not in style yet, and conducted his band very tersely, without a wand. The chorus was weird, too, always standing at attention with their arms at their sides and all the songs sounding like marches, which made their immobility ever more curious. His hits included "The Yellow Rose of Texas," a traditional American folk song from the 1850s and "The Colonel Bogey March" from the 1957 Alec Guinness movie *The Bridge over the River Kwai*, which was whistled, not sung.

AND HERE NOW THE NEWS…

The way News was presented on TV in the 60s was very different from today, especially earlier in the decade. Of course, one big difference is that we didn't have multiple channels dedicated to it, glitzy graphics ("Chyrons," named after the company that produced them and I worked in a few years) and numerous live action reports. The earliest News program I remember my father watching, in the early 60s, was a local news channel hosted by a guy named John Tilden. John literally just read the news, with no graphics behind him, and no live video reports. There would be reporters out in the field that would telephone him on-air to make reports. The Network news was more sophisticated, with live reports. My father watched Walter Cronkite (1916-2009), on CBS, and I watched him too as I got older. There were no graphics behind "Uncle Wally," as people called him, but he appeared at a desk in the center of a newsroom filled with desks and teletype machines, with people walking around, occasionally ripping some new developments off the teletypes. The teletypes provided a constant background noise, like da-da-da-da-da, that made the viewer perceive that fresh news was constantly being transmitted in. Also, at times a page ripped from a teletype would be handed to Walter, who would announce, "this just in," and immediately read it.

I found the News boring. I wasn't interested in politics then, and, as already noted, I became numb to the constant stream of news about Vietnam battles and their casualties. Then, local news at least became exciting: the Eyewitness News format was introduced, and with it banter and jokes amongst the News team. Finally, local News became entertaining. What made Howard Stern successful in later years—not knowing what silly thing would come out of his mouth next—made local News successful in the late 60s.

In NYC, Eyewitness News premiered on ABC in 1968. Its opening theme song was a very busy instrumental from the 1967 movie *Cool Hand Luke* by Lalo Shifrin and its closing theme song was the beautiful, sleepy instrumental "Forgotten Dreams" (1954), by Leroy Anderson, who also wrote "The Syncopated Clock" (1945), used for 25 years as the intro to *The Late Show*, and the great Christmas Classic *Sleigh Ride* (1948). Eyewitness News starred at the time the acerbic Roger Grimsby and more dignified Bill Buetel as co-anchors. One famous gaffe that my brother and I probably just remember was a promo for the News that aired without Grimsby knowing, where he was lying back smoking a cigarette, finally noticed he was on air, and quickly dropped the cigarette, saying "We're on?" and then trying to recover himself. Geraldo Rivera got his big break on this program, but worked hard for it. He was always sent on dangerous assignments, in which one I remember that he and his camera team were being trapped from escaping some compound, but managed their way out. Rose Ann Scamardella was an early female reporter, who looked like a soccer mom, and became famous (or infamous) by being lampooned by Gilda Radner on *Saturday Night Live* on multiple occasions in the 70s under the name "Roseanne Roseannadanna." The weatherman, Tex Antoine, was the real comedian of the bunch. [Incidentally, he had to make do without a bluescreen behind him; instead there was a permanent map of the United States in which he wrote the temperatures and illustrated the high-pressure areas with a marker.] Ol' Tex was always good for a joke, until in 1976 he stated just after a story about the attempted rape of an eight-year-old girl, "With rape so predominant in the news lately, it is well to remember the words of Confucius: 'If rape is inevitable, lie back and enjoy it'." From that moment, Tex was gone; Roger Grimsby had to make the subsequent apology. Five days later Grimsby, being the smart-ass he was, introduced Antoine's replacement, Storm Field, with "Lie back, relax and enjoy the weather with Storm Field."

STEVEN MANDELI

4 MUSIC AND STYLE

Music and style changed so much from 1960 to 1969. In the early 60s we retained much from the 50s, but by 1969 so much had changed. I don't think any decade had this much change. For example, teenage fashions between 1950 and 1959 were not drastically different, but between 1960 and 1969 (miniskirts!) they were. The 50s did see a music revolution with rock-and-roll, but compare the 50s-style and early-60s-style rock-and-roll to the acid rock of the late 60s (just what Jimmie Hendrix alone could do with an electric guitar!) and you can agree there is a tremendous difference. Let's take a look at the music and style I experienced in the 60s…

MY DAD's MUSIC

The first music I heard was the music my dad played. My mom liked music, but wasn't that into it as my dad. My dad was 31 when the 60s began and 41 when they ended, so his record collection wasn't quite "hip." He had bought a lot of records the previous decade and they reflected the conservative, adult style of that period, pre-rock-and-roll. Some examples:

- "I'm Walking Behind You" (1953) – Eddie Fisher (Star Wars' Carrie Fisher's dad)
- "The Tennessee Waltz" (1950) – Patti Page
- "Goodnight Irene" (1950) – The Weavers
- "Que Sera, Sera (Whatever will be, will be)" (1956)—from the Alfred Hitchcock film *The Man Who Knew Too Much* (1956)
- "Vaya Con Dios (Go with God)" (1953) – Les Paul and Mary Ford
- "The Yellow Rose of Texas" (1955) – Mitch Miller
- "Marianne" – The Easy Riders (1956) – A calypso song
- "(How Much) is That Doggie in the Window" (1953) – Patti Page
- "Gonna get Along Without You Now" (1956) – Patience and Prudence. There would be many covers of this song, including a disco version by Vio-

la Wills in 1979.

All of the above were purchased as 10-inch 78-RPM records. The singers noted are the covers my father bought. This is important to note as in the 50s successful songs immediately had many covers made by many different artists. All of the above were very successful; many were long-time No. 1 hits. In fact, the Mitch Miller (yes, *him* again) hit above knocked Bill Haley's "(We're Gonna) Rock Around The Clock" from the top of the Best Sellers chart in the U.S.

My father played the above records throughout the 60s and beyond, so they became very familiar to me. Some I liked better than others; for example, when I was young, I loved "(How Much) is That Doggie in the Window," as it actually had dogs barking in it.

My father of course bought records in the 60s, this time 12-inch 33-RPM "LP" (Long Playing) records, but in the 60s he bought a lot of German *Schlagers*. According to *Wikipedia*, *Shlagers* were "a style of popular music prevalent in Central and Northern Europe, and Southeast Europe…The style emerged in Europe after the Second World War, partly as a backlash against American rock and roll, and uses simple patterns of music. Typical *schlager* tracks are either sweet, highly sentimental ballads with a simple, catchy melody or light pop tunes. Lyrics typically center on love, relationships and feelings…Musically, *schlager* bears similarities to styles such as easy listening music." In particular, *German* and *Austrian schlagers* (he had both), which reached their peak of popularity in the 60s in those countries, are considered by Germans to be "their Country Music and in fact American Country and TexMex are both major elements in the Schlager culture."

I always considered these "Schlagers" as German folk music, and it appears I was basically right. Though I only knew a smattering of German, I knew they were sentimental and harkened to the "old homeland (*heimat*)," exactly in those words in one song I remember. My father was born and raised in Romania, but in a German town. When he missed "home," he would play these syrupy songs. My brother and I would laugh at them and be embarrassed by them (especially when my dad set his record player to "full blast"), but he was just being sentimental about his childhood, as I am now in writing this book.

MY EARLY FAVORITES

Of course, I heard plenty of music outside of my home, on AM radios and in Muzak (though it wasn't called that then), movies, TV, etc. I liked the happy tunes, like Petula Clark's "My Love" (1965). Miss Clark, CBE (1932-   ) was a powerhouse singer that was part of a "gentle" British invasion of music that actually was an international invasion. Her "My Love" album is said to "[encapsulate] the sound of popular music in the mid 1960s." Note the term "popular music." This essentially meant non-rock-and-roll music.

I also enjoyed pretty music. One of my favorites (and still beautiful to me) was "More (Theme from *Mondo Cane*)" (1962). As a friend of mine puts it, "More" was a theme from a film completely incongruous to it. As "More" is arguably one of the most beautiful movie themes of all time, the movie it was a theme to, *Mondo Cane* (Italian for "Dog World") was an ugly documentary film with the apparent point to shock the audience as to how backward and animalistic humanity (then called "Mankind") was, all around the world. [BTW, I liked the film as an adult, but it would have frightened me in 1962.]

I liked The Beach Boys pretty much (who didn't?), who filled the 60s with cool-sounding hits, as well as Jan and Dean who sang exactly like them, though it is said it was the other way around. I actually remember listening to, on our little AM radio, "Hey Little Cobra" (1963), by The Rip Chords. I also actually remember listening to "See You In September" (1966) by The Happenings. The Turtles' haunting "Happy Together" (1967) was a favorite of mine, as was another "haunting" classic, "California Dreaming" (1965), by The Mamas & the Poppas. I also enjoyed a hit song that was an instrumental (in the 60s we had hit songs that were instrumentals), "Telstar" (1962), by The Tornados but also The Ventures. I probably liked that song because it was upbeat, electronic, and about the first communications satellite. I loved "Elusive Butterfly" (1966) by Bob Lind, as did many others; it was not only a hit for Lind but covered many times in many ways. It still almost makes me cry. I liked pop rock music in general, as long as it was happy and peppy (or awesomely sentimental and cool).

An enormously successful group of the 60s (in fact, called "the most popular band before the Beatles") that sang more "traditional" 50s-like music was Frankie Valli and the Four Seasons, which thankfully is still popular today in part because of the Broadway hit *Jersey Boys* and also because Frankie still performs (and is still fabulous!). Frankie's signature falsetto voice led Top Ten songs that brought us through the 60s—"Sherry" and "Big Girls Don't Cry" (1962); "Walk Like a Man" and "Candy Girl" (1963); "Dawn (Go Away)," "Ronnie," "Rag Doll," and "Save It for Me" (1964); "Let's Hang On!" (1965), "Working my Way Back to You," "Tell it to the Rain" and "I've Got You Under My Skin" (1966), "C'mon, Marianne" (1967), and Frankie's solo outing in 1967, "I Can't Take My Eyes Off of You." Four of the aforementioned hits reached #1 on the charts, with Frankie's solo coming close at #2. A similar falsetto was used by Lou Christie, not as successful as Frankie, but to great effect, in "Lightnin' Strikes" (1965, #1), "Rhapsody in the Rain" (1966) and "I'm Gonna Make You Mine" (1969).

What I didn't care for much were The Beatles(!). I certainly liked some of their tunes, especially the earlier, simpler ones, like "I Wanna Hold Your Hand" (1963), but I felt that too much fuss was made over them. I had older, female, cousins that simply adored them and spoke of them constantly, and I guess I kind of rebelled against that. I love The Beatles, but I never became a super-fan. However, they changed music forever and were the most successful band ever, with estimated sales of 178 million records in the U.S. and over 800 million physical/digital albums worldwide. They have had more number-one albums on the British charts and sold more singles in the UK than any other act. As of this writing, they hold the record for most number-one hits on the Hot 100 chart with twenty.

America's answer to the Beatles were The Monkees, though one of its members, Davy Jones, was British. The Monkees was actually thought of as a TV show (about a band) *before* the Beatles became insanely popular, in 1962, but the creator failed sell the show. Because of the popularity of the Beatles, selling the show became easier later in the 60s. Originally *The Monkees* TV show was to star an existing band, but it was decided to create a new band. The first Monkees single ("Last Train to Clarksville") was released right before the series, and became a #1 hit. Their sitcom series did well during its short run from 1966-68 and the Monkees band continued to play until 1971. The Monkees have sold more than 75 million records worldwide and had international hits, including the above and "Pleasant Valley Sunday," "Daydream Believer," and "I'm a Believer." At their peak in 1967, the band outsold the Beatles and the Rolling Stones combined.

I don't think I bought any albums for myself in the 60s, but of course I bugged my parents for some children's fare. One was the aforementioned Batman album of 1966. During the time my brother and I attended the Queens Nautical Cadets (which I will talk of later), my parents would have some time without us monsters and occasionally they surprised us with something good. One night in 66 they announced they had two surprises for us—they had ordered a Color TV and they had gotten The Batman Album!

The Batman Album was weird, but my brother and I enjoyed it. Most of it wasn't music from the show but contained original compositions by Neil Hefti (1922-2008), who had written the Batman theme and later scored both the *Odd Couple* movie and TV series. The compositions were quirky, some with sound effects, but the whole thing did seem like Batman.

Shortly later I wanted the Green Hornet album. This crime-fighting duo had to have an album as well, and thus it was made. The Green Hornet Theme was composed and executed by the great Al Hirt (1922-99), trumpeter extraordinaire and band leader. That was on the album, but the rest of the tracks seemed liked recycled elevator music, each with Green Hornet-type titles.

"POPULAR" MUSIC

They now call it just "pop" music, and it's top-40 stuff now, but in the 60s it was more traditional, conservative music as opposed to rock-and-roll, rock, and the other new forms of music coming out. That *didn't* mean it was like the slow music of the 50s. In fact, the line that separated "Popular" music from "soft rock" could be quite thin.

One genre within popular music was Easy Listening. This would include

Instrumentals with strong strings by orchestras such as *101 Strings*. In the NY area, WPAT (Paterson, NJ) would play this kind of music all the time, and it was always the station playing in our local barber shop. Hence, my brother and I always referred to this stringy music as "Barber Shop Music."

Annunzio Paolo Mantovani (1905-1980) was the conductor of a string-rich orchestra (using cascading strings) much popular in the 50s and 60s and even into the 70s. Personally, his renditions of "Greensleeves" and "Stranger in Paradise" are always moving to me.

One master of 60s pop would include a man who you have probably never heard of but you have probably heard his work—Burt Kaempfert (1923-80). Burt graced us with "Strangers in the Night," the number 1 hit sung by Frank Sinatra in 1966; "Danke Schoen" (1962), Wayne Newton's signature song; "L-O-V-E," recorded by the late great Nat King Cole in 1966; "A Swingin' Safari" (1962), and the happy tunes "Afrikaan Beat" and "That Happy Feeling" (both 1962).

Herb Alpert (1935-   ) was a pop music icon in the 60s, highly successful with his "Tijuana Brass" band. His music, to me, was the "sound of the 60s," at least for popular music. Over his career he produced five No. 1 albums and 29 albums total on the Billboard Album chart, 14 of them platinum and 15 gold. He had 19 Top Ten singles in the 60s alone. His Number 1 hits of the 60s were: "A Taste of Honey" (1965), "Casino Royale" (1967), the awesome theme composed by Burt Bacharach for the "unofficial" James Bond comedic movie of the same year and title starring David Niven as the "real" James Bond; "A Banda (Ah Bahn-da)" (1967), and "This Guy's in Love with You" (1968). Other popular favorites include the humorous songs "Tijuana Taxi" (1965) and "Spanish Flea" (1966).

Another successful icon of 60s music that was a big contributor to its "sound" was Burt Bacharach (1928-   ), a composer, songwriter, record producer, pianist, and singer. Together with lyricists like Hal David (1921-2012), Burt composed many hits specifically for many great performers in the 60s—including "Please Stay" (The Drifters, 1961), "Baby It's You" (The Shirelles, 1961), "Only Love Can Break a Heart" (Gene Pitney, 1962), "Take it Easy on Yourself" (Jerry Butler, 1962), "Don't Make Me Over" (Dionne Warwick, 1962), "Blue on Blue" (Bobby Vinton, 1963), "(They Long to Be) Close to You" (1963, recorded by The Carpenters in 1970, who made it a #1 single), "Anyone Who Had a Heart" (Dionne Warwick, 1963), "Walk on By" (Dionne Warwick, 1964), "What the World Needs Now Is Love" (Jackie DeShannon, 1965), "What's New Pussycat" (Tom Jones, 1965), "Alfie" (1966, a big hit for Dionne Warwick in 1967), "Casino Royale" (Herb Alpert & The Tijuana Brass, 1967, for the movie of the same name), "The Look of Love" (Dusty Springfield, 1967, also for *Casino Royale*), "I Say a Little Prayer" (Dionne Warwick, 1967), "One Less Bell to Answer" (1967, made into a #2 hit in 1970 by The Fifth Dimension), "Do You Know the Way to San Jose" (1968, Dionne Warwick), "This Guy's in Love with You" (1968, performed and sung by Herb

Alpert) "I'll Never Fall in Love Again" (1969, Dionne Warwick) and "Raindrops Keep Fallin' on My Head" (1969, BJ Thomas, for the movie *Butch Cassidy and the Sundance Kid* and to which my sister and her Kindergarten class danced to circa 1971).

And that's just a *partial* list of Burt's work in the 60s. His hits *preceded* the 60s as well (including one for Perry Como in 1958), and went through the 70s, 80s, and 90s. As of 2014, Bacharach had written 73 US and 52 UK Top 40 hits. Unfortunately, many younger people may only know him for his brief appearances in all three *Austin Powers* movies (1997, 1999 and 2002).

Bobby Darrin (1936-73) performed in a range of musical genres, including jazz, pop, rock-and-roll, folk, swing, and country. His 1958 song "Splish, Splash" was a rock 'n roll hit that reached #3 in 1958, and his song "Dream Lover" was also a rock 'n roll hit, in 1959. But in that same year he also sang "Mack the Knife," which reached #1 and won a Grammy Award in 1960. It was a jazzy number from a German *opera*. He followed it with "Beyond the Sea," which also charted well. In the 60s he continued with jazzy and folksy records.

A lot of old-fashioned crooners did well in the 60s, like Dean Martin, Frank Sinatra, and even Jim Neighbors (1930-2017), who played Gomer Pyle in the TV series *Gomer Pyle, U.S.M.C.* (1964-69). Frank Sinatra vocalized 32 albums released in the 60s. This includes a number one hit, "Strangers in the Night" (as noted above, composed by Bert Kaempfert) in 1966 and another #1 in 1967 with his daughter Nancy ("Something Stupid"). He also did well with "My Way" in 1969. Dean Martin sang a lot on his show, and sold 21 albums of his crooning in the 60s. His signature tune, "Everybody Loves Somebody," knocked the Beatles' "A Hard Day's Night" off number one in the United States in 1964. Jim Neighbors recorded 28 albums in his career; two of them went gold in the 60s (1966 and 1968).

There were many, many other popular crooners of the 60s, who may have not had many hits but sold a fair amount of records anyway and always found their way to the variety shows.

FOLK MUSIC AT SCHOOL

Folk music was popular in the early 60s and accepted by many people, even my parochial school teachers. They were simple, gentle, and had good messages (or so it seemed) that were in sync with Catholic values (peace, love, etc.). One of the favorite folk groups of my teachers was Peter, Paul and Mary (and not because of their Catholic-sounding names).

A number of this trio's songs were played in class. This included "Puff the Magic Dragon" (1963), about childhood innocence and not marijuana, as some had suggested. Also included was "If I had a Hammer" (1962), a hit of the trio actually written by Pete Seeger years previous, in 1949. Another favorite was "Where Have All the Flowers Gone?" (1962), also written by Pete Seeger. Yet another was "Blowin' in the Wind" (1963), written by Bob Dylan in 1962.

Bob Dylan (1941-) wrote songs about social unrest in the 60s that were adopted as anthems by the civil rights and anti-war movements. "Blowin' in the Wind" was adapted by him from "No More Auction Block," an African-American spiritual sung by former slaves who fled to Canada after Britain abolished slavery in 1833. Dylan also wrote and sang "The Times They Are a-Changin'" in 1964, an anthem for the rapid change going on in the 60s, this one inspired by 18th and 19th century Irish and Scottish ballads.

Another folk song played in school was "Both Sides Now" (1967), sung by Judy Collins and written by Joni Mitchel. Another, a bit later, was Gordon Lightfoot's beautiful "If You Could Read My Mind" (1970).

Yet another song they played was "Michael Row the Boat Ashore," not exactly a folk song but another African-American spiritual, from the Civil War days.

MOTOWN AND RHYTHM & BLUES

Motown was a record company founded by Berry Gordy Jr. (1929-) in 1959, though not actually named "Motown" until 1960. "Motown" was short for "Motor City," as Detroit was called when it was the center of auto manufacturing in the US, as it was in the 60s. In the 60s, Motown and its subsidiary labels were the most successful proponents of what came to be known as the Motown Sound, a style of "pop" soul music, or Rhythm and Blues. This "sound" gave us great, successful music by African-American bands and singers that is a major part of the 60s musical tapestry.

"Shop Around," the Miracles' first number 1 R&B hit, peaked at number two on the Billboard Hot 100 in 1960, with one million records sold. On April 14, 1960, Motown and subsidiary label Tamla Records merged into a new company called Motown Record Corporation. A year later, the Marvelettes scored Tamla's first US number-one pop hit, "Please Mr. Postman." By the mid-1960s, the company, with the help of songwriters and producers such as "Smokey" Robinson, had become a major force in the music industry. From 1961 to 1971, Motown had 110 top 10 hits. Top artists on the Motown label during this period included the Supremes (initially including Diana Ross), the Four Tops, and the Jackson 5, while Stevie Wonder, Marvin Gaye, the Marvelettes, and the Miracles had hits on the Tamla label. Another label of Motown, which Gordy named after himself, featured the Temptations, the Contours, and Martha and the Vandellas. Yet another label, called V.I.P., included groups such as the Velvelettes and the Spinners, while the Soul label included such groups as Gladys Knight and the Pips.

The significance of Motown in the 60s was no less than historic. In a decade of racial tension, and segregation still being enforced in areas, it gave us music that was enjoyed by all, white and black, and not just in the US, but world-wide. Smokey Robinson: "I would come to the South in the early days of Motown and the audiences would be segregated. Then they started to get the Motown music and we would go back and the audiences were integrated and the kids were dancing together and holding hands."

THE INVASION

The "British Invasion" was the occurrence in the mid-60s when rock and pop music acts from the United Kingdom, as well as other aspects of British culture, became popular in the United States. The major pop and rock groups such as the Beatles, Rolling Stones, the Dave Clark Five, the Kinks, Herman's Hermits, the Animals, and the Who were at the forefront of the invasion, but the invasion included many others. The first song that from Britain reached #1 in the U.S. was the aforementioned instrumental "Telstar" in 1962, played by The Tornados but written and produced by Joe Meek, who was anything but like his surname, having anger issues and paranoid delusions that culminated in him killing his landlady and then himself in 1967.

Petula Clark, whose song "My Love" that I enjoyed so much when it came out in 1966, brought a number of pop hits to the U.S. in the mid-60s, including: "Downtown" (1965), "I Know a Place" (1965), "I Couldn't Live Without Your Love" (1966), and "Colour My World" (1967), all in the top 50 in the US.

Also mentioned previously for her lusty rendition of "The Look of Love" (1967) was the incredible pop star Dusty Springfield (AKA Mary O'Brien; 1939-99). She sang an early invasion hit, "I Only Want To Be With You" (1963), an upbeat, likeable song, to be later covered by many others, including the Bay City Rollers (1976) and Nicolette Larsen (1982). Later, she sang, "Wishin' and Hopin'" (1964), "I Just Don't Know What to Do with Myself" (1964), "You Don't Have to Say You Love Me" (1966; one of my favorites), and "Son of a Preacher Man" (1968). From *Wikipedia*: "With her distinctive sensual mezzo-soprano sound, she was an important blue-eyed soul singer and at her peak was one of the most successful British female performers, with six top 20 singles on the United States Billboard Hot 100 and sixteen on the United Kingdom Singles Chart from 1963 to 1989... International polls have named Springfield among the best female rock artists of all time." She was also described as "the finest white soul singer of her era." Springfield experienced a career slump for several years. However, in collaboration with the Pet Shop Boys, she returned to the Top 10 of the UK and US charts in 1987 with "What Have I Done to Deserve This?" Unfortunately, she developed breast cancer during her comeback and died from it in 1999.

Other groups that were part of the British Invasion included Peter and Gordon, who sang "A World Without Love" (1964), #1 in the UK and #12 in the US. The Animals provided us with the international #1 hit, "The House of the Rising Sun" (1964). Herman's Hermits gave us the UK #1 hit, "I'm Into Something Good" (1964, written by the US's husband-wife team of Carole King and Gerry Goffin), the US #1 hit, "Mrs. Brown, You've Got a Lovely

Daughter" (1965), and another US #1 hit, "I'm Henery the Eighth, I Am" (1965). The Troggs gave us a US #1 hit, "Wild Thing" (1965). Donovan gave us the US #1 hit "Sunshine Superman" in 1966 as well as the #2 hit, "Mellow Yellow" in that same year. "Lulu" provided us with "To Sir, With Love" in 1967, a US #1 hit from the movie of the same name. Chad and Jeremy gave us "A Summer Song" in 1964, a US #7 hit. Gerry and the Pacemakers gave us "Don't Let the Sun Catch You Crying," #4 in the US in 1964, as well as "Ferry Cross The Mersey" in 1965, which hit #6 in the US. Tom Jones gave us the vocals for the Burt Bacharach – Hal David tune "What's Up, Pussycat?" in 1965 from the movie of the same name, reaching #3 in the US. Jonathan King gave us the quizzical but beautiful "Everyone's Gone to the Moon" in 1964, which reached #4 in the UK and #17 in the US. He also discovered and named the band Genesis.

King was sentenced to 7 years in prison in 2001 for having sexually assaulted five boys, aged 14 and 15, in the 1980s. He was released on parole in March 2005.

COUNTRY MUSIC

Country music gained popularity in the 1960s. Many older-generation listeners turned to country music as the mainstream grew "rocky." Greats like Johnny Cash (1932-2003) thrived in the 60s with people of all ages, including my father's generation, and indeed some of my friends' dads were into Johnny's music.

But before Johnny there were early successes in country music in the 60s. One of my favorites at the time was "King of the Road" (1964), a catchy tune about the life of a wandering hobo written and performed by Roger Miller (1936-92). It was highly successful, reaching #1 in Country and Easy Listening, and peaking at #4 in the Billboard Top 100. Eddy Arnold had 8 #1 country albums in the 60s, including the highly successful "I Want to Go With You" album that did well also on Easy Listening charts. Other greats included Ray Price, Tammy Wynette and Charley Pride.

One of my favorites and popular with my family was Glen Campbell (1936-2017). His hits in the 60s included "Gentle on my Mind" (1967), "By the Time I Get to Phoenix" (1967), "Wichita Lineman" (1968), "Galveston" (1969) and "True Grit" (1969), for the John Wayne movie *True Grit* (1969), which Mr. Campbell also starred in. Many of Glen's songs did extremely well on the Country charts, but also did well on Billboard, showing a great general appeal. In 1969 Glen got his own variety show, the *Glen Campbell Goodtime Hour* (1969-72), which was regular viewing at my house.

One of my personal country favorites from the 60s is Canadian/New Zealander Gale Garnett (1942-   ). Her hit song, "We'll Sing in the Sunshine" (1964) was considered Country, Pop, and Folk, reaching #4 on Billboard. I also have to mention Country and Pop singer Bobbi Martin, whose delicious if outdated theme of the dedicated housewife, "For the Love of Him," reached #1 in Easy Listening in early 1970.

But back to Johnny Cash, the "Man in Black," who has been described as "one of the most influential musicians of the 20th century and one of the best-selling music artists of all time, having sold more than 90 million records worldwide." Although primarily remembered as a country music icon, his sound also embraced rock and roll, rockabilly, blues, folk, and gospel. Cash won the rare honor of multiple inductions in the Country Music, Rock and Roll, and Gospel Music Halls of Fame. His #1 country hits in the 60s, which also did well on Billboard, were "Ring of Fire" (1963), "Understand Your Man" (1964), "Folsom Prison Blues" (1968; live from Folsom Prison), "Daddy Sang Bass" (1968), and "A Boy Name Sue" (1969). And these hits from the 60s are just a slice of a decades-long career.

MUSIC TAKES ACID

The late 60s saw a different kind of music arrive, and I wasn't very fond of it at the time. It has been known as "acid" rock or "psychedelic" rock, as it was related to drug experiences. As already noted, drugs concerned me, so I didn't really like these songs at all, though admittedly I do like some now and consider them classics.

The "good" songs, in my humble opinion, included "White Rabbit" (1967) by Jefferson Airplane (with the great lyric, "Feed your head!") and "Purple Haze" by The Jimmie Hendrix Experience in that same year.

Jim Morrison and the Doors shot to prominence with a No. 1 hit in 1967, "Light My Fire." In 1968 this song was beautifully reinvented by blind singer-songwriter Jose Feliciano (probably best-known for the Christmas classic "Feliz Navidad"), who made it a hit again (No. 3). His rendition sparked re-interest in the Doors version, which once again made the Billboard Hot 100. The Doors attained notoriety when performing the song live on *The Ed Sullivan Show* broadcast on September 17, 1967. They were told by a producer to change their lyric, "girl we couldn't get much *higher*" to "girl, we couldn't get much *better*," to remove the possible drug reference, which the sponsors didn't like. The band promised to make this change, then ignored it when performing live. Ed Sullivan was pissed and never had them appear on his show again, despite the fact that they had been in negotiations to do six shows.

There were more hits by the Doors, but Jim got himself into scrapes with the law due to his alcoholism and drug addiction. He was found dead by his girlfriend Pamela Courson in a Paris apartment bathtub on July 3, 1971. There was no autopsy performed and the cause of death was recorded as "natural causes," but 40 years later singer Marianne Faithfull claimed her drug-dealing ex-boyfriend "killed Morrison" by giving him heroin which was "too strong." Morrison died at the age of 27, as did his girlfriend three years later. He belongs to the infamous "27 Club," which includes an unusually large number of musicians and artists who died at that age, usually of overdoses, alcoholism, homicide and suicide. It includes Brian Jones, Jimi Hendrix, Janis Joplin, Kurt Cobain, Amy Winehouse, and Anton Yelchin, among many others; a total of 70 have been identified thus far.

The Grateful Dead started in 1965 and played a mixture of musical styles, including rock, psychedelia, and even just jams. Among other venues, they played at countercultural figure Ken Kesey's "acid tests," parties that centered on the use of LSD, or "acid." Audio engineer and chemist Owsley Stanley, known as the "Acid King," whose acid supplied the "tests," became the band's financial backer in 1966, buying them sound equipment as well and renting a house for them.

Ron "Pigpen" McKernan, one of the band's founders, played keyboards and harmonica for the Dead until shortly before his death in 1973 at the age of 27 (yes, another member of the Club). He died from complications from liver damage brought on by alcoholism. Keyboardist Brent Mydland died of a drug overdose in 1990. Founding member Jerry Garcia died in 1995, from a number of conditions, after struggling with drug addiction for years. The remaining Dead and new Dead have a loyal fan base known as "deadheads" that make them popular to this day.

Well-established bands got into the acid movement. The Beatles did, in their "Revolver" album (1966) and "Yellow Submarine" (1969), the latter of which was also a movie in 1968 that was odd but not bad—though at the time it was in theaters you couldn't catch me dead there (my older female cousins, though, talked about the movie incessantly and I think they saw it many times). "Strawberry Fields Forever" and "Penny Lane" were psychedelic singles released together by The Beatles in 1967 and premiered to American audiences as early "videos" on *The Ed Sullivan Show* (which I distinctly remember) and I am told *The Hollywood Palace* as well. Even the seemingly squeaky-clean Beach Boys got into the act, with "Good Vibrations" (1966), a classic some have called one of the best rock-and-roll songs of all time. It was the result of the Beach Boys' Brian Wilson's foray into psychedelic drugs.

THEMES AND INCIDENTAL MUSIC

Themes for TV and Movies were awesome in the 60s. Consider the theme for the classic western *The Magnificent Seven* (1960, by Elmer Bernstein), repeated in the 2016 re-make and used for years in Marlboro cigarettes commercials, the "Marlboro Man" enjoying a smoke after a long day of cattle driving. Other incredible movie themes and scores included those from *Breakfast at Tiffany's* (1961 – including "Moon River," by Henry Mancini), *Lawrence of Arabia* (1962, by Maurice Jarre), *The Pink Panther* (1963, by Henry Mancini), *Doctor Zhivago* (1965, by Maurice Jarre), *The Sound of Music* (1965, by Rodgers & Hammerstein), and the Bond movies of the 60s—*Dr. No* (1962, by Monty Norman, composer of the original James Bond theme), *From Russia With Love* (1963, by

John Barry), *Goldfinger* (1964, theme powerfully sung by Shirley Bassey, music by John Barry), *Thunderball* (1965, John Barry again), *You Only Live Twice* (1967, John Barry), and *On Her Majesty's Secret Service* (1969, guess what?—John Barry).

Television shows also had impressive themes. A lot of care was put into composing these. The themes were rousing if they needed to be, funny if that was applicable, etc. I already have raved about the theme to the *Avengers*. The theme for the *Prisoner* was great as well, but there were so many, much too many to mention here.

"Incidental music," or background music, is the music played in media like TV to provide a certain mood that enhances a scene. 60s television loved incidental music, and it was used fluently. Watch a modern show and listen for background music. You might hear something, you might not. When you hear something it probably will be low-key. In the 60s you will be barraged with music, and not low-key. Just listen to one episode of the original *Star Trek*. Each episode was rich in incidental music. In fact, fans will buy CDs of this incidental music (I did!). As a comparison, *Star Trek: The Next Generation* (1987-1994) has much more low-key background music, with only some of it popular with fans and marketable. Incidental music was certainly at a pinnacle in the 60s, in my opinion.

A lot of Jazz found its way into incidental music in movies and television, especially in the early 60s. *Take Five* was a Jazz piece composed by Paul Desmond and originally performed by the Dave Brubeck Quartet. When originally released in 1959, it didn't make any chart records, but when re-released in 1961 it became the best-selling jazz single—ever. This piece itself found its way in many movies and TV shows, including NBC's Today Show in the early 60s. *A Charlie Brown Christmas* (1965) featured a jazz score by pianist Vince Guaraldi. My favorite TV show of all time, *The Twilight Zone*, used Jazz frequently, and quite honestly turned me on to Jazz. The episode "Dead Man's Shoes" (1962) had an awesome soundtrack of Jazz music. "A Passage for Trumpet" (1960), starring Jack Klugman, was about a washed-out alcoholic Jazz trumpeter, with many Jazz bits seemingly played by Klugman.

A great contributor to *Twilight Zone* incidental music, though not Jazz, was the Academy-award winning American composer Bernard Herrmann (1911-75). Mr. Herrmann provided incredible soundtracks to Hitchcock's *Psycho*, *North by Northwest*, *The Man Who Knew Too Much*, and *Vertigo*. He also composed scores for many other movies, including *Citizen Kane*, *The Day the Earth Stood Still*, *Fahrenheit 451* (my favorite), *Cape Fear*, and *Taxi Driver*.

I actually looked forward to some of the music found in commercials. A lot of times these were pretty, such as the little ditty used for Chock full 'o Nuts coffee ("Chock full 'o Nuts is that heavenly coffee, heavenly coffee, heavenly coffee… Chock full 'o Nuts is that heavenly coffee, better coffee a millionaire's money can't buy"). I of course love the Marlboro commercial. I also liked the wonderfully hum-drum music used for Colt 45 malt liquor, which had previously been used by genius 60s comic Ernie Kovacs (1919-62) in his *Nairobi Trio* skits, the tune being "Solfeggio" by Robert Maxwell. [The Nairobi Trio were two men and a woman, including Ernie Kovacs and often his wife, with gorilla masks on and wearing bowler hats and overcoats; the comedy was in how they reacted to each other sneakily hitting each other on the head.]

MUSIC NOTES

Notice I didn't say "musical notes." These are just general notes I'd like to make about 60s music.

First of all, I wasn't as much "into" 60s music as I was 60s television. I didn't get a stereo portable radio until 1970, the beginning of my teen years, and a portable cassette player until 1971. Around that time I really got into music, and would make decent recordings with my cassette player from my radio. I had attempted to record music from our six-transistor AM radio in the 60s into our ancient mini reel-to-reel Aiwa tape recorder, but the results were disastrous. As for buying records, I really didn't have much money for that.

There was a lot of music in the 60s that I discovered in the 70s, and recorded it, to my delight. Some of my favorite bands began in the 60s or just missed the decade—Genesis (1967), The Moody Blues (1967), and ELO (1970). In the 80s I had money and bought many albums of my favorites. [I did love the Moody Blues' "Nights in White Satin" (1967) when it first appeared.]

There is one thing I'd definitely like to say about how music was produced in the 60s as opposed to later. In the 60s "stereo" meant "stereo." You would hear different parts of a recording on the left and right channels. Sometimes it was as obvious as the instrumental part on one side and the vocal part on the other. Nowadays 60s music and more modern music is re-mixed basically into one channel, whether you have a 5.1 or 7.1 sound system or not. I don't understand this. I think true stereo was great. You could adjust your balance and hear different "sides" to the music. Now balance does seemingly nothing. It appears that modern music must be loud on all channels, with no separation. As a result, newer-mixed 60s songs are generally lousy mixes, louder and clearer than what we had before, but the same on all channels.

I also don't understand the modern fascination with vinyl records. Purists would claim that without digitalization music sounds better, but quite honestly I think there are very few people on this Earth that could tell a difference. Vinyl wears down, like it always did. The more you play a vinyl record, the more you destroy its fidelity, and there was never a good way to eliminate static created by dust.

Be that as it may, the music of the 60s was rich and varied, much more than later decades. I am not saying it was "better" per se, but it possessed originality that we generally no longer see. Maybe it's all been done before, and originality is not something to expect as much. I don't know, but all genres of 60s music sound great to me, and it will always take me back…

STEVEN MANDELI

WHAT I MISSED – INCLUDING WOODSTOCK

Because of my young age, I missed a lot. I know people who went to Woodstock (actually in Bethel, NY) in August 1969 and had a unique experience. All the major bands were there, especially the folk and acid rock ones—Arlo Guthrie, Joan Baez, Santana, The Grateful Dead, Janis Joplin, The Who, Jefferson Airplane, Crosby, Stills, Nash and Young (CSNY), and Jimi Hendrix, just to give you a sample. It was three days of 24 hours each of rock music and whatever you were imbibing and popping. I am told some of the acts sucked—Janis Joplin was too stoned to make a decent performance, as were The Grateful Dead, and Jimi Hendrix's band didn't handle well playing 9:00 on a Monday morning that was supposed to see the concert already ended (and indeed many fans had already left). The health hazards from lack of enough toilets and running water are mythic. But it was an Experience.

Even if I was older I don't think I would have gone to something like Woodstock. In fact, my brother was near 18 and didn't but I know people about the same age who did, and said it was a great time. Of course, memory fades a bit after half a century...

I missed the whole hippie counterculture movement, which at the time I was OK with missing as hippies and their drugs worried me. As I said, I wasn't into acid rock, though I recognize some of it now as great. As for the hippies, they seemingly disappeared, and ended up blending in with "The Establishment." A statement back then was that nobody wants to live past thirty because by then you would become part of that Establishment. Curiously, there was no rash of suicides of people aged 29 in the 60s or 70s or any time.

By the way, I finally did get to Woodstock—in September 2017. The area has been well-kept, and is in fact beautiful. On July 1, 2006, Bethel Woods Center for the Arts opened on the site of the original Woodstock Festival and hosted the New York Philharmonic. CSNY closed out the inaugural season in August 2006, bringing them back to Bethel for the first time since the original festival. The Museum in the Center is fascinating to anyone interested in Woodstock and the period of the late 60s. Concerts continue in the Center to this day, and have included performers like: Chicago; America; Bob Dylan; Lynyrd Skynyrd with The Marshall Tucker Band; Earth, Wind & Fire; Arlo Guthrie; Richie Havens; and many more.

STYLE

Style changed incredibly in the 60s, I would say more than any other decade. Looking at what was considered fashionable for young men and women's clothing from 1960 and comparing it with 1969 one sees an extraordinary difference. Hair length for men went from very short to very long in the 60s, to the consternation of many parents, including mine. Women's skirt lengths changed in the opposite direction, from long to short. Cars changed enormously from 1960 to 1969. Home décor did as well, if you wanted to keep "modern." It was generally difficult to keep up if you were concerned with being conceived as modern, or "mod" as it came to be called. Let's look at what changed so much in style in the 60s.

WOMEN'S FASHION IN THE EARLY 60s

First of all I'd like to say that I liked women's fashion throughout the 60s, though the early 60s was less "revealing." Women looked great in the styles of the early 60s, with black high heels being standard and not associated to foot fetishes, as in our day. I have researched (lovingly) what the heck is the difference between "high heels" and "stilettos" but I am still confused and don't really care. Suffice it to say that all stilettos have a high heel and what we generally call "high heels," certainly in the context of the 60s, are high heeled shoes with a thin heel that was raised off the ground at a "reasonable" distance and was usually black. This to me provides a very nice look at women's feet, even though they are uncomfortable (I hear) and unnatural and just simply bizarre if you think too much about them.

Women now use pantyhose, a combination of panties and stockings, and when wearing pants might wear "knee-highs" or simply socks. When women wore dresses and skirts in the early 60s, which they mostly wore, they wore stockings. As dresses got shorter, there were titillating times when a woman wearing stockings crossed her legs and you could possibly see the tops of the stockings. But I digress! Though pantyhose was invented before the 60s (patented in 1956) and were manufactured to a limited degree in the 60s, more women wore stockings than pantyhose throughout the 60s. In 1970, U.S. sales of pantyhose exceeded stockings for the first time, and it has remained that way since then.

So, continuing in our "dressing" of the woman of the early 60s, we have the black high heels so far and stockings. Of course, we need panties added as well, and a bra. Though bras are optional today, they remained with women through most of the 60s. Bras in fact became very stylish and enhanced a woman's...upper assets. The bullet bra (also known as a torpedo or cone bra), a carryover from the 50s, made breasts come to a point. This looked quite sexy and it was pretty much the best that could be done in a time that women's nipples surely could not show through.

Girdles were considered essential garments by many women from about 1920 to the late 1960s. They created a rigid, controlled figure that was seen as eminently respectable and modest. Constructed in the 60s of elasticized fabric and fastened with hook and eye closures (that I helped my mom with many times), most open-bottom girdles extended from the waist to the upper thighs. They included suspender clips to hold up stockings.

Add to the above a rather conservative shirt and skirt (no further up than the knees), or a pretty, flared-out dress, and a picture begins to form. The picture is not complete, however, even though it may seem to be; women still wore hats and white gloves a lot. A famous hat of the early 60s was the "pillbox," made popular by Jacqueline Kennedy, First Lady of President John F. Kennedy. Unfortunately she was wearing one when her husband was assassinated on November 22, 1963, and its popularity reportedly diminished after that.

Of course there were options in women's clothing. Women could wear pants, for example. Capri pants, pants longer than shorts but not reaching the calf, had been around awhile but tight-fitting ones were made popular by Mary Tyler Moore (1936-2017) in the early 60s in her character of Laura Petrie in *The Dick Van Dyke Show* (1961-66).

And of course women weren't slaves to fashion in the house and wore simple things like housedresses, though these could be stylish, too. Jeans could be worn as well, though not as common as today.

Age made a huge difference in what women wore, more so than today. In the 60s there was the "old lady" style. I am not defining what "old" is, as it varies from individual to individual. But "old ladies" had their own style. They wore "old" tie-shoes that were fashionable in a prior age and plain long dresses (when I think of one of my grandmothers, I always see a navy-blue dress with white spots). They wore their own hats, and were fonder of kerchiefs than younger people. They just looked completely different from everyone else.

MEN'S FASHION IN THE EARLY 60s

Men's fashion in the early 60s was neat but boring. It was boring because it didn't have much variety, and business wear today is incredibly similar. Suits and ties were a must for business, but were worn in leisure time as well, like in my aforementioned "Sunday Best." Suits tightened up, maybe too much, in the 60s from the 50s. Gone were the baggy oversized trousers (enjoyed by some today) and jackets. Gone were the big ties, replaced by skinny ones. To get an idea of what this looked like, take a look at Rod Serling in any episode of the *Twilight Zone*. He looks uncomfortably tight.

On their way out were Fedora hats. They were so common in the 20th century, but were losing favor in the 60s. In the early sixties you would still see a lot, but not on every male. They made appearances on people throughout the 60s, but died out a lot by the end of the decade. There were some hangers-on, of course, like Frank Sinatra, and Dallas Cowboys head coach Tom Landry. Tom always wore that hat, well after the 60s, and in fact it became his trademark.

The question, "boxers or briefs" was easily answered. Boys wore briefs and men wore boxers.

Some men still wore garter belts to keep non-elastic socks up. This was more of a fancy thing, nothing I ever wore. Interestingly, they were also used for comic relief. In a 60s TV show if a man had his trousers down they would show him wearing the garter belt holding up their socks. Though almost nobody used them anymore, the image was just funnier.

WOMEN'S FASHION OF THE LATE SIXTIES

In the late 60s, the girdle was generally supplanted by the pantyhose. Pantyhose replaced girdles for many women who had used the girdle essentially as a means of holding up stockings. Those who wanted more control purchased "control top" pantyhose. Alas, stockings faded away.

But with the rise of the miniskirt (pun intended) stockings could no longer be an option, as they barely made it to the hemline. Indeed, may mini-skirted females wore no stockings at all. Some had the legs for miniskirts while some didn't, but *cest la vie*.

Many claimed to have "invented" the miniskirt, and why not? But it wasn't a patentable thing, so it didn't matter. They popped up rather quickly, in Britain, around 1965 and by 1967 were very popular in the US. In 1968 I would say they were even more popular. Already in 1969, however, designers were working on the anti-mini—the "maxi," which became popular in the 70s.

"Go-go" boots went well with miniskirts, as these high boots that made the scene in the mid-60s covered the leg almost up to the knees, so that the combo resulted in only exposing the knee and thigh. The low-heeled boots were made of patent leather or plastic and were further popularized by a go-go-boot-wearing Nancy Sinatra (Frank's daughter) in a video of the 1966 song "These Boots Are Made for Walkin'" which actually hit #1 on the charts.

A new kind of pants came out for both men and women—bell-bottoms. Borrowing from the style of pants worn by sailors, these had a flare on the bottom cuffs that looked like a bell. The hippies seemed to like these first, but they spread to the mainstream in the 70s. For quite some time people like myself wore them.

And then there was the Bikini. This two-piece swimsuit was actually designed by a French engineer, Louis Réard, back in 1946, addressing (by undressing) a fabric shortage after World War II. He named the swimsuit after Bikini Atoll, where the US had initiated its first peace-time nuclear weapons test. Réard hoped his swimsuit's revealing style would create an "explosive commercial and cultural reaction" similar to the explosion at Bikini Atoll.

Though invented back in the 40s, women weren't exactly wearing them everywhere shortly thereafter. They were simply too risqué, especially for the US. Remember that the Hayes Code was not abandoned by the U.S. until the mid-60s, and it did not allow for navels to be shown in films. Early American films to feature Bikinis only showed ones that were quite modest, covering up that nasty navel. One of the most stunning appearances of a woman in a movie wearing a Bikini, navel exposed, was Ursula Andress (1936-   ) in the first Bond movie, *Dr. No* (1962). It wasn't until the late 60s in the US that many young women were wearing bikinis. In 1967 *Time* magazine wrote that "65% of the young set had…gone over [to bikinis]". And bikinis "improved" in the 60s, to be all the more revealing, with technology once again coming through. In the 60s DuPont introduced Lycra (DuPont's name for spandex), which expanded the range of novelty fabrics available to designers which meant suits could be made to fit like a second skin, without heavy linings. "The advent of Lycra allowed more women to wear a bikini," wrote Kelly Killoren Bensimon in *The Bikini Book*. "It didn't sag, it didn't bag, and it concealed and revealed." Increased reliance on stretch fabric led to simplified construction and allowed designers to create the *string bikini*, but not to be enjoyed until the 70s.

MEN'S FASHION OF THE LATE SIXTIES

In the late 60s men still wore their boring suits and skinny ties. There were more choices though for what to wear in their leisure. Polo shirts, for example, were worn by everybody, and not just people playing polo or golf. V-neck shirts were popular. I wore both of these kinds of shirts and thought they were pretty cool.

I reported in my diary in 1969 that my brother bought a Safari jacket. These began to come into style in the late 60s and unfortunately well into the 70s. As their name implied, these jackets were originally designed to wear when going on safari in the African bush. Outside of that environment, they were rather odd.

Then came the Nehru jacket. This hip-length tailored coat with a mandarin collar named after Indian Prime Minister Jawaharlal Nehru entered the fashion scene in the US in the late 60s and promised to be the new suit jacket or formal wear. I remember my dad driving through Manhattan, stuck in traffic, and my hearing over and over again on a loudspeaker from a department store that the Nehru jacket, in their display window, was "the look of the future." I was actually excited over this, thinking that indeed the old jackets and ties would go the way of the dinosaur. Well, the Nehru jacket went that way, in the early 70s. In fact, even by then it was already a joke. My High School freshman English teacher wore one to class in 1971 and we laughed at it.

Young people wanted to look like the Beatles. They wore Nehru jackets for a time, as well as pointy shoes, which I did get and thought were awesome. Fortunately my parents did appreciate generally what we wanted (except the length of our hair—see below), whether they understood it or not. One day my mom surprised me with a large medallion on a long chain, something "cool people" wore in the late 60s. But I don't think I ever wore it…

HAIR

On July 22, 1969 (I remember because it was the day after the first moon landing), my brother had a terrible argument with our father over the length of his hair, which was fashionably long for that time. My father won the argument, and my brother got a haircut. Not many years earlier, my brother and I had argued with my mother to get a crew cut, a very, very short cut. She refused, and we settled for what was called a "semi-crew cut," which left hair a bit longer. Thus summarizes the quick change in hair length in the 60s, brought about by (who else?) The Beatles.

In the late 60s and thereafter if our hair was too long my parents would say we were beginning to look like Beatles. Interestingly, many years later we watched an old video of the Beatles and asked my mom how they looked. They said they looked like nice young men; they dressed neatly and their hair was neat.

For girls it was the opposite. My father would never allow short hair on his daughter. My mother would struggle with her hair, especially when she was very young and seemed to always get playdoh or gum in it. I have to admit I always liked the same on my daughters.

The "beehive" hairdo, named such because it resembled a beehive, was very popular in the 60s with women. A beehive could look nice or ridiculous. When they added about a foot or more of height they looked ridiculous. Examples of ridiculous would be what "Yeoman Rand" (Grace Lee Whitney) wore in the first season of *Star Trek*. Another would be Marge Simpson's and Amy Winehouse's, or even what the girls in the 80s band the B52s wore ("B52" was another name for the beehive, as it resembled the front cone of a B52 bomber).

My mom and many other women would get "permanents" that looked like beehives. Maybe they weren't "beehives" per se, but the permanents produced "big" hair. This was achieved at the cost of spending hours at a beauty parlor, with chemicals applied to hair and the hair heated in conical hair dryers. The chemicals softened the inner structure of the hair and made it swell, stretch and soften, molding around the shape of the form the head was in. I hated when my mom got a "perm." It made her hair smell terrible.

MAKEUP

"The 1950s look continued into the 1960s – the elegant eyes, pale pink hues and loads of powder," according to glamourdaze.com. "However," the website continues, "the London fashion explosion brought with it the London Look and a revolution in hairstyling (Vidal Sassoon) and Makeup (Mary Quant Cosmetics), and all eyes for a time turned to the fashionable scenes of Carnaby Street and Portabello Road in London. Yardley of London tapped into the new youth look and their firm experienced a whole new lease [on] life with iconic 1960s models Twiggy and Jean Shrimpton modeling their makeup products under the banner of The London Look. English Model and Beatles [*again!*] chick Pattie Boyd wrote a Letter from London column in the American teen magazine *16*. Teens from across the USA eagerly read about her exploits and followed her Beauty and Hair Tutorials. There were three distinct looks in the 1960s, the classic, the mod and the hippy. The mod look is the cosmetic look most remembered from this beauty era."

One of the focuses of the "mod look" was eyelashes. Eyeliner was "the most important makeup tool" and was even doubled-up at the end of the eyelid. False eyelashes were very popular, both on top of the eyelid and on bottom. These are in fact what I remember most of make-up used in the 60s. Singer Dusty Springfield, in my opinion, is one of the celebrities who wore these well.

Twiggy (Lesley Lawson, 1949-   ), by the way, though a fashion icon of the 60s, was often the butt of jokes as she was so skinny, hence the name. But in recent years Twiggy has spoken out against the trend of waif-thin models, explaining that her own thin weight as a teenager was natural for her.

STYLES OF HIPPIES

Hippie "fashion," if it can be called that, was deliberately different from "The Establishment." As such, it was sloppy, casual, bum-like, and yet colorful, assumedly to remind them of their psychedelic experiences. Anything that was different from Western Civilization was embraced, such as Native-American clothing. In defiance of "corporate culture," much hippie clothing was self-made and hippies often purchased their clothes from flea markets and second-hand shops. As part of a unisex trend, male and female hippies had their hair the same long length, and they wore the same plain blue jeans, often bell-bottoms. Some hippie women wore long, full dresses and skirts as if in defiance of miniskirts. No matter where they walked, they preferred to wear sandals, moccasins or nothing on their feet at all. Hippie men often wore beards; women often wore no makeup. Some also did not wear bras, which would come into the mainstream in the next decade. Hippies wore Native American jewelry, head scarves, headbands and long beaded necklaces. Hippie homes, vehicles and other possessions were often decorated with psychedelic art, again in conjunction with their psychedelic experiences.

5 DEALING WITH ANCIENT TECHNOLOGY

Technology of our present time would be almost totally incomprehensible to even an Engineer of the 60s. I studied electrical engineering in college in the 70s and worked as an electrical engineer from the late 70s to mid-90s (when I switched to programming and IT) and I can tell you from my relatively expert point of view that the electronics we casually use today could not have been imagined by us in the 70s, 80s or even 90s. This great advancement is of course even more pronounced going back to the 60s. We used radios, TVs and computers (though computers only in business) in the 60s, but they would be almost unrecognizable to a 60s person in their present forms. And, of course, we have technologies that did not exist in the 60s, even ubiquitous ones so ingrained in our culture such as the internet.

I'm sure you have heard of the processing power of our miniature microprocessor-based (computers on chips of silicon) gadgets compared to the feeble processing power of old computers that took up large rooms. A smartphone, for example, has more processing power and memory than one of the large IBMs of the 60s that were deemed machines of marvel back in that time. And those computers had little, if any, communication with other computers that could extend their limited knowledge. Now our smartphones tell us many things that they don't locally "know" via WI-FI and cellular networks, extracting (and sending) information from the thousands of computers tied similarly into the tremendous "cloud" of information that we call the internet.

In the 60s we watched movies like *2001: A Space Odyssey* and imagined that in that time we would live in a wonderful age of "manned" space exploration and space stations and colonies. Well, we didn't do so bad in that area despite never developing lunar or planetary colonies or huge space stations as depicted in that epic film; our robots have explored Mars quite well and we have visited and studied every planet in the solar system with our robot craft. We have visited other heavenly bodies as well, including asteroids and comets, planetary moons, and even the disgracefully-downgraded "dwarf planet" Pluto, as well as beyond (such as the "Kuiper Belt Object" Ultima Thule, about a billion miles farther than Pluto). We haven't built a huge, rotating space station, but we did build, in a united effort of humanity, a pretty impressive space station that has been constantly occupied for many years. And with the Hubble Space Telescope and other space observatories, utilizing new technologies, we have looked at galaxies that are almost literally from the beginning of time and discovered planets in other "solar" systems that, according to a smartphone app I check regularly, amount at the time of this writing to no less than 3,663 total *confirmed* planets, a growing number of them *in the habitable zone and thus prime for life*. And that number is *guaranteed* to be out-of-date when you read this.

While audiences in 1968 oohed and ahhed at the beautifully filmed spaceships and space station in *2001*, there was a device used in that movie that got less attention—the Newspad. It was being watched by the astronauts on the mission to Jupiter as they ate some unpalatable-looking space meal. This superthin iPad-like device was not explained in the movie, but was described in its novelization, released concurrently, to be a source of news, from any place in the world. Thus, a current-day marvel was accurately predicted, an internet-driven tablet.

My personal experiences in electrical engineering included incredible advancements in computer memory and processing power. I was blessed to work with microprocessors that, though they were relatively primitive by today's standards, paved the way for the incredibly capable devices of today, including the Mac PC I am typing at now. I also saw advances and was involved in non-computer technologies well before they were available to the public. For example, I saw high-resolution (though not as high as modern times) miniature cameras and displays in the early 80s. I saw a small plasma display back in the early 90s. I worked with GPS when it was for military aircraft only, and the constellation of GPS satellites were not all launched yet; I saw that technology mature from something clunky when it was first introduced to the commercial world to something that just works, without complication, on my smartphone and in my car.

But enough about me. Let's take a look at the devices that existed in the 60s and we still use today—and some we don't.

TELEVISION

To say television was different in the 60s, in terms of technology, is an incredible understatement. All of us are familiar with CRT TVs—"Picture tubes." They have been replaced very quickly by flatscreen technologies, including plasma (itself almost phased out), LCD (no longer manufactured in new TVs without LED or QLED backlighting) and OLED (no backlighting required). Of course, in the 60s CRT technology was the only TV display technology available and there was nothing else in sight to replace it. Oh, we imagined flatscreen TVs coming to us one day, like the convincing one in the movie *Fahrenheit 451* (1966) and even the bridge viewscreen in *Star Trek*, the original 60s series. There was talk of "wall TVs" and some fun poked at the concept. In an episode of *The Dean Martin Show* aired in the late 60s, an unfortunate couple's wall TV breaks down (ignoring the fact that flatscreen TVs don't generally break down because they are solid state—more on that below) and their entire wall has to be taken to the shop (again, see below). Ha, ha.

Almost all Americans had *one TV* in the sixties, and from 1966 onward many bought color sets. Before 1966 very few people had color sets and for good reason—they were expensive and there was little color programming. But starting in the Fall Season of 1966 almost all network programming was transmitted in color; in fact the "full name" of shows had the words "in color" appended to them (e.g., "*Batman*—In Color"). [Commercials were a mixed bag of color and black-and-white and at least one show I remember—*Peyton Place*—was still in black-and-white.] Keep in mind we also had independent and public TV stations that lagged a couple of years before they were broadcast in color.

The first color set we bought, though good for the period, wasn't very good. First of all, it didn't just turn on in color—it sat useless for a few weeks before a service guy had to turn the color on (no idea if this was standard procedure, or we got a lemon). Then, when the color worked, it seemed to work well, but only until you changed the channel. You had to manually adjust the color controls ("color" and "tint") for each station. Each station's color signals were different—NBC's was the strongest, CBS the weakest and ABC somewhere in-between. The key to getting the right colors, it was told, was to adjust the color controls so that faces looked flesh-colored (yes, it was a white-centric world, and not many blacks were on TV then).

So the above adjusting was added to the already ridiculous adjusting for black-and-white sets. Before cable/satellite with digital technology, the pictures you got were pretty terrible as received by even nearby transmitters. Signals bounced off of buildings and other objects, so you got "ghost" images. And if you weren't near a transmitter you watched your shows through "snow," annoying white specks that filled your screen. If you had a "rabbit-ear" antenna, you could mess with orienting its two antennas and the mysterious adjustment knob on it, but good luck with that. Many of us had crazy-looking roof antennas to give us better reception (and got broken legs or worse putting the darn things on the roof), but they weren't perfect either. I aimed ours at the Empire State Building transmitter and at times reception still sucked. So, in summary, add color adjustment to all that. Don't forget to add some horizontal and vertical sync issues that would often crop up and had to be corrected manually.

And after all that, you still got a low-resolution picture, on a curved picture tube far from square—in fact our color TV was curved like a pair of parentheses on its sides, leading to all kinds of distortion.

Keeping all the above in mind, if you wanted to watch something at 8 PM you'd better start up that TV, which took about a minute to "warm up" enough to show a picture, change to your station, and get ready to make your adjustments well in advance of 8 PM!

The other issue with 60s TVs was that they required maintenance. They were made with vacuum tubes (the largest being the picture tube itself), which had fairly limited lifetimes. Tubes would burn out and have to be replaced; depending on which one failed, you would get a different result. It could be something you could ignore for awhile, but if it involved something like the aforementioned horizontal or vertical sync, there would no longer be a way to adjust those. Or, a tube could fail that made you lose your picture completely. Fortunately, sometimes tubes didn't completely fail at first, so literally banging on your TV could make them temporarily work. Ever see someone, especially on the older side, bang on a device that was failing, in an attempt to fix it? This action went back to vacuum tube-based electronics. There is actually science to this—banging a device vibrates a vacuum tube which in turn loosens "stuck" electrons in that device and lets it work a while longer, sometimes even weeks.

If you were a DIY kind of person, you would open the back of your TV and see what tube was dark—when vacuum tubes worked, their filament would be lit. You took the tube to a place that had a tube tester, plugged it into that tester, verified it didn't work, and bought and installed a replacement. Tubes were in sockets and were easily removed and inserted. If you were a real industrious person, like one of my fathers-in-law, you took out one tube at a time while the TV was working, wrote what part number it was and noted the symptom that occurred on your TV. Then you bought a full set of replacement tubes for your TV and when something bad happened you just looked it up on your list of symptoms and replaced it with the correct replacement tube. I still have his 1947 Emerson TV, complete with a shoebox filled with replacement tubes, a list and schematic.

If you weren't that kind of person, and maybe you just didn't like sticking your hand into TV sets with dangerous high-voltage power supplies (needed to energize the picture tube), you called the TV Repairman. He would come to your house like the doctor who made house calls, except his bag was even bigger as it contained every vacuum tube known to Man. He could fix your TV in your home, on the spot. I remember having one over when banging the TV didn't resolve the blank picture issue too well anymore. When he come over the picture was working but then went dark, and I told him he just had to bang the TV on the side to fix it. That led to a good laugh for all the adults, though I wasn't trying to be funny.

Unfortunately, TV Repairmen weren't always successful in repairing your TV at home, and they would announce the dreaded words, "I'm afraid I'm going to have to take it to the shop." These were indeed very frightening words, as if your best buddy was going to the hospital. But at times they actually had to do some real troubleshooting! The only thing worse was them telling you that the picture tube blew. That meant you had to get a new TV (exciting if you were a kid, and didn't have to pay for it—a new TV maybe meant a color one or a black-and-white with a better picture).

Until Plasma and LCD technology, the first flatscreen technologies, a broken picture tube was still a reason to buy a new TV. Though TVs moved to solid state (transistor-based) technology after the 60s, the picture tube was the last vestige of vacuum tube technology in any electronic device, the last troublesome component. TVs were not completely solid state until that CRT went away.

One more thing about ancient 60s TVs: the sound sucked! Pictures got better in later decades but the sound didn't. We had stereos in the 60s but not stereo TV—those didn't come around until about the 80s. This was a well-known shortfall of the TV—all concentration was put on the picture but not audio. We did have a work-around in the 70s though, for special telecasts. They were known as *simulcasts*. TV audio was sent synchronously to a TV and your stereo system; so you turned the TV volume down to zero and cranked up the stereo. This was awesome! Unfortunately, they did not do these simulcasts often. The first may have been for the TV premiere of the movie *Earthquake* (1974), which was shown in the theatres with something called *Sensurround*—low frequencies of sound that mimicked the rumbles of earthquakes.

In the 80s TV programs were transmitted in stereo but I didn't have a stereo TV. The answer: a stereo VCR with outputs I connected to my stereo sound system. Again, the TV volume was set down to zero and the stereo was cranked up.

Interestingly, I still crank my flatscreen volume down to zero and turn up the volume on my 7.1 sound system.

RADIO

AM radio was still King in the 60s, as it had been for decades, though of course TV had replaced Radio for entertainment programming the previous decade. For music, AM was what was most available. Though FM technology (the terrestrial broadcast standard for music still in use today) had been established for some time, most of us didn't have FM radios in the 60s. In fact, listenership of FM stations did not exceed that of AM stations until 1978. So, the crackly, low-fidelity monophonic AM stations are what we tuned to for our top-40 music. In fact, when FM came around it didn't direct itself to the top-40's: it was album-oriented, a source for groupies to listen to choice cuts of their favorite bands that didn't make it to the top-40 and even entire albums by them. I can refer you to George Carlin to educate you on the difference between AM and FM radio broadcasting in that period. He performed an excellent bit, available on YouTube, comparing the raucous AM programming to the cool, seemingly drug-induced sedateness of FM programming.

We didn't feel cheated of course with our AM radios and their programming. With the use of solid-state electronics radios got smaller and lighter so that you could bring them anywhere (even put them in your pocket—but you would need a large pocket). In the 50s there were portable radios of course, but they were bigger and heavier, and suffered the maintenance issues that TVs did with their vacuum tube technology. One that my mom got my dad for a

Christmas in that decade was given to me years later by her for me to examine to my heart's content as part of my research into electronics (and it was broken anyway). I was amazed at how small the circuit area was, with its vacuum tubes. The majority of real estate used by the large lunchbox-sized portable was two humungous batteries. They were called "lantern batteries" because they were originally used for…well, electric lanterns. That was where all the weight came from.

So we were happy with what was called "transistor" radios. The transistors were the solid-state (as opposed to gaseous) equivalent of vacuum tubes—tiny in comparison with much lower power requirements and much better longevity. In fact, you didn't repair a transistor radio, you just got a new one. The transistor radio battery was odd-shaped but small—the 9-volt battery, less common now than back then but amazingly still in use for limited items.

The quality of the radio was based for some time on how many transistors it had. Think of the equivalent as a comparison of memory (chips that contain the equivalent of transistors) between computers. The most common was the six-transistor radio, and they were proudly advertised as much. Then "better" radios were introduced, with more transistors. Unfortunately, some off-brand manufacturers just added useless transistors to their radios to advertise they were "better." Then it was no longer allowed to advertise the radios by the number of transistors they had.

AM or FM, radios were hard to tune. There was no frequency locking as we have now. You just tuned them for the least static and crosstalk from other stations. This was not always easy to do.

RECORD PLAYERS

You can read about the marvelous research in the 60s into providing taped music to homes via audio compact cassettes and cars as well as homes with 8-track tape cartridges, but throughout the 60s most of us only had record players to play pre-recorded music on. The 60s were the last decade that the majority of the population only had vinyl available for this, and record players remained popular until CDs replaced them in the 80s and 90s. CDs of course were mostly replaced by streaming music in the 21st century, but then there was also the current curious development of the resurgence of vinyl.

Our record player/home radio/sound system throughout the 60s was my dad's Zenith Cobra-Matic (so-called because its tone arm was intentionally shaped like a snake). It was mono, but my father did once rig up another speaker for it. It was an AM radio and record player, supporting all existing record formats—10" 78 RPM (pre-1960 old-standard singles), 12" 33-1/3 RPM ("Long Playing" or "LP" standard), 7" 45 RPM (new standard singles), and even one planned LP standard—16-2/3—which never made it because of poor fidelity (but used by us for entertainment reasons, making singers sound all like baritones). It played all of these with a stainless-steel stylus—a step above the sewing needles used for that purpose when my parents were young and a step below the crystal stylus.

The fidelity wasn't great on the Cobra-Matic but you could crank it up a bit. One of its best features was that you could stack quite a number of records on the spool so that you could listen to music unattended for quite a while. If you stacked too many, though, the record you were playing would slip on the record under it, causing its rotation speed to vary and therefore making recorded singers sound drunk. When records were played one at a time they held onto the felt platter well, but they didn't hold onto other records that well. Still, my dad liked to stack them up, especially the large and heavy 78's which spun the fastest, and when the next record smacked down on the one just finished playing it would go *plunk*.

As noted above with the useless 16-2/3 speed, we kids would change the speeds to the wrong ones for hilarious effects. There was nothing to prevent that, so we did it. Raising the RPM to 78 changed any singing on a 33-1/3 record into *a cappella* chipmunks. You could also spin a record on the platter manually, for interesting results, and, when the fad came about that hidden messages could be heard when music was reversed, you could manually spin them backward. We also gave dizzying rides to objects or even insects on the platter.

Many speak of the truer sound you get from analog sources, like records, but the darn things were dust magnets and it was impossible to get the dust completely off the record and stylus. Dust equaled crackling, especially for low-volume passages. Years later they developed electronic filters that got rid of those effects supposedly without affecting the original sound but CDs eliminated that problem for good.

Each time you played a record, you deteriorated it. If you really liked a record, you deteriorated it more quickly and at some point had to get another copy. The Cobra-Matic's steel stylus would degrade a record quicker than a record player with a crystal stylus, but not badly. The worst record players ever in that era were the *Kenner* Close and Play record players for children, which actually came out in the early 70s. My sister had one. It had a steel stylus that gorged on vinyl. My sister's favorite records were filled with white circles of scraped away vinyl and they sounded awful. Actually, they never sounded good on the Close and Play as that toy had no electronic amplification. It had batteries to rotate the platter and the sound came from the stylus just following the grooves in the record and vibrating. It was basically a battery-operated Victrola!

PHONES

Well, we have come a long way with this one, right? Many of you may not even have a telephone anymore, using smartphones only and no landlines. I still have a wireless "dumb" phone in my house which I personally never use, but it's not tied to a landline.

Phones were big, heavy things and in more than one murder mystery were used to kill people by bonking them on the head with one. Actually, in the 60s they got lighter and "daintier," but not everyone had a new phone. My grandparent's phone was extremely heavy, and just holding its receiver for awhile could make your arm sore.

Most people in the 60s had the good, old-fashioned "rotary" phones with a dial, and if you had a pushbutton one it still took about as long to get connected as they dialed out in the same way, with a series of pulses. It took quite a while to "dial" a number, and in old TV shows and movies you will notice that almost every time the actor would "cheat" by dialing less than seven numbers to avoid slowing down the action. A question at the time as popular as the one of which way you hang your toilet paper was whether you kept your finger in the hole as the dial went back to the home position for every number. Telemarketers and any person who dialed numbers all day would have achy fingers from the practice of dialing, especially if the dialer was metal, like the old-fashioned ones were. In fact, they would often dial with pencils in the hole, eraser side down.

The raucous phone sounds of the 60s have passed into memory, as we don't hear them anymore unless we seek out MP3s of them on nostalgic web sites. Certainly we don't hear the dial sound anymore, or the nasty "dial tone" of that time. Even nastier than the dial tone was the "busy signal" you got when the person you were calling was on the phone already—it couldn't have been a nastier sound. Of course, in an era without voicemail or its predecessor, "answering machines," you just had to keep calling until that person was off the phone. My father was convinced that if you left the handset off the "switch-hook" (which the handset lie on when you "hung up" the phone) you would be connected to whom you were calling, but alas that's not the way it worked.

Back then, long-distance was a big deal—costly and lousy. There were no satellites for phone communications yet, and the technology used was standard old copper telephone cables—referred now as POTS, Plain Old Telephone Service. POTS was an analog system, though early modems and Fax machines could use that system—at incredibly slow data rates, of course. Without satellites or cell towers, all transmissions were done through the copper cables, without digital technology. There were cables that stretched oceans, and they worked, but not too well. Again, watching an old movie or TV show, you can hear people speaking loudly on a long-distance call because the fidelity was so bad.

Most people had one phone in the house in the 60s, and that's why entire large cities like New York, with all its five boroughs, could get away with having only one area code—212. Long Island's non-NYC counties had another—516—which long later was split into 516 and 631, and shortly will have yet another.

Phones were "dumb," but they still did the job for voice communications and blissfully if you were not at work or home you were unreachable. We did have pay phones, the old kind that had accordion doors and could be totally closed, but they were filthy and a lot of times broken by vandals, and, at least in some parts of NYC, sometimes used as shelters by the homeless or employed as offices for drug dealers.

"HOUSEWIFE" APPLIANCES

My mother was a housewife. She occasionally worked at menial jobs to help out, but she was basically what was defined as a housewife, or *homemaker* as is the PC term (though they didn't *make* homes). She had no problem with this position in life, as far as I know, and she was very good at it—we ate well, she was a great shopper, she kept the house clean, and kept us in clean clothes. It's a thankless job and the "pay" is lousy, but she seemed to enjoy caring for us and keeping things spotless.

I'm sure, though, there were some chores that she was not very fond of. Even with modern home washing machines and dryers, doing laundry still sucks. We didn't have a washing machine until 1966, and we didn't have a dryer until well after the decade. My mother didn't like "wasting" money at the Laundromat, so she did it all by hand prior to 66, using a *washboard* in the kitchen sink. The washboard was a rectangular wooden frame in which there were mounted a series of ridges or corrugations for the clothing to be rubbed upon. That was it. My poor mom. Laundry was painstaking work indeed. And even when she got the washing machine, she did small jobs and items like underwear still with the washboard as she claimed they came out cleaner.

Without a dryer, my mom usually hung out the wash on a clothesline, affixing the clothes to the line with wooden clothespins, some that just pushed the clothes into the line and others that had a spring that made it easier to attach. She had two setups that my dad devised. One was in the cellar; its disadvantage was that it wasn't very long and it didn't give the clothes a fresh smell while its advantage was that being inside rain was not anything to worry about. My mother preferred the line that went from the bedroom window outside to a pole—it was a long line that allowed the fresh natural elements to dry the clothes and make them smell nice. And, she didn't have to stick her body out the window, for the bedroom window faced the backyard, and right outside the window there was a fire escape landing to stand on (which always worried me when I watched her stand on it). Unfortunately, if it rained she would run to the clothesline and take all the clothes off it and put them on the bed and anywhere else that would accommodate them.

We had a gas stove. There was nothing else to cook with, as microwave ovens did not become common or affordable until years later (and were known at first as "radar ranges," since their technology was based on radars). You might think that gas stoves haven't changed much, but there are improvements. My mom didn't even have a timer to work with. Lighting the burner was dangerous. They didn't have a self-cleaning feature, and they had to be cleaned with caustic substances. My grandmother didn't wear gloves while cleaning her oven, and got that substance on a finger, which burned it, got it infected, and eventually her finger had to be amputated.

Refrigerators (still referred by my parents as "iceboxes") have gotten better, too, though they worked just fine then. We would have loved an automatic icemaker, but it wasn't time for that yet.

My mom would have loved a dishwasher, but they were also not common or cheap. Of course, when they were, she got one.

CARS

My father's first new car was a 1956 Chevy Bel-Air. It was a great car, but cars got out-of-date quickly in the 60s. In 1968, the 56 was still running and looking good, but it was hopelessly out of style. My father bought a new Chevy Impala in that year, which was very exciting, but we all shed a tear on July 1, 1968 when the Bel-Air was towed to a junkyard that was the only one we could find that would not charge us for the tow.

The 56 was 3,300 lbs. of awesome metal. To say it was "solid" is an understatement. The hood, the trunk and doors were all heavy metal; to close any of these you had to slam them hard. It was all that metal that saved you and your car in a collision. It was also a beautiful car, though as I stated in its later years it looked so old that quite honestly I was ashamed of being in it. It had a two-tone flat finish, and its tailfins were just right, streamlined enough but not outrageous like some cars from the early sixties.

It was regal yet simple. It had a V-6 that guzzled gasoline, but no-one cared when you could fill up for five bucks. No troublesome computer or catalytic converter. Simple AM radio and analog clock (which only intermittently worked). Instrument panel with barely more than a speedometer (the needle of which in those days would quiver and shake, which added to the illusion of speed). Lots of room, huge trunk space. You got flats more often then because the tires had tubes in them, but flats could be fixed in a few minutes (ever see *Christmas Story*?). Cars then were so easy to maintain, because they were so simple. Carburetors could be a bit temperamental, but you could work with them.

There wasn't any power steering, power brakes, power door locks, power seats, power windows, or power *anything*. The most important of these things was power steering. Manual steering made you have to turn the wheel a lot, and at slow speeds that was quite a chore. Parking involved turning with great force, hand over hand. It hurt your arms worse than lifting an old phone. Making sharp turns wasn't easy either, and involved turning and turning and spinning the wheel. Even keeping your car straight on the road involved moving the wheel back and forth (another thing you can see in old shows and movies). There was some play in the wheel, and bored drivers would play with the wheel a bit just to make things a little interesting.

There was no air conditioning, at least for us normal folks. There used to be a triangular window in front of the regular front windows that would swivel open as much as you desired and would provide a nice breeze of fresh air, cooled down by the speed of the vehicle, so you could cool off without opening the regular windows. I remember that at high speeds it made a kind of whistle—even when completely closed—oh well.

There were some safety issues with a car like the 56, but I'll cover them in another chapter…

The 68 Impala, virtually indistinguishable from the 68 Bel Air, was awesome. It was about 1,000 lbs. even heavier than the 56 Bel Air, but gas prices were still not a problem. We called it "the boat;" it was huge. And it was fast, equipped with a V-8. It also was sleeker, *cooler* than the old Bel Air. In fact, it was literally cooler, having *air conditioning*! It was also safer, having lap belts and a cushioned dashboard.

It had power steering, and my dad went through the difficulties that all drivers back then had getting used to it. He couldn't play with the wheel anymore—at least without moving back and forth on the road.

We loved that car. It was my dad's favorite, I think. Some schmuck stole it in the first half of the 70s, and my dad got a used 69. But we all missed the 68.

TYPEWRITERS – A DEAD TECHNOLOGY BETTER OFF DEAD

Despite the above title, I used to *love* typewriters. I loved them because they put my words in print. I used to write all sorts of stuff just to see how it looked typed. I also wrote stories with them and term papers for school.

In the 60s there were good portable typewrites, even the mechanical ones, and you could opt for a fancy electric one. I never got an electric one. I had requested a typewriter one Christmas and my father couldn't see why you would buy a version that required electricity when you could buy one that worked without it.

As stated, I loved typewriters but they could be a pain, mechanical or electrical. The big problem with typewriters is that there was no good way to correct mistakes. If the mistake was big enough, you had no choice but to type the page over. If you wanted to shuffle things around a bit or make simple modifications, a simple task using a word processor, again you just had to retype. You could make minor corrections with correcting tape or "white-out"/"liquid paper" (a fabulous invention by the mom of a Monkee—the band, that is—Michael Nesmith), which both covered mistakes and you could type on them (blowing on white-out applied to a page to dry it was a common sight in offices). Then there came onion skin paper, which was *erasable*, using a simple pencil eraser, but that was not a problem-free solution. First, the paper was very thin and an underline could cut right through your page (I guess not the worst thing in the world). Second, pencil erasures did not mix well with the mechanical workings of a typewriter, which seemed to suck them in and cause jams, a problem anyway with typewriters.

Yep, typewriters were cool, but I don't miss them.

DISAPPOINTING TECHNOLOGY

I personally found a lot of the technology of the 60s disappointing. This was particularly true with toys and gadgets. While I am amazed at the high-tech in modern toys and gadgets, I found when I got something in the 60s it almost always didn't live up to the hype.

I bought what was advertised as a "calculator" in 1969 via mail-order. When it finally arrived I was confused how such a device came in a thin package. When I opened up the package I found out the disappointing truth—it was basically an abacus with a metal stylus. It could do what an abacus could, but I had actually thought it would do it automatically! I really was so disappointed. Still, I reported in my diary on October 4, 1969 some excitement over its delivery and reported that it somehow was a "machine," though I exhibited frustration on how to use it:

> I received through the mail my CALCULATOR, which I sent away for over a week ago. My CALCULATOR is a small "machine" which actually adds, subtracts, multiplies, and <u>aids</u> division. Most of my morning was used up trying to see how to use it. Now I only know how to add (I think).

I got a "computer" for Christmas 1968, called "Digi-Comp 1." It had looked great in the ads, like something out of *Star Trek*. But when I opened the box I only saw pieces of plastic, metal rods, short plastic tubes and elastic bands. I put the darn thing together. The instructions said that like a computer, I could count down in binary from 111 to 000 (7 to 0 for you base-10 fans), in a "game" called Missile Countdown, as well as play other, very simple, "computer games" (I would imagine the first). I "played" these by moving a plastic piece in and out. I think it was "programmed" by moving the plastic tubes. It was unexciting, but it did teach me binary math. Interestingly, I have found this gadget to be quite popular on the internet and a number of people who work in IT, like myself, have fond memories of it (I had been disappointed, but it was fun to build and have it do the simple things it did). It is so popular that the $5 toy is still available in an updated version for $49. There is even a "Friends of Digicomp" Yahoo group.

Next I got an "electronic" computer from Radio Shack—how could I go wrong with that? I soldered together a number of interesting electronic components, and it had a battery! This thing *had to* work. I turned on the switch and…nothing happened. I pushed a pushbutton and a small meter moved. It turned out to be a basic analog computer, that supposedly could multiply if you selected two numbers on separate dials and then selected a third dial until you saw the meter center, and read the result on the third dial. Alas, this never really worked.

I bought a radio kit as well, which really looked like it would work great. Unfortunately, it needed to be "grounded" with a stake that was supposed to be inserted literally in the ground. I couldn't get the darn thing to work. Then, one evening I wrapped a long ground wire around our vertical steam pipe (don't see those much anymore!) and I heard things come out of the speaker. The radio *basically* worked, but it worked like crap!

Speaking of radio, I was excited by the possibility of recording music from it after my brother got a tape recorder for Christmas in 1964. However, when we tried the results were extremely disappointing—the fidelity was just awful. The first song we tried it with was the aforementioned early favorite of mine, "Hey Little Cobra." Our radios and recorders were too primitive for this objective. We wouldn't be able to record much, anyway, as the small reels on the recorder only held minutes each. By the way, I tried recording from TV as well, with disastrous results. But I had a lot of fun with that recorder, and I'd love to find the tapes we made of ourselves so many years ago, including of my grandpa.

We were all excited when we got walkie-talkies in the late 60s. But we soon found out their range was practically nil. I reported in my diary on November 9, 1969 an experiment to prove out their range. We went to visit relatives by car while my brother stayed home. I expected to lose range somewhere on the way—but we were out of range already before we reached the car! This was an improvement, though, over a previous set of "walkie-talkies" we had in the early 60s—what looked like two phone handsets, connected by a long wire to each other. That in itself was barely an improvement over the old cup and string technology.

At the same time I got Digi-Comp 1—Christmas 1968—I got a "robot"— Zobor the Zeroid. It had been excellently advertised by toymaker Ideal, making the thing look like it had a mind of its own. Actually, it was motorized and ran on batteries but could only move in a straight line. There was a plastic ramp that you could aim it to that moved a switch on the bottom that made it go in reverse, which actually looked pretty cool. The robot's case was its robot home, which was also cool. There were different attachments for the "hands" and it had rubber bands inside so you could pull back an arm and let it go in a swift motion. Zobor was the "bronze transporter"; Zintar was the "silver explorer" and Zerak the "blue destroyer." I recently unearthed Zobor and will hold on to it.

I got a 90-power Tasco Telescope for Christmas 1969 that at first turned out to be a disappointment because I misinterpreted what "90-power" meant, but it turned out to be pretty cool. I proudly reported in my diary when my dad ordered it on November 24, 1969 from Abraham and Strauss, COD, because it cost $29.99—perhaps my most expensive Christmas present ever. It arrived on December 11.

[That same Christmas I also got a toy that quite honestly wasn't disappointing at all. It was the Hasbro Amazamatic car. You "programmed" a course for this car by inserting pre-cut cards into it. You also got blank cards that you could use to program your own course, though I never became an expert at that.

PAST COMPLACENCE

I tried to come up with an expression that would be opposite to "Future Shock" and this was it. *Future Shock* was a fascinating book from 1970 by futurist Alvin Toffler (1928-2016). It really opened my eyes to something fresh. According to Mr. Toffler himself, "Future Shock" is "the social paralysis induced by rapid technological change." This is something that Toffler discovered in the 60s, when technology was rapidly changing, though not anywhere near the rate that it is now. One of the changes that Mr. Toffler wrote to some great length about was the movement to disposable items. This movement was great in the 60s, but we also clung to the old as well, and had many things repaired instead of replacing them. Thus, my Aunt still used in that decade a mechanical sewing machine, that used her own foot power via a large metal plate that she pedaled. Thus, my mom, when she already had a washing machine, still used a washboard to clean underwear. Thus, things like teabags were re-used in my house. Thus, a fan was used instead of an air conditioner because it wasn't "hot enough" for the AC. Thus, when my mother had an electric sewing machine she would still do a lot of sewing by hand, such as in darning socks. Thus, ripped shirts and pants weren't thrown away but patched. Thus, paper grocery bags were recycled as trash bags and small paper bags as lunch bags. Etc., etc.

If something could be repaired, it was. Certainly TVs and other electronics were. But minor disposable items snuck their way in. Instead of keeping fountain pens for years and refilling them with ink, we bought throw-away pens and disposed of them when they ran out of ink. Instead of refilling nice, monogramed metal cigarette lighters, we started buying disposable ones. Instead of using removable-blade razors, we bought cartridge razors, the entire head assembly ("cartridge") being removed and disposed of, instead of just the blade; then we bought completely disposable razors. Instead of using cloth diapers and having them cleaned by a Service or by ourselves, we bought disposable ones. And thus, at least for small items, we became a disposable society. Later, more towards the present, almost everything has become disposable—certainly electronics. With technology getting better at its current rate, chances are after just a few years we are better off with a new item because it is so much more advanced and convenient.

6 ANCIENT MEDICINE

In 1962 I was hospitalized for ten days for an ear infection. Yep, you read that right. I was only five years old and the horror of those ten days will never leave my mind. Aside from being in pain from the infection, and having pus and blood draining out of my ears constantly, I had to deal with staying in a hospital every night without my parents or brother—there were no overnight parent stays back then. Instead, I had a very nasty nurse "care" for me—she yelled at me and held my nose as she forced medicine down my throat. Once I resisted so much that I spilled medicine everywhere—and the nurse said that I would have to sit in it, she would not clean it up. When my mother found out about this she was pissed at that nurse.

To be hospitalized, and for so long, for an ear infection undoubtedly sounds absurd. But keep in mind that antibiotics were not so plentiful then, nor in so many varieties. Basically all we had in 1962 were penicillin and some varieties of penicillin. Penicillin had just become available to the general public in 1945, after it saved many lives during World War II. It had been invented years earlier, but for some time there were problems mass-producing it.

My infection did not respond to penicillin and its varieties that had been approved by the FDA at that time. My doctor suggested a new antibiotic still in trials. My parents signed a release form, in desperation, so that I could try it. Fortunately for me, it cured my infection. Only "bleeding edge" drug technology saved me from becoming deaf or even worse.

Of course, misuse of penicillin and other antibiotics that were developed in the 60s through 80s created the "superbugs" of today that require much stronger antibiotics. But even without superbugs, the 60s clearly were not the best time to get an infection. I barely scraped through, though I have a nice scar on my eardrum to show for it.

Nowadays, we also have a simple solution that prevents people, especially kids, from getting ear infections—temporary tubes pierced through the eardrum. But—not invented yet.

Just as my luck would have it, I also needed my tonsils out that same year. Back then doctors loved to take out tonsils. Any persistent sore throat was enough for them to do it. They were just itching to send you to the hospital—for a few days at least—to snip those pesky things off. While they were at it, they took out the adenoids, too, no matter how healthy they were. Hey, they were in there anyway…

Let me tell you how horrible this simple surgery was back then. For one thing, hospitals were more disturbing than today, if that can be believed. Somehow the electronics make them more palatable to me, and there were none then. There just seemed to be all kinds of needles and sharp and skinny things to stick in you—no miniature cameras. But the worst thing was the smell—the smell of ether. That smell permeated the entire hospital, and it was the most sickening of odors. But that was the anesthetic of the day, and its odor travelled everywhere.

So, at the age of five, I was affixed onto a gurney with tight leather straps into a very austere operating room. [On the way there, the "Theme from a Summer Place" played, a hit from two years previous that unfortunately I still relate to that operation.] The surgeon put a funnel to my mouth, I assume with a screen in front of it, and poured liquid ether into it. I gagged, and the surgeon said, "That's right. That's what you are supposed to do." Then I passed out.

When I awoke, I vomited. That's what ether does to you—make you vomit. I felt awful. I got better, but on the day I waited for my parents to bring me home, I felt sick again, holding myself back from vomiting (eventually losing that battle) because I thought the hospital would then not let me go home (hey, I was five). Fortunately they took me home, where I then endured the Chicken Pox.

Speaking of childhood diseases, there were many then to endure as they hadn't developed vaccinations for them yet. At the age of five, I got pretty much all of them—including Chicken Pox, Rubella (German Measles) and Mumps. They all sucked. Chicken Pox and Rubella made you feel sick and itchy. Mumps is an infection and swelling of glands near your temples. When I would lie my head down on either side, it felt like that side weighed a ton—in fact, I related it at the time to "treasure chests" in the sides of my head that were weighing me down.

My brother, on the other hand, never seemed to get sick. And back then, my parents tried to make him sick. Doctors wanted childhood diseases to inflict children, so they wouldn't get them as adults, when they would have more serious ramifications. So my parents would take my drinking glass that I used while I was sick and give it to my brother to get him sick—which never worked.

There were some inoculations back then, but for diseases that now have been almost literally wiped off the face of the Earth. For example, there was the polio vaccine, for which we were not only inoculated for but given boosters. The "boosters," to make them easy on us kids, came in the form of sugar cubes that had the nasty medicine inside. They distributed these things to us in school.

The other inoculation was for smallpox. They inoculated you for smallpox by injecting live cowpox virus into you, to literally give you cowpox. But it was much better to give you cowpox than smallpox, and having cowpox immunized you against smallpox. Cowpox just gave you one big mother of a boil at the site of injection. You waited for it to get crusty and fall off. It did leave you a scar, which everyone past a certain age can show you. Of course, they don't immunize people anymore for smallpox, at least not in developed countries.

All this talk of sickness brings me to the doctors of the period. Our family doctor was, let's say, Dr. Sturgeon (of course, though long dead, I'm not providing his real name). Dr. Sturgeon was carefully selected by my parents to be our family doctor. He met three requirements: (1) He lived and had his office diagonally across the street; (2) He was Austrian, so like my German and Austrian parents he could speak "in code" in front of us kids; and (3) He was Jewish (though there was plenty of anti-Semitism back in that day, there was pro-Semitism as well for certain fields, like doctors and lawyers). As said, he lived where he worked—he owned a two-family house where his office was downstairs and his apartment upstairs.

Dr. Sturgeon had office hours, but no appointments. You just walked into his office, if you were able, and waited for him to become available. If you were not able to visit him, outside of his office and hospital hours, he would come to you—yes, he made house calls. He balked sometimes about the house calls, but he always came anyway, with his black bag.

Dr. Sturgeon believed in cash. During most of the 60s, his fee for an office visit was $5. And he had a great stash of free samples in his closet. Not a bad deal, for even then. Dr. Sturgeon didn't have office personnel but also didn't ask for money. When all was said and done at the end of the visit, it was understood that it was time to pay. If you lost track of things, he would signal time for payment by taking out his wallet—which was stacked with a huge wad of $5 bills.

One thing I hated about Sturgeon was that he was old school—i.e., Vienna Medical School. He had some odd ways about him. For example, he believed greatly that temperature could only be taken accurately by anal means—at any age. If you had diarrhea, he believed in diagnosis by smell—he would put his gloved finger up your butt, move it around, and take it out, smelling what was on the glove, while he squished it with his fingers. I swear I saw him do that and then say, "OK. Normal." He was also inappropriate at times (like the smelly finger wasn't). He would like to check out testicles (I hope for hernias) and then ask, "So, do you have a girlfriend?" I swear, as a kid, with my mother in the room, he asked me if I "jerk." I had no idea what he was talking about. He explained, "Do you let something out at night?" I really didn't get it. My mother said, "No."

MISSING MEDICAL TECHNOLOGIES

There is much medical technology we have today that we take for granted and wasn't available for us in the 60s. Let's take for example the status of present-day treatments for heart disease in the 60s:

- Coronary Bypass—In development
- Portable defibrillators—In development
- Angioplasty—In development
- Stents—Not developed and used until 1986
- Implantable pacemakers—In development
- Heart transplants—The first on a human was done in 1967 and kept the patient alive 18 days; they now extend life an average of 15 years

So, things looked pretty grim if you had heart disease in the 60s—there was basically nothing that could be done about it. People walked around with so-called "weak hearts" or even were bedridden with heart ailments until they died. If you didn't die from a heart attack you most likely remained severely debilitated the rest of your life.

And there was plenty to give you heart disease—rampant drinking, freedom to smoke anywhere, an ignorance of the effects of eating fatty foods, and lack of exercise. In the 60s, it was not uncommon for Americans to die of heart attacks in their 40s and 50s. As a kid I heard about it all the time. It was often sudden and unexpected.

According to the National Institute of Health (NIH), between 1970 and 2005 the life expectancy of the average American increased by 6.6 years; 4.7 years—over 70%—of the increase is due to reductions in deaths from cardiovascular disease.

Strokes were another relatively frequent danger. Again according to the NIH, the death rate from stroke, the third most common cause of death, has declined by about 75 percent since the early 1960s. Risk factors have been clearly demonstrated to prevent strokes and heart disease—high blood pressure, elevated serum cholesterol, smoking, obesity, diabetes, and physical inactivity. Addressing these factors via diet, exercise, and medication has saved many lives since the 60s.

What about the diagnostic tools we "enjoy" today? In the 60s you could get an x-ray to see what was ailing you. That's about it. CAT scans weren't introduced until the next decade, MRIs the decade after that (and not in common use until about the 1990s). Ultrasound wasn't available. Very often in the 60s doctors didn't know what was wrong with you until they cut into you. They resorted to "exploratory surgery." I can hardly think of two more frightening words together.

THE FLU

I had horrible bouts with the flu in the 60s and 70s. Flu vaccinations, though started in the US military in the 40s, were not commonplace in the 60s like today, nor as cheap, covered by insurance, nor as safe. The "Hong Kong" influenza pandemic of 1968-69, caused by an H3N2 influenza virus, resulted in roughly 34,000 deaths in the U.S.

In my diary entry of November 2, 1968, I noted that a kid in my class threw up right before we left to go home. My response at the time was, "I laughed my head off." The next day we couldn't get anybody to clean his desk, though the floor had been cleaned. We pushed the desk out into the hallway, "because it stunk and the teacher didn't want us to get the virus, or whatever disease [he] had."

In my diary entry of December 16, 1968, I noted that students and teachers as well were afflicted with the virus and on January 5, 1969 I reported that my entire family was sick.

Though I don't see a note in History of a flu pandemic the following year, my diary did indeed record sickness in my family. Everybody was sick from Christmas Eve to the end of the year of 1969. I even recorded its transmission path on December 26, 1969:

> Daddy caught this disease in the shop where he works and gave it to mommy. Mommy gave it to Helen Marie [my sister], and she gave it to me, and Johnny is getting it from me.

Thus, we were all sick as the decade came to a close...

THE BIG "C"

There have been certainly major advances in the treatment of cancer since the 60s, including anti-cancer drugs, better chemotherapy (with much fewer side effects), better targeted radiation, immunotherapy, hormone therapy and early detection made possible by better diagnostic tools. But the death rate for cancer dropped only 5 percent from 1950 to 2005. In contrast, the death rate for heart disease dropped 64 percent in that time, and for flu and pneumonia, it fell 58 percent. Longer life expectancy may be a contributing factor to this, as cancer rates and mortality rates increase significantly with age; more than three out of five cancers are diagnosed in people aged 65 and over. The life expectancy in 1960 was only 69.7 years; in 2010 it rose to 78.7. I also cannot help to think that environmental factors have kept cancer rates from falling much.

To be fair it should be noted that cancer treatment is getting better all the time, especially in the current decade. Being diagnosed with any cancer at any stage still provides hope for the patient, as new research is going on constantly and breakthroughs are being made. A friend of mine was told to not look up his condition of aggressive stage 3 lung cancer on the internet as news there on treatment would already be out-of-date when he read it and it would upset him. His cancer spread to his lymph nodes and brain, but after chemo and radiation he is now cancer-free; it is expected to return in a few years or so, but research continues and he has gained years more of life…

Of course, it matters what kind of cancer you get. Great strides have been made for certain cancers. The 5-year survival rate in the US for prostate cancer is 99%. Leukemia, practically a death sentence for both adults and children in the 60s (especially prior to chemo and radiation treatments for it that didn't start until 1962), now has an average five-year survival rate of 57% in the US for adults, with a 60 to 85% rate for children under 15. Age-adjusted deaths from breast cancer, the most common form of cancer in women, rose slightly from 31.4 per 100,000 women in 1975 to 33.2 in 1989 but since then has declined steadily to 20.5 in 2014.

SMOKING

"Tobacco is a poison to the young, and is far more hurtful to the adult than is generally supposed. It may be stated, as a rule, that there are few persons who use it habitually that do not suffer injury from it. The injury is mainly caused by…nicotine."

The above is not from a modern source, or even from the 60s. It is from *Hutchinson's Physiology and Hygiene* by Joseph C. Hutchison, MD, published in 1895. Fortunately for the tobacco companies, people took heed to advertising instead of medical texts.

Anybody who has seen *Mad Men* and similar shows that take place in the 60s know how universal smoking was then. I hardly ever saw my father without a cigarette, and he wasn't the only one. Even my paternal grandfather smoked in his 80s; in my diary I record that his gift from us on Father's Day 1969 (when he was nearly 83 years old) was a card and cigarettes.

Many doctors smoked then. Other doctors, like Dr. Hutchison above, said it wasn't good for you, or that it would "stunt your growth" (rather appropriate as pregnant women who smoke statistically give birth to babies with low birth weights). But the link to cancer was bandied about for years in the 20th century. As early as 1929 there was a German study linking lung cancer (among the rarest forms of cancer before smoking) to smoking. But not until 1964 did the United States Surgeon General announce the relationship between smoking and cancer. And I remember that announcement.

I was watching Saturday morning cartoons when a special announcement was made concerning the above Surgeon General statement. My dad worked Saturday mornings, and I was afraid I was going to get cancer from him when he lit up when he got home. When he did get home I hid in my parents' bedroom to stay away from him and his dangerous smoke. He had a talk with me that assuaged my fear somehow. I think basically he said that I wouldn't get cancer if I didn't smoke myself. I was fine with that.

In 1986 it was demonstrated that passive smoking was also harmful.

It was impossible to get away from cigarette smoke then, and we all just got used to it. We actually tolerated it to a high degree, though there were exceptions for me. In cars on cold days my father would smoke with us there, and the windows closed. The smell of the vinyl seats that were standard issue in cars, combined with the cigarette smoke, would make me nauseous. Just thinking about that smell makes me queasy.

It's interesting how intolerable cigarette smoke is to me now considering how generally tolerable it was to me in the past. In 2002 my family and I visited Austria and Germany. You could smoke anywhere. We ate dinner in a small diner, where people were eating and smoking and some just drinking and smoking. It was cold outside, so the windows were closed. It was nauseating to all of us, so we opened a window. We were chastised for letting cold air in and the waitress shut the window.

RUGGED INDIVIDUALISM

We didn't run to hospital emergency rooms that quickly when we got hurt or sick. There were probably some times when we should have. Though I didn't play rugged sports, I sure fell a lot, off my bike (and helmets weren't available yet) and even down my stoop. No matter what bruise, cut, or lump I got (on my head), it was always taken care of at home. Sometimes that wasn't good, like when I got a nasty infection on my arm that I hurt when running down concrete stairs in a park, but even then we didn't go to a doctor or hospital. Hydrogen Peroxide to clean wounds and ice to bring down lumps, together with the popular Band-Aid, were all we needed.

I never saw my grandfather go to a doctor. Once he got a bloody nose that just wouldn't stop bleeding, so we brought Dr. Sturgeon *to him* (after balking about having to make a house call). The doctor said he should go to the hospital. My grandfather steadfastly refused, over and over again. My grandfather said that people only went to the hospital to die. So he didn't go. His nose stopped bleeding.

In 1973 his wife, my grandmother, had a heart attack and went to the hospital. She died that same day. My grandfather died in 1975, in his bed at home.

Once as a kid I had brown urine. It concerned me, and I showed my mother. She said I would have to see a doctor *if it happened again*. It didn't.

Another time when I was small I woke up shaking, fairly violently. If that ever happened with one of my kids, I would have taken them to a hospital immediately. My parents gave me tea and we waited some time. I remember them looking concerned but they weren't quite ready to bring me to a hospital. Indeed, after some time passed the tremors went away, and I went back to sleep. They never returned—ever. To this day why that happened back then is a mystery to me.

I witnessed my dad doing something foolish on a trip to the park once, squirting lighter fluid from its metal can onto a coal fire that appeared to be dying out. Flames rushed up the stream to the can and the can exploded in his hand. His hand was cut pretty badly—I never saw anyone bleed like he did before. He took it calmly, though, applying pressure with a piece of cloth, and the barbeque continued. His bleeding eventually stopped and he never sought stitches.

We never went to emergency rooms, in fact, in the 60s. Never.

PRIMITIVE WAYS TO HELP MENTAL ILLNESS AND DEVELOPMENTAL DISABILITIES

Around 1960 my father had issues with anxiety. When he explained his condition to a NYC doctor recommended by a family friend, the doctor gave him a handful of pills and told him to take them together and take a walk in Central Park with my mom. The pills didn't make him feel more relaxed—they made him sick. My mother worried about getting him home. But they did get home, and my father didn't go back to a doctor about anxiety anymore. Fortunately, it passed.

In all fairness, much progress was made for mental illness in the 1960s. Since the development of effective antipsychotic drugs in the 50s, such as Chlorpromazine (trade name Thorazine), there was a great push for deinstitutionalization of mentally ill patients, moving them from an asylum-based mental care system to community-oriented care. Antipsychotics were a major factor in reducing the number of people living in institutions in the US, from about 0.3% in 1955 (over 500,000 total) to about 0.04% in 1996 (less than 100,000 total), just about one-tenth that of 1955.

In addition, after centuries of abuse, patients were given rights under the Community Mental Health Act (CMHA) of 1963, and strict standards were passed so that only individuals "who posed an imminent danger to themselves or someone else" could be committed to state psychiatric hospitals. This Act led to considerable deinstitutionalization.

Unfortunately the CMHA was only a partial success. Only half of the mental health centers it proposed were built, and even those were not fully funded. Not all communities had the facilities or expertise to deal with the mentally ill. In many cases, patients wound up in adult homes, back with their families, in anonymous shelters or even homeless.

Thorazine was no panacea, either, though it was fairly safe and effective. It produced a lethargy so bad that Thorazine patients became known as having the "Thorazine shuffle," a foot-dragging stride of walk. The long-term use of antipsychotics in general is associated with side effects such as involuntary movement disorders, increase in size of male breasts, and increased blood pressure, obesity and other metabolic problems. They are also associated with increased mortality in elderly people with dementia.

Depression in the 60s was treated medicinally by Monoamine Oxidase Inhibitors (MAOIs). Unfortunately, these drugs had an extreme side effect—death—in patients who ate foods and drank beverages containing Tyramine. Tyramine occurs widely in plants and animals. It can be found in meats that are potentially spoiled or pickled, aged, smoked, fermented, or marinated; most pork; chocolate; alcoholic beverages; most cheeses; yogurt; soy; bananas; pineapple; figs; eggplants; plums; raspberries; peanuts; cocoanuts; processed meats and more. Because of this, safer alternatives have been prescribed since the 70s.

Because of the medications developed, Electroconvulsive therapy (ECT, or "shock treatment") actually saw a decline in the 60s. The use of ECT has *increased* since the 70s (and continues to this day) because of improved treatment delivery methods, increased safety and comfort measures, and enhanced anesthesia management. ECT is considered the most effective treatment for severe mental illness and is also considered an extremely safe treatment. It can cause severe memory loss, however.

Though in the US the 60s were the last decade of its use, Insulin Shock therapy was used for treatment of schizophrenia by injecting large doses of insulin in patients in order to produce daily comas over several weeks. After about 50 or 60 comas, or earlier if the psychiatrist thought that the maximum benefit had been achieved, the dose of insulin was rapidly reduced before treatment was stopped. Courses of up to 2 years have been documented. Seizures sometimes occurred before or during the coma. Many patients would be tossing, rolling, moaning, twitching, having spasms or thrashing around. Some psychiatrists regarded the seizures as therapeutic and patients were sometimes also given Electroconvulsive therapy or cardiazol/metrazol convulsive therapy during the coma, or on the day of the week when they didn't have insulin treatment.

Unfortunately, the treatment of mental health had a bad reputation from the mid-60s to the late 70s. From "Mental Health in New York State 1945-1998," by Bonita Weddle, Coordinator of Electronic Records at NY State Archives:

> From the mid-1960's onward, the problems associated with the slow development of community mental health centers, the inherent shortcomings of the centers themselves, and excessively optimistic discharge policies became increasingly apparent. Politicians and the general public were increasingly critical of the poorly planned revolution in mental health treatment and policy…society's opinions about mental health and psychiatry changed dramatically as a result of the intense cultural, political, and social ferment that characterized the latter half of the 1960's and early 1970's. People on opposite ends of the political spectrum denounced the very concept of

mental health. Psychiatrists, who had formerly been seen as compassionate experts, were instead frequently denounced as ruthless oppressors bent on singling out and crushing the individuality of those who rejected the dominant values of society... Extremist right-wing organizations had long denounced mental health programs as covert attempts to facilitate the spread of Soviet communism, and their attacks increased as psychiatrists and others voiced their support for the civil rights and anti-war movements, anti-poverty programs, and other causes. By the late 1960's and early 1970's, mainstream conservatives, who were increasingly convinced that the mental health field was composed almost exclusively of their political enemies, were also suspicious of psychiatry...

The writings of scholars outside of the psychiatric profession gave added force to the assault on psychiatric legitimacy, and their influence is to this day evident within a number of academic disciplines. In 1965, the English translation of French philosopher Michel Foucault's "Madness and Civilization" first appeared. Foucault argued that the altruism that had been associated with psychiatry since the eighteenth century was a facade: psychiatrists were not humane helpers of the mentally ill but coercive figures seeking to force asylum inmates to internalize the moral discipline of bourgeois society...He asserted that the function of insane asylums and prisons is to compel the compliance of those who resist integration into the state's moral and behavioral regime.

Ms. Weddle goes on to say that from the early 60s onward writers and filmmakers took a harsh view of psychiatrists, in novels such as *One Flew Over the Cuckoo's Nest* (1962; screen adaptation in 1975), *A Fine Madness* (1964) and the film *Diary of a Mad Housewife* (1970). Indeed, I can add to that list *Frances* (1982), which showed how easily one could be institutionalized in the 1940s and lobotomized to cure a supposed mental illness.

Along with the Movement to deinstitutionalize the mentally ill in the 60s, there was a similar Movement to deinstitutionalize the developmentally disabled as well. However, in the 60s there were still many developmentally disabled patients in institutions. And not until 1980 was there a law, the Civil Rights of Institutionalized Persons Act, to protect the rights of these people as well as those in nursing homes, mental health facilities, and in correctional facilities. However, not even this law protects people in private facilities.

Willowbrook State School was a state-supported institution for children with intellectual disability located in the Willowbrook neighborhood on Staten Island in NYC from 1947 until 1987. Though designed for 4,000 people, by

1965 it had a population of 6,000. At the time, it was the biggest state-run institution for people with mental disabilities in the United States. Notorious conditions created by overcrowding, budget cuts and just plain indifference caused NY Senator Robert Kennedy to refer to Willowbrook in 1965 as a "snake pit." Too slowly did the deplorable conditions there get the attention of the media. In November 1971, The *Staten Island Advance* published a series of articles detailing the horrible conditions at the school. Following these articles, in January 1972, Geraldo Rivera, the previously-mentioned reporter from Eyewitness News, NY, began a series of programs that shook the conscience of New York State and the nation and inspired parents and others to take legal action.

I remember Rivera's reports from inside Willowbrook. In his first visit, unannounced, patients were lying or sitting on floors, in various degrees of undress, many naked. The floors were covered in urine and feces, many patients sitting on their own excrement or smeared with it. It was crowded, and everyone appeared to be on their own, not being helped by any staff (Rivera, in fact, reported that there was only one staff member for 50 children). The howling ("mournful wail," as Rivera described) of the patients struck my soul. It was at the time the scariest stuff on TV, and it was real.

Rivera went back announced, and lo and behold conditions were vastly better. But on another unannounced visit, things were just like the first visit. Rivera also reported on physical and sexual abuse of residents by members of the school's staff.

The history of Willowbrook was even worse than this. The disabled children were used as human guinea pigs on research into how hepatitis was spread. One of these studies involved feeding live hepatitis virus to sixty healthy children.

STEVEN MANDELI

7 SAFETY

Though I have written about what a "safe" time the 60s appeared to be, at least in terms of crime and terrorism, it was really not a "safe" period to live in. I have already covered the "ancient" medicine of those days which made living more precarious than now, exacerbated by the acceptance of smoking anywhere, but there were a lot of other things that made it an unsafe world. I've also already covered the historical events such as the Cuban Missile Crisis of 62 that almost led to nuclear annihilation (at least the closest we got to it), but there were a lot of everyday things that made the 60s less safe than today.

CARS AND TRAFFIC SAFETY

As noted previously, cars were solidly built—both our 56 and 68 Chevy's were like trucks. But there is a lot more to safety than solidity. The 56 had no crash safety devices. It certainly didn't have any air bags, but incredibly it also didn't have any seat restraints—even lap belts. It also wasn't built for safety—no collapsible fenders or other "safe" construction features, though all that metal did provide some protection. Unfortunately, the dashboards were metal, too, and there was nothing to restrain you from flying into them.

I remember actually sitting in the front bench seat right next to my dad, who was driving, unrestrained and happy (though I preferred the window seat, which my brother always got—grr). I imagine that at times I was a pain in the ass, and could have disturbed my dad while driving as he was right next to me. It behooves me that I could do this and it was acceptable and legal. But wait—my sister was born in 66 and was held when she was a baby by my mom in the front or back bench seats with neither restrained. There were no child seats and no lap belts to attach them to. Damn!

But we can add to this dangerous scenario. We lived in NYC, which since the gas shortages of the early 70s has had a 50 MPH speed limit on highways, with the rest of Long Island stuck at the double-nickel—55 MPH. But in the 60s the speed limit was generally 65.

We can add even more danger. Keep in mind that alcohol flowed freely in the 1960s (no party was complete without lots of booze) and it essentially wasn't against the law to drink and drive. There were no DUI or DWI laws and certainly no sobriety checkpoints. There wasn't even a breathalyzer to test your BAC.

[Side note. Even in the early 80's you got away with drinking and driving. I was a foolish young man then and had a drunk driving incident in which my car was damaged but stuck in a ditch. I was *happy* to see a police car to help me out (no cellphones). They did, calling a tow truck on their radio to pull my car out. I thanked them all and drove home.]

But I can paint an even less safe picture. Roads weren't lit like today. Even the Long Island Expressway did not have lights outside of Queens until sometime in the eighties. I know—I travelled that road at night going to graduate school in the early eighties (I didn't just drink in excess then). That road did have reflectors at that time, but they weren't around in the 60s. [The LIE wasn't "completely around" in the 60s, either, I should note, as its construction spanned from the 50s to 1973.]

The lights on highways that did exist in the 60s were relatively poor—utilizing incandescent or old florescent technology. Signs were lit by lights—the green reflective signs did not exist yet. And the darn signs were *small*—with black letters on white backgrounds.

Quite a grim picture of traffic safety, eh? It's a wonder that most of us survived.

What about traffic lights? Now they hang in the middle of a street. Then they were affixed to poles on the sidewalks. Obviously, they were harder to see.

In Queens there weren't enough traffic lights. There were stop signs everywhere, even in major intersections. They weren't replaced with traffic lights unless there were major accidents occurring at that intersection. Then, *viola!* traffic lights.

In 1968 the National Safety Council implemented the Buckle Up for Safety campaign. TV was suddenly filled with PSAs to "buckle up for safety." Jingle writer Richard Trentlage (1928–2016), composer of the famous Oscar Meyer jingle ("Oh, I'd love to be an Oscar Mayer Wiener, that is what I truly wish to be…") adapted the musical number "Buckle down Winsocki" from the 1943 musical motion picture *Best Foot Forward* (starring Lucille Ball) into the following catchy tune:

Buckle up for safety, buckle up.
Buckle up for safety, always buckle up.
Pull your seat belts snug, give an extra tug,
Buckle up for safety, buckle up.

Buckle up for safety, buckle up.

Buckle up for safety, always buckle up.
Show the world you care by the belt you wear,
Buckle up for safety when you're driving, buckle up.

Buckle up for safety, buckle up.
Buckle up for safety, always buckle up.
Put your mind at ease, tell your riders please,
Get your seat belts buckled, everybody buckle up.

The PSA sternly added, "If you *don't* have seat belts *get* them. If you *do* have seat belts *use* them."

Unfortunately, seat belt use was optional for a long time. The very first law requiring seat belt usage for drivers and front seat passengers wasn't until 1970, and that was in Australia. Slowly, the US states enacted these laws much later. The National Highway Traffic Safety Administration (NHTSA), which conducts the National Occupant Protection Use Survey (NOPUS) annually, reveals that seat belt use was only 14% in the first year of its study, 1983. It reports usage in 2010 as 85%.

DANGEROUS SUBSTANCES

One of the most dangerous substances due to its ubiquity was cigarette smoke. Almost everyone smoked and they could smoke anywhere. So secondhand smoke was a major problem, and would continue to be well beyond the 60s. But there were other dangerous substances that were everywhere.

It is now well-known and has been known for a long time that asbestos is dangerous, causing many cases of deadly mesothelioma per year. In a decade like the 60s asbestos was used everywhere—including apartment buildings, homes and schools. We had it in our basement insulating the steam pipes. In fact, my father told me that *his father* put it there.

According to Asbestos.com, asbestos was "once was lauded for its versatility, recognized for its heat resistance, tensile strength and insulating properties, and used for everything from fire-proof vests to home and commercial construction." Homes and apartments built before 1980 often are filled with asbestos, needing only normal wear and tear with age to dislodge particles and send them airborne. Asbestos can be found in floor tiles, roofs, furnaces, plumbing, appliances, fireplaces and window caulking, leaving most everyone vulnerable.

Asbestos removal has been going on for decades, but it still exists in hidden places where it has not been noticed. However, in the 60s, it wasn't being removed anywhere—it was being *installed*.

The insecticide DDT was used widely used for decades. Fortunately, in 1962, the groundbreaking book *Silent Spring*, penned by American biologist Rachel Carson, was published. It described the environmental impacts and effects on human health of indiscriminate DDT spraying in the US. The book claimed that DDT and other pesticides had been shown to cause cancer and that their agricultural use was a threat to wildlife, particularly birds. Its publication resulted in a large public outcry that eventually led, in 1972, to a ban on the agricultural use of DDT in the US.

We have a lot to thank Rachel for, but a lot of people had been exposed to DDT before 1972 and died from it. The 60s was the last decade of its use in the US, but one can only assume, because of population growth, that the 60s was the peak decade of its exposure to humans.

In the 50s people started talking about and recognizing pollution. In the 60s and 70s Congress started to *do* something about it. The first federal legislation to actually pertain to controlling air pollution, for example, was the Clean Air Act of 1963. But like the situation with DDT, one can assume that the 60s was one of the most polluted decades in the US.

For me, education about pollution started in the late 60s. In High School in the early 70s I first learned of Rachel Carson's book—in Speech class (it wasn't covered anywhere else).

Hollywood fortunately joined the bandwagon, just after the 60s, and showed us ecological nightmares. In a 1971 episode of the TV series *The Name of the Game*, an early directorial effort by Steven Spielberg, we are shown Los Angeles in the year 2017 as an air-polluted wasteland wherein people have to live underground. The episode, simply titled, "LA 2017," concerned me. I would be 60 then, I thought—old, but dying? In 1973, the movie *Soylent Green* appeared, and showed us what NY would be like in 2022. One of my favorite movies, starring both Charlton Heston and Edward G. Robinson (in his last role), it showed a miserable overcrowded world where the temperature is always high, even at night in the 90s, due to the greenhouse effect—a term bandied about a lot now but something new to most people in 1973. A less memorable but still important movie, *Silent Running* (1972), showed a future where all flora on Earth has died and the only existing flora is safe in pressurized domes on a spaceship orbiting Saturn. These portrayals from 1971, 1972 and 1973 showed that we were certainly worried about the long-tern effects of pollution in the 60s-70s terminator. These cautionary tales may have indeed inspired some legislation.

A simple form of air pollution occurred regularly in my neighborhood in the 60s. There was a large apartment building across the street that still used an incinerator to burn its garbage. Admittedly as a kid I thought it was fun to see the ashes float down to the ground, like snow. But it obviously wasn't good for us.

Soft drinks were extremely popular in the 60s, especially with kids. They are still popular today, but there is now a health consciousness that keep many away from soft drinks and giving them to their kids. My granddaughter, for example, has never tasted a soft drink because my daughter has never allowed her to—she has only drank formula, water and juice. Non-diet soft drinks are filled with sugar, which leads to a number of possible medical issues such as obesity and tooth decay. Though I wasn't obese as a child (now I am), I sure had trouble with tooth decay. Yearly visits to the dentist would reveal large amounts of cavities, sometimes about 5 or 6. At that time my sugar intake was high, between soft drinks and candy. The "candy" was anywhere from sugary (candy bars) to flavored sugar (powder candy) to pure sugar (rock candy).

"Diet" soft drinks at the time were much less common than now, as modern "sweet" artificial sweeteners were not developed yet. Diet Rite was the first soft drink made without sugar, and was introduced for dietetic consumers only in 1958, but in 1962 was marketed for the general public. Diet Rite was sweetened with cyclamates and saccharin. In 1963, the Coca Cola company introduced their own diet soda, Tab. [Remember when Marty McFly asked for a Tab in 1955 in *Back to the Future*? Tab was still available in 1985, his own time, though Diet Coke had been introduced by then.] This was sweetened with cyclamates only.

For kids, soft drinks like Tab sucked; I thought it was awful. Cyclamates were not very sweet at all, not near as sugary as modern sweeteners such as NutraSweet. They were definitely only for serious dieters. So, most people drank the bad sugary stuff. As it turned out, research in the 60s indicated cyclamates caused cancer—at least in mice. The FDA banned it in 1969. Diet Rite and Tab had to be reformulated, as well as diet snacks that used the stuff. My poor mom had to deal without some of those snacks at the time, and we were frightened that she may have gotten cancer from them. As it turned out better studies made later indicated that the original studies were wrong. Though the ban on cyclamates still exists in the US today, other countries that had banned them now allow their use and the countries that never banned them still use them—though I have no idea why, as there are better sweeteners around.

As for saccharin, which got used in diet sodas after cyclamates were banned, that too got a bad rep as being a possible carcinogen in studies performed on rodents, but it was never banned. Warning labels were required for a time but those were no longer required after December 2010, when the EPA removed saccharin from its list of hazardous substances. By the way, that's what *Sweet 'n Low* is made from.

So, in summary, people who insisted on drinking diet soft drinks in the 60s, as horrible as they were, did indeed reap health benefits over regular sugary soft drinks. And those terrible diet snacks that my mom ate that had the consistency of Styrofoam and very little sugary taste did her no harm after all.

DANGEROUS TOYS

A lot of toys popular in the 60s were actually quite dangerous. Let me give you some examples.

The Creepy Crawlers Thing Maker was first introduced by Mattel in 1964, and it was so "cool" I had to get it right away (probably the next Christmas). It was essentially a heating plate that you plugged into the wall (with a very short cord, so I would plug into a kitchen outlet and play with it by the stove). Onto this miniature "hot plate" you put metal dies of all sorts of creepy animals—bugs and reptiles, essentially. You squeezed a substance in a plastic tube called "plastigoop" into it, which came in a variety of colors. There was no on-off switch; it started heating up as soon as it was plugged in. The heat (reportedly 390 degrees) would harden the plastigoop into the mold of the creature. To find out if it was "ready," you were supplied a pin to stick into the hardening goop. When it was ready, you picked up the tray with tongs provided that you squeezed together to fit into slots on the metal mold and you moved that mold onto a plastic tray provided that you had filled with water. The mold would be cooled (eventually) by the water, and you pried the plastic creature with the pin out of the mold. *Voila!*

Though I never received major burns from this contraption, I sometimes burned myself, as I was dealing with high temperatures at close proximity to my hands and face. To make things even more interesting, you got safety pins to hold on the surface of the still-hot plastigoop so half would be embedded. This made for fine jewelry, which I presented once to my teacher and she wore it all day! [I was unhappy, though, that she didn't wear it ever again.]

Mattel made a safer version of this out of plastic with lower temperatures for the next decade but it didn't work as well.

The Kenner Easy-Bake Oven baked treats using the heat from two 100-watt incandescent (the old kind) bulbs, which is a lot of heat! Incredibly, the now-defunct Kenner sold millions of these throughout the years and complaints about burns weren't made (at least legally) until this century, and this toy, albeit in a safer version, continues to be sold this day.

Hasbro's Lite Brite was a square box with holes throughout it that one could insert different-colored plastic pegs in and used the good-old fashioned (hot) incandescent bulb, plugged into the wall, to light them up from the inside. Hasbro got rid of the light bulb as soon as technology allowed, using LEDs, but now perhaps the safest form of this toy is now available—an app on the iPad.

In the late 60s it was time for a chemistry set—and just in time, as they were losing popularity because they were reputed to be dangerous (pshaw!). I had a love/hate relationship with mine. The chemicals did scare me, but I liked the tricks they could do. For example, there were two clear chemicals that mixed together would turn red—and as you continued to mix them they became clear again. You could also have the mix start out clear and just shake it to turn red; shake it again, and it returned to clear. I always imagined, though, that if I mixed the "wrong" stuff together, I would cause an explosion. Once while just making a mixture to clean a test tube, the mixture itself bubbled out of the test tube like a volcano (well, not quite, but it was scary). We once found an ancient chemistry set in the cellar. I bet that had really dangerous stuff in it. We disposed of it immediately—carefully.

Many toys were dangerous because they used lead paint. As we now know, lead is very toxic, affecting almost every organ and system in the body, of most concern to a child's developing brain. It is considered a "highly poisonous metal," especially when ingested, to a lesser extent through inhalation, and occasionally just through direct contact. A small amount of ingested lead (1%) will be stored in bones, and the rest will be excreted by an adult but only about a third of lead will be excreted by a child.

The Toy Safety Act of 1969 removed lead paint from toys. This was obviously too late for us children in the 60s. And lead paint wasn't just used in toys.

SAFETY IN THE WORKPLACE

The Occupational Safety and Health Administration (OSHA) was not created until 1970. The 60s were a dangerous time for workers, though many were pushing for worker safety in that decade, indeed resulting in the formation of OSHA right after it ended.

I remember that working conditions for my father, who was a machinist, were uncomfortable and dangerous. The summers were very hot, with only some fans to provide warm breezes. He bundled up to survive the cold winters in the machine shop. He had at least a few injuries in his career, including getting small pieces of metal in his eyes and his fingers; his finger once developed a tumor around the metal and the tumor had to be removed.

There were a number of incidents in the 60s that pushed for formation of a federal watchdog for worker safety, the history of which can be found on the Department of Labor website. In January 1968, President Johnson called on Congress to enact a job safety and health program, stating that it was "the shame of a modern industrial nation" that each year more than 14,000 workers were killed and 2.2 million injured on the job. Citing inadequate standards, lagging research, poor enforcement of laws, shortages of safety and health personnel, and a patchwork of ineffective Federal laws, Johnson argued that a comprehensive new law was needed. Congressional committee hearings on the Johnson proposal began in February 1968. Secretary of Labor Wirtz, who led off the hearings, compared the industrial toll at home to the military toll in Vietnam—and claimed that 3 of 4 teenagers entering the work force would probably suffer one minor disabling injury or more during their work life.

Despite the above, the 1968 proposal failed to pass Congress.

In 1967, it was revealed that almost a hundred uranium miners, an abnormally high number, had died of lung cancer since the 1940s. Up to a thousand more such deaths were expected. In 1947, when large-scale uranium mining was getting underway, the Atomic Energy Commission discovered that radiation levels in uranium mines were dangerously high. The Commission, in cooperation with the Public Health Service, began a long-term health study of the miners. A number of Federal agencies had limited jurisdiction over uranium mines, but none had clear responsibility for them, and there was very little enforcement.

In 1968, a mine explosion killed 68 men in Farmington, WV. This spurred Congress to pass the Coal Mine Health and Safety Act of 1969.

In the context of Federal action, President Richard Nixon presented his version of a comprehensive job safety and health program to Congress in August 1969. Buried in the battle of witnesses for and against the Nixon proposal were some thought-provoking comments by Irving Selikoff. He described the suffering of construction workers who succumbed to asbestosis (which can develop into lung cancer, mesothelioma, and pulmonary heart disease) from applying asbestos insulation to buildings. Refusing to blame any one group, he said that no-one was to blame—and that the deaths were "impersonal, technological," but that "we have all failed."

Again according to Asbestos.com, the properties of asbestos were so desired that, "The United States military mandated its use in every branch of service. Asbestos was a perfect blend to make things better – except it was highly toxic, too. Today asbestos is a known cause of mesothelioma cancer, is banned in more than 50 countries (*not the U.S.*), and its use has been dramatically restricted in others…More than 75 different types of jobs in America have been known to expose workers to asbestos, according to the National Institute for Occupational Health and Safety. At the same time, an estimated 30 percent of all mesothelioma cases are military veterans, an indication of where the worst damage has been done. Occupations in the construction industry have been hit the hardest, according to the National Institute for Occupational Safety and Health. Plumbers, pipefitters, steam fitters and electricians were the most vulnerable to asbestos-related diseases. The occurrence in both the shipbuilding and the electrical power industries also has been abnormally high."

Life in the 1960s: The True Story

8 WHAT WE DID WITH OURSELVES

No internet. No personal computers. No smartphones. No video game consoles. No Blu-Ray/Blu-Ray 3D/DVD players or even VCRs. Since there was no internet, there were no Facebook pages to maintain, no Wikipedia to look things up, no YouTube to browse through, no twitter accounts to follow, no instant access to porn (not that I ever look), I could go on and on. We had TV (up to 25 inches diagonal or so, and in the first half of the decade in glorious black-and-white), but could watch only three networks with one channel each, two local stations, and one PBS station (without even *Sesame Street* until 1969!), for a total of seven channels. We could listen to music in STEREO from a radio or a record player, but we of course couldn't download music. So what the heck *did we do with ourselves*?

THE WORLD OUTSIDE

My mother hated seeing us kids inside our house when it was a nice day outside, especially if we were just goofing around or watching TV (just another form of goofing around), so she always encouraged us to play outside.

I'm sure sickos existed back then but apparently not as much as now (and certainly not as well-advertised as now), so we kids would, in apparent safety, go to different places in our neighborhood and outside of it all day, sunrise to sundown if we wanted, outside of school hours. We would walk, ride our bikes, catch a bus or subway, and go somewhere interesting and fun. We sure didn't ask our parents to take us there, unless it was *really far away*—for me, New Jersey, upstate NY or "out on the island" as we used to call Long Island (pronounced "Long Guyland"). We certainly didn't have "play dates" to bother our parents to drive us to; we just got to Jimmy Smith's house however it was best to get there—preferably by walking or bike, because buses and subways cost 15 cents, a lot of money back then that could be used for better things like a comic book or three candy bars or a slice of pizza.

We had good reason to be outside and go places. First, we didn't have all that stuff that we have now to keep us entertained at home. Second, most of us didn't have air conditioners until later in the decade, and even then it was only for one room, and our parents would put it selfishly in their bedroom. On hot days, it was cooler to be outside—and if you were lucky enough to get money to see a movie, you got to sit for hours (in the case of a double-feature, with intermission) in the theater, which *was* awesomely air conditioned. Third, why would you hang out with your mom and/or dad when you could run amok outside?

So, we went to movies (to see one and cool off), public pools (to see girls in bathing suits and cool off), and wherever to fancy our interests. Now that isn't to say that we never stayed right by our homes. We could play and do all sorts of mischief there too—and when doing mischief, just making sure our moms didn't catch us as they stuck their heads out the window to tell us to come up to eat or simply to converse with people as they stopped by (my mom would do her ironing at the picture window we had and, if she saw a friend, stick her head out the window and have a conversation).

So what did we do outside? We played stickball in the street, stoopball by the…stoop, killed ants with concentrated sunlight from a magnifying glass, played with "outside" toys (like plastic soldiers) in the dirt, and played *War*.

We loved to play *War*. We saw a lot of war on TV and the movies, and we heard war stories from many of our dads, who might have served in World War II or the Korean "Conflict." We played the squeaky clean "war" we saw on TV, which amazingly never had blood. So much for realism. War wasn't hell in those days—it was kind of fun, at least on TV. Heck, they made a hit comedy about a Prisoner of War camp on *Hogan's Heroes*—and it was very funny.

World War II was our favorite war. It was the one portrayed the most on TV and the movies. The Good Guys and the Bad Guys were clearly delineated—no shades of grey. And the Nazis were evil, no doubt about that, so they deserved to die. Korea just wasn't exciting enough. And as for Vietnam, no-one knew what that was in the early sixties and as that new "conflict" continued, it just became a short segment covered by the likes of Walter Cronkite daily. Body counts, ho-hum. [No offense to the brave men who died there; I'm just saying the news accounts of the battles became so commonplace.]

We played *War* with whatever we had. Every boy had toy guns—cap guns (which used loadable strips of paper with actual blisters of gunpowder on them and made a nice sparky noise), machine guns, air rifles, BB guns (though then you could shoot your eye out!), you name it. If we didn't have toy guns sticks would do. If we didn't have that we just pretended.

We also sometimes had war accessories, like plastic helmets. I knew one kid who was lucky enough to have his dad's actual helmet. There were ammo belts too, and other fun War stuff.

Playing War led to (surprise!) fights often. The fights were over whether you were "killed" or not. Nobody liked being killed, which meant you had to play dead and be out of the game, so we fought over who was killed in a battle. That could actually lead to real fisticuffs. Hey, we took our wars seriously.

We pretended a lot in our outside play, and used our imaginations. We also built things to play with—like scooters, out of wooden boxes. It was neat to invade our dads' workshops and nail something together for play. In fact, the act of driving nails through wood was fun in itself and expended loads of youthful energy and pent up frustrations.

But not all that we did outside was play—there was work to be done, too! My brother was an avid collector of all sorts of creatures—creatures that had to be fed. So, many bright and hot Summer mornings were spent in search of food for things like frogs and toads which were caught during trips to the Park. The "food" was bugs, bugs of all kinds.

Now it should be said that my brother, a fan of Reptiles and Amphibians, cared most for the former and he had a snake to feed (an incredible capture made near a resort we stayed at in upstate NY). The frogs were important because they were the *snake's* food. So it was a food chain we were supporting.

Having a snake was special. It was special because people were disgusted by them and watching a snake eat a frog whole was the ultimate in disgusting (translate "disgusting" into "cool" for boys). So, if we really liked somebody enough to bring them into our basement (AKA Inner Sanctum) to see the snake eat (you didn't think our mom would let a snake in her house!), they were in for a treat. As I said, it would eat the frog whole, unhinging its jaw to accommodate its amphibious treat. There would be some bubbles of blood, and hopeless resisting on the amphibian's part, which made it all the more exciting. And it was a *slow* process. Toward the end you would only see the still-extant frog's legs sticking out of the snake's mouth, jerking hopelessly. And at the end you would just see the frog's outline in the snake's stomach, which would slowly, ever slowly, diminish in size...

Who needs a thousand channels of TV!

I was less interested in animals than my brother, but, doing everything he did, I endured the heat to get those bugs from our backyard gardens and other people's backyard gardens. I also usually went with him to the pet shop to get food for our other animals, such as the tropical fish. It's interesting that most that sticks out of my mind of those days is the oppressive summer heat.

Now I can't say I had no interest in animals, but my interest was basically in torturing insects and killing them, due to some innate prepubescent desire to be mean to them. Maybe it was the heat. As noted above, frying an ant with the concentrated sunlight from a magnifying glass was widely practiced and socially acceptable. I went further. For example, I had an ant cemetery. I used flakes of lead paint (which might explain some mental issues) that was coming off of buildings (with a little prying) and used them as gravestones. I put them in an empty shoebox that I filled with dirt. One might say it was quite respectable of me to inter ants this way, but, you see, I was the one that squished them all to death in the first place!

Some of my cruelty to insects was for science's sake. I put ants and little bugs into plastic capsules that we got out of gumball machines (and had small choking hazard toys in them) and threw them up in the air as hard as I could to see if they would survive. They always did, until I squished them. I was very much into the Space Race and thought this was my contribution to the Reentry problem.

I hurt or killed animals of a higher zoological class than insects, but they were the victims of accidents. I didn't know that tying a string around a cat's neck to give it a "collar" so I could walk it would almost hang the cat. I didn't know that chasing chickens at my grandparents' farm in Austria would result in a dead chick that I had stepped on and a broken leg of another, larger, chicken that I had also accidentally stepped on. I didn't know at that same place that if I threw gravel into the air I would kill two birds in a flock that was flying by. Yes, I killed two birds with one throw of multiple stones.

I have a bird now and two dogs and all are still well, after a number of years living with me. So, no need to worry about further accidents. I do kill insects in my house, though.

DAYS IN THE PARK

We had wonderful weekends in the Park. For my brother and I there was only one park that was worth the trip—Alley Pond Park, only 20 minutes away. This wasn't a playground—this was nature. Alley Pond had two marvelously muddy ponds stocked with carp, lots of grass and trees, little pavement, and nature trails. It abounded with wooden picnic tables and barbeque pits made out of stone. It was a place you could catch frogs and toads (AKA "snake food") and maybe even something exciting (we tried to catch a mole once but only succeeded in drowning it in its underground lair). We fished in the ponds and caught carp and an occasional goldfish.

Almost every weekend, my dad would ask us where we wanted to go on Saturday and we always answered, "Alley Pond," to which he would reply, "Again?" But he would take us, the whole family, sometimes with friends and cousins too.

We would have barbeques in the park, though we didn't use the stone ones there—they were too "dirty," my dad would say. We brought our own grill. I loved the barbeque, because when it was done I would conduct my pyrotechnic experiments. These "experiments" usually just involved how much smoke I could create with dried leaves on the grill. Sometimes those leaves fell out of the grill, and I started little fires on the ground, but they were easily stomped out.

To this day the smell of charcoal burning reminds me of happy times in Alley Pond. My wife, though, having been raised in the 'burbs, doesn't understand having barbeques in the park—she always had them in her backyard. How boring! Nowadays I always see groups of people having barbeques in the park in large groups and they really look like they are enjoying themselves. My wife says they are there because they don't have houses. I think it is more of a cultural thing, because they seem mostly Hispanic. But they got the right idea—barbequing in the park is fun!

FISHING

We fished in those muddy ponds in Alley Pond Park, and actually took the small carp home. They would start dying on the way home, and the "lucky" that made it would die in a pail in our bathroom usually by morning. I have no idea why we brought these fish home (I think we actually considered we could keep them alive), and they sure smelled up the bathroom.

Being in NYC not far from the East River and Astoria Park, we would fish in the East River. Fortunately there was a metal fence on a sunken concrete wall that separated us from the river as the river was quite nasty. The rocks that bordered it had all sorts of garbage on them (I imagine also human remains) and live rats. We never caught anything worth a damn—only slimy eels.

In the South Bronx there was Orchard Beach, another favorite of local fishermen. We fished on a bridge over very shallow water that was an inlet of Long Island Sound. The biting was good—for the mosquitos. I never again encountered so many of those bloodsuckers until I visited Alaska many years later.

By Throg's Neck Bridge, in the vicinity of Fort Totten, there was an artificial narrow peninsula of boulders that jutted out into Long Island Sound. We assumed that these boulders originated from the construction of the Throg's Neck bridge in the early 60s. In either event, in the late 60s and early 70s we trekked out onto these boulders to do some fishing. The fishing wasn't great, but it was a great male bonding experience for dad, my brother and me. Troublesome were the rats and yellow jackets that loved those boulders; I wasn't as good as my dad and brother in ignoring them.

A nicer fishing destination was the New Croton Reservoir in Westchester, NY. This reservoir provided water to much of NYC. NYC always had a reputation for good water, and looking at this lake one could see why. It was pristine in appearance, the water looking clear enough to drink before filtering. Speaking of male bonding, this was the ultimate place for that in the late 60s and early 70s, with my brother and father joining me; the "girls" were always left home. We fished illegally, as you needed a special license to fish at this lake, but the worst that happened was having a state policeman saying we couldn't fish there, us leaving, and then returning. One thing I didn't like about this pretty spot were the caterpillars that appeared one time. They were everywhere, hanging on to every branch. I avoided them like the plague, but upon my bath at home I noticed one had gotten into my undershirt, and had been crawling in there for hours.

In the late 60s we used to fish on a boat owned by one of my father's friends in Center Moriches, Long Island. We caught a little of everything, including flounder and crabs. Center Moriches was a long trip for us; we would take the Long Island Expressway until it ended (it was not completed at the time) and then take a local road to Sunrise Highway to make it the rest of the way. It was worth it, though; I loved fishing on a boat. I remember getting seasick only once.

The best fishing was probably upstate, in the Catskills (see "VACATION" below). We were allowed to fish in a privately-stocked artificial lake. At one time we had a friend with us who caught a bass so big he had it mounted (which we would chuckle about—it wasn't that big). Once at sunset we noticed birds flying in the trees, after the birds should have quieted down for the night. The mystery was solved when we noted they were bats.

SUMMER NIGHTS

Summer nights were fantastic. Since for the most part of the 60s we didn't have air conditioners, everyone spent a fair amount of time outside in the Summer. We kids played just as we did during the daytime, though a little more carefully since our parents were outside too.

Our parents had a ball as well. This was a time of socializing. The streets were filled with people babbling about almost everything. This was a blue-collar neighborhood, so all the men got a break from their back-breaking jobs in the heat and the women got a break from the drudgery of housework in the heat. Men like my father didn't bother changing from their work garb though they tended to take off their shirts on those hot nights, revealing the now-infamous "wife beater" undershirts, the sleeveless form-fitting ones. Men didn't generally wear shorts—the long pants they wore during the day served well at night too.

My dad, like many men of the era, had the ubiquitous cigarette in his mouth and beer can in his hand; I don't think I would recognize him without those accouterments. When he ran out of cigarettes he just sent for more—my brother or I were the delivery boys. As noted above, we didn't have to worry about being minors—the local candy stores where we got the cigs knew us and that we didn't personally smoke them. As for beer replenishing, anybody could be asked to go upstairs and get another from the "icebox" (it was really a refrigerator, but old names still stuck), or my dad would actually get one himself on the way back from pissing out previously imbibed beer.

Our parents would sit on their stoops, often with others, and passers-by would stop to talk, until they all went to bed. It was really a wonderful thing when I think about it. We knew the whole neighborhood and they knew us. In the early 60s we didn't even have fences out front, so we kids had a lot of space to play in and people had a lot of space to hang around and talk. Then one day some idiot put up a fence, followed by another, until almost everyone had one. We and a next-door neighbor were literally the last holdouts.

Before the fences, conversation groups would get so large sometimes that people would bring out beach chairs to the sidewalk and sit in them, in basically a circle. Such meetings became epic. There was a lot of laughter and yes, the beer was flowing. Sometimes I joined in, though it was generally adults-only. The conversation only got a little dirty at times.

Now, living in suburbia, I see nothing like this. I only see neighbors when I come and go.

WINTER DAYS

Winter days were a lot of fun for kids as well. I do see plenty of kids enjoying winter nowadays, but a lot of it is in parks, supervised by parents. We had more fun without parents, in the streets. Of course, snow was a good reason for war games—snowball fights. They got pretty nasty, too. We would fight each other until somebody told us to leave their yard, and then we would go to another. Peacetime activities included building forts and shelters, and generating stockpiles of snowballs for the next war.

One winter, while snowball fighting with a group across the street, using cars as battlements, we covered the melted, mushy snow in the part of the street next to the curb with fresh snow so it didn't look like mushy snow. We then goaded them to cross the street and run after us by making nasty remarks about their parents or whatever. They fell for it, and stepped in a curb-height's worth of slush. The plan was perfectly executed. Of course they were angry and I ran like hell.

Of course, our parents did take us to parks for sled riding and other wholesome activities, and we enjoyed them. They are among my fondest of memories.

SUNDAYS & CHURCH

A lot of people actually attended church on Sunday regularly in those days, in our case the Roman Catholic Church. Every Sunday Mass was occupied beyond capacity; my brother and I would arrive a little late and have to stand, which he preferred I think because then we didn't have to kneel. In Summer it was hot; all they had to cool us down with were huge electric fans at front which were not very effective. Most people fanned themselves with any paper they could get their hands on. Mercifully, Masses had "Summer schedules" of only a half-hour duration. But even that was hard for people to handle. Often, people would faint—very often, in fact. But the Masses would always continue.

There were rules then that don't exist now. For example, we couldn't have eaten since the prior Midnight because our stomachs had to be empty to receive Communion. That made me very hungry at Mass. In fact, at times I got sick and threw up. Another rule was that men could not wear hats (popular all year at the time) in church while women *had* to keep their heads covered. And, of course, we were always dressed in our Sunday Best (see below).

One thing that was annoying in the early 60s was that the Mass was spoken in Latin, and the priest did not face his audience. This made things impersonal and you couldn't understand what was being said without a cheat sheet. I must say that Latin is a beautiful language but difficult to say and understand. Fortunately Vatican II occurred in the period 1962-1965 and starting in 1966 around the world we heard Masses in our own language—with the priest facing us.

Amazingly, there were no bathrooms available in church. Once I had a very bad stomach ache and my brother embarrassingly had to ask an usher for me to use a bathroom. They let me use one in the rectory, where the priests lived. I always wondered how the rest of the people "held it" during a normal Mass of nearly an hour. They couldn't all have gone to the rectory. Bathrooms were certainly scarcer in public places then. Of course, just watching 60s TV shows you would know we never had to go to a bathroom—nice people at least don't do that.

Outside of going to Mass, Sunday was a special day when people would walk around in their aforementioned "Sunday Best," which for men and boys was a suit. No matter what we did or where we went we wore a suit. A lot of times we just walked around, like check out the construction of my neighborhood's first strip mall, which to me was an amazing thing. In the NYC area (and in others, like LA), almost everybody went to a place called Robert Hall to get those suits, where the selection was enormous and the prices discounted. Robert Hall, in fact, was one of the pioneering warehouse-type retailers in the U.S. It operated for many years, but went bankrupt in 1977.

The women and girls dressed up in nice pink and frilly things, especially in Spring. They even wore white gloves. Everybody looked good on Sunday.

VACATION

We didn't have a lot of money for vacation. But my father did stock up money from unused sick days and Christmas (not "Holiday") bonuses. On occasion, we actually went somewhere for vacation.

One place we went to was "The Sunshine Valley House" in the Catskills of upstate NY. The reason we went there is because it had a German theme and it was operated by a friend of my father's, Karl Schwarzenegger. Of course, that last name may sound familiar to you, as it was shared by Arnold Schwarzenegger, actor and former governor of California. Interestingly enough, Karl's son was an "Arnold Schwarzenegger," who was a kid at the time we visited and for some time later we thought he was THE Arnold Schwarzenegger. Well, he wasn't, but many, many years later I learned on the internet that his father Karl was indeed a cousin of the famous Arnold, and in fact the future "Governator" had visited the Sunshine Valley House on a number of occasions.

The Sunshine Valley House was basically a bed-and-breakfast. The rooms had no TV, unusual at the time, but from what I have seen on the internet continues today (though under a different name). We loved our time there, as it was basically in the middle of nowhere, in unspoiled nature. We fished a lot, played some old geezer games like shuffle board, and frolicked in their pool. At night they would have German dancers in their clubhouse, which I would ignore while reading a comic book. My brother caught his snake there, which would give us years of enjoyment.

Of course, nothing is perfect. My sister would throw up on the way there, in the back of our 68 Chevy Impala. I would have horrible hay fever allergy symptoms, since we spent so much time outside and there was literally a lot of hay around. We even went to a doctor in town for me, who really had nothing to suggest, and said hay fever was just a nuisance for me right now but I would definitely develop asthma as an adult. I didn't. We met a nice older couple who we clicked with on their last night there for hours. The man showed us card tricks that amazed me. They exchanged numbers with us and it certainly looked like we made new friends who we would see again. The next morning we found out they died in a car accident on their way home.

All in all, though, I have fond memories of the Sunshine Valley House. There was one particular evening that provided a really nice memory with my father. We had gone there on this occasion with a family that was friends of ours (and one of our tenants), and one night we all played Monopoly. The father of the other family was clearly winning, which pleased him a little too much, and he got pretty obnoxious about it. I was losing, and not happy. At one point I just threw the game board down, its game pieces and faux money flying everywhere. The "winner" was pissed. He said to me, "If I were your father I'd give you a nice whooping in the ass." My father took me outside, and I was worried about the "whooping" I would get. Outside, he paused a bit, and then told me I shouldn't have done that, it was only a game. We stood outside for a few minutes and then just went back in. My father decided apparently that the incident wasn't worth a "whooping."

I must admit I was very sad every time we left that place. Karl Schwarzenegger always played a farewell song over the loudspeaker when a guest left. The goodbyes were sometimes long, and it would be played again and again, if need be. The song was "Auf Wiederseh'n, Sweetheart," sung in English by the great Vera Lynn (1917-   ) in 1952 and a chorus of English Soldiers and Airmen. It literally translates to something more than goodbye, but more like, "until we see (each other) again," like *au revoir*. It always nearly brings a tear to my eye.

We had a very special vacation in 1965, when I was seven. In that year we travelled to Austria and Germany. This was certainly a big deal then, as most people weren't traveling by plane for vacation. And it was a *jet*, which made my father very proud. The airline was Swissair, which at the time, typical of many airlines, was very much concentrated on customer comfort. Back then, there were no "flight attendants," but Stewardesses, all female and all attractive. They would fuss over us kids, pinning wings for the airline on our suits (which were almost required wear for plane travel). Meals were actual meals, and served on real plates.

This was the first time any member of my family flew on an airplane. My mom and brother sat with me, as there were three seats on each side, but my dad was alone on the aisle seat across from us. He was nervous as hell. I felt bad for him.

When we landed in Vienna we were picked up by my mother's dad, who was cold in demeanor. I couldn't believe this was my maternal grandfather, as he made no fuss over my mother. But he was still angry over my mother's decision to leave home and go to America in 1946, almost twenty years prior, when she was just 19 years old. He came with another guy who would drive us, in the first small car I ever saw, to our mom's home town.

On the way there he was stopped by a traffic cop, for some unknown reason. My dad tried to bribe him with American money, but he would have no part in that. Instead, he accepted a bribe from the driver in Austrian money, which in those pre-Euro days was in Schillings.

The arrival at my mom's home in lower Austria, near the Hungarian border, was completely different from the meeting of her father at the airport. Her mother and my mom cried, which confused me at the time because it was the first time I saw adults cry when happy to see each other.

We generally had a good time in Austria, staying with my grandparents, though I knew almost no German at all. My brother knew more, and would be able to converse with the kids well enough to get basic points across, like where he could catch frogs (which they couldn't understand why anyone would want to).

Of course, we missed TV, and I missed feather beds (they used hay filler, which I was allergic to). But things could have been worse—my grandparents had installed a modern bathroom just before we arrived, just because we were visiting.

One day a rooster attacked me, which made my grandmother very angry, and the next dinner we had she proudly exclaimed that the rooster who attacked me was now on the dinner plate. I was shocked, and felt too upset to eat it—besides, rooster meat is tough anyway. My family in general also caused a pig to die, as my grandparents decided to slaughter a pig in our honor. My brother and I were not allowed to be witnesses to the slaughter, but when we awoke we saw the pig carcasses hanging from a line, with blood everywhere.

My relationship with my maternal grandfather was onerous. He loved me, but was so angry at us Americans. He showed me a bug on his crops and claimed that the Americans had airdropped these in boxes during WWII. I have never heard of this, but why would he lie about it?

Life in the 1960s: The True Story

In 1965, just 20 years after WWII, some people just did not accept us very well. When we spoke English some would utter curses in German. On a train ride to Germany, to visit relations of my father, I had to use the bathroom, and in the process stepped on an old man's (or seemed so at the time) foot. He gestured to hit me, which my father stopped. [Then, when I got to the bathroom, I was dismayed that the "toilet" was simply an opening to the tracks, which I was afraid to fall through.]

In Germany, my father's relatives gave us a tour of a bombed-out city. I was aghast. I asked innocently, "Who did this?" to which one of the relatives responded, "You Americans." I felt so bad. I did not know yet the history of WWII and who started it.

Since Hungary was just a few miles away from my mom's town, we decided to visit the border. At that time the border was the Iron Curtain, and guarded by Soviet army in guard towers. We looked across the border, and then noticed the Soviet soldiers pointing their guns at us. We quickly ran to our car.

PLAYING GAMES

Of course, we usually stayed at home and didn't *always* play outside. It did rain at times, and sometimes we just wanted to stay inside. And, believe it or not, even without video games there were things to do.

For one thing, there were board games. *Monopoly* was one of my favorites, though back then there was only one variety—as of this writing, according to the Monopoly wiki (yes, there is one), there are 1,332 varieties of Monopoly, not including the PC versions. There is everything from the .com version to the Zoo-opoly version. We just had the one, but it was great. The realism wasn't always quite "up there," with rents and houses going for ridiculous sums ($200 for a house on Boardwalk, while real houses averaged about $15K!), though if passing "GO" happened weekly, $200 wasn't bad.

Monopoly games could become mythic. They could last for hours or even days. Sometimes we wrote down our board positions, cash, and properties and continued a game weeks later. Ah, the deals that went on when things were close and also not so close! Who needed *Shark Tank*?

Another favorite was the *Game of Life*, which started with the decade. This was a more realistic game, but still a lot of fun. And it had a three-dimensional board, with buildings and bridges. In this game, *after you got "married,"* you got "kids," which were pegs you stuck into your car playing piece that had holes in it to accommodate them. There were only six holes, so if you had more, you just laid them between their peg sisters and brothers. You wanted kids, because each player had to give you $500 when you got one. They didn't cost you anything after that, which is where realism went out the window. Your objective was to go through the normal path of life or take a chance of becoming a *tycoon*. Like Monopoly, whoever ended up with the most money at the end won. Unlike Monopoly you only went around the board once, and the game had a definite end in a reasonable amount of time.

The Game of Life had a famous spokesman—television personality Art Linkletter (1912-2010). He was such a good spokesman they put his picture on the box, with a testimonial stating, "I heartily endorse this game." And his picture was on the highest denomination of money—$100,000.

We played other games, of course, including card games. A favorite of ours was *War* (sense a common theme?). It was played with an ordinary deck, and I only played with one other player at a time, usually my brother. The deck was divided evenly between us; in turn, each revealed the top card of our decks – this was a "battle" – and the player with the higher card took both of the cards played and moved them to the bottom of their deck. If any cards played were the same (regardless of suit), then there was a "war"—both of us placed the next three cards of our pile face down and then another card face-up. The owner of the higher face-up card won the war and added all the cards on the table to the bottom of his deck. If the face-up cards were again equal then the battle repeated with another set of face-down/up cards. This repeated until one card was higher than the opponent's. The objective was to get all the cards, with your opponent left with none. No, I don't know what this had to do with war and it was pure random chance, not strategy.

My brother and I played "wars" in another way. We each got a huge (or at the time it seemed that way) plastic ship. Mine was an aircraft carrier called "Mighty Matilda" that moved slowly on the floor on battery power. It was one of the neatest toys I ever had. It came with tiny naval figures of different sorts that I could line up meticulously on the deck. It also had plastic aircraft I could line up on the deck and also move between upper and lower decks with mechanical elevators. Add to that spring-loaded missiles and you had a complete functional modern aircraft carrier!

My brother had "Big Cesar," a toy Roman galley ship. It moved, too, a bit more impressively, as the oars moved back and forth as it did. It came too with plastic figures, though lesser in number but larger than mine. Most had impressive spears.

We would have anachronistic battles between the two, which my brother, even with an ancient vessel with inferior technology, would always manage to win. I remember one time bugging my brother to have a war, and he just wasn't in the mood. But I persisted. He finally gave in, and we battled—for about 60 seconds. He knocked down all my meticulously lined up figures with one of his soldier's spears. I was annoyed, but it was kind of a fair fight; unarmed seamen were no match against giant soldiers with giant spears.

The two mighty ships succumbed to what many 60s toys succumbed to—battery leakage. Batteries were terribly made back then. If you left them in toys that remained unused for a time they leaked acid all over them and destroyed them. Thus was the fate of our ships in not too long a time—they were grounded by battery acid.

Interestingly, years later I would work as an Engineer on one of those aircraft that I positioned so carefully on that aircraft deck…

BUILDING AND CONSTRUCTING

Another thing we were fond of doing at home was constructing model kits. The fun was in the construction, but it carried on later as you played with them. My brother and I had constructed dozens each. For me they included fantasy spacecraft (Starship *Enterprise, 2001: A Space Odyssey* Moon bus) and real spacecraft (Apollo Lunar Module), war machines (of course), an underwater research lab (Sealab), a model of the human heart, and many superheroes. My brother loved building models of horror figures, like the Wolfman, Phantom of the Opera, The Creature (From the Black Lagoon), King Kong and Godzilla, but also of superheroes, too, like Batman. The horror figure models, made by Aurora Plastics Corporation (defunct since 1969), were invariably a buck apiece—not bad.

Though I liked building models, I had little patience in doing it. I usually didn't bother painting them (which my brother did), and I insisted on building them in one sitting. They were glued together using "Airplane Glue," a stringy, smelly adhesive that got itself on a lot of unwanted places like your fingers and was difficult to get off. It was supposed to be used in a "well-ventilated area," but I never really bothered with that and I kind of liked the smell anyway. At some point kids were not supposed to be allowed to buy it because some got addicted to sniffing it ("It looks like I picked the wrong day to stop sniffing glue!"—*Airplane*, 1980), but I don't think I ever had any problem purchasing it, just like I never had a problem buying my father cigarettes at that time. I certainly didn't sniff it, but it was hard not to succumb to its vapors, which made me unpleasantly light-headed (don't know why anyone would want to feel that way) and just "out-of-it." It was said to kill brain cells, especially when sniffed. Such were the dangers of model building. By the way, the paint I avoided smelled funky, too.

I liked constructing things in general. They always called me a "little Engineer," and that is what I would later become. I loved constructing buildings. I used to have a toy that was just a collection of white plastic bricks and some doors and windows, and I would make wonderful things with them. Then came Lego, and I was in Nirvana. I loved making all kinds of constructions with Lego. Unfortunately, Lego was not a cheap toy, and thus my building supplies were relatively limited.

There was also the Erector Set—I made airplanes and robots and all kinds of good stuff with that. And I got a motorized version—though I never got the gear chain to rotate anything. I think it was literally impossible. At least for me.

One of the most awesome construction toys was the *Kenner* Girder and Panel Building Set. It had a board with evenly spaced holes in it that you inserted red plastic "girders" into. You connected the vertical girders together with horizontal ones, creating a "floor," and you built upward to higher floors by inserting vertical girders into the tops of vertical girders below them, and again adding horizontal girders to the second-floor girders, and so on. Thus, you created the skeletal structure of a building. Then, you could add "walls" to the building by snapping into pegs on the outside girders thin plastic panels (which eventually cracked) containing translucent "windows." Square navy-blue roof panels—some with translucent skylight domes molded into them—were snapped onto the topmost girders to complete your building. How truly awesome does that sound? I would have hours upon hours of fun building "skyscrapers" that reached up to the top of my head. It was also fun having "Godzilla" (me) destroy them.

As if the above wasn't enough, *Kenner* also came up with the ultimate construction toy: the *Bridge and Turnpike* set. It used the same girders as above, but with roadway sections instead of the walls. With it you could create bridges and turnpikes, just as the name said. I was obsessed with this toy. I would get enlightened during car trips with ideas for it. My fantasy was to reconstruct a roadway like Grand Central Parkway in Queens in its "grand" completeness. This was true Nirvana.

BROTHER SCIENTISTS

My brother and I were obsessed scientists, though in different directions. He was into animals and the microscopic world while I was into the macroscopic world of space. So, he got a microscope and I got a telescope. I enjoyed both, however.

The telescope literally opened me up to a whole new universe. Not only could I see Jupiter and four of its moons, but I could almost literally see an ant crawling on a brick across the street. I could also nose in on neighbors, and see perhaps what they were watching on TV. In later years, as puberty struck, I used it to spy on a woman who sunned herself in the backyard. It was a marvelous instrument indeed.

So was the microscope. We put everything under that thing and were never disappointed. Some of those things were disgusting, like snot—but even the disgusting was worthy of serious research.

My brother was truly the biologist. He even had a dissecting kit. And he got icky things in formaldehyde to practice on. So together we would open up a "pickled" frog and look at its inner workings, which in all honesty always just looked like blood and goo. In retrospect it seems kind of weird to think we dissected things for fun and had scalpels and other dissection tools, but it was interesting and harmless. What we dissected came to us dead already. Why let a good, preserved dead animal go to waste?

LITERARY PURSUITS

I spent a lot of time reading comic books, and collecting them. My favorites were DC Comics (as opposed to Marvel). So, I liked Superman, Batman, Justice League, and other DC titles. But I *loved* DC's Legion of Super-Heroes. I guess I liked them best because they lived exactly one thousand years in the future, tying in with my fascination with the future and science fiction in general. And the Legion had about 30 different teen-aged heroes, all with a unique special power or set of powers. Some of these were admittedly silly, like Matter-Eater Lad, whose power was that he could eat anything, including the hardest steel. This hero hailed from the planet "Bismoll," I'm sure not a coincidence that it was similar to the name of the product Pepto-Bismol, used to ease heartburn and indigestion. Another silly one was Bouncing Boy (a healthy baby would be said to be "bouncing," so a bouncing boy would be a healthy baby boy), an ordinary human of the 30th century who, after accidentally drinking a super-plastic formula he believed was a soda pop, gained the power to inflate like a giant ball and bounce around. But I loved the futuristic exploits of the Legion. As time went by I would fall in love with the female heroes, who had sexy costumes and were drawn deliciously.

I could not get enough of comic books. I remember always begging my mom for the 12 cents to buy one (rarely would I get the "80-page Giant" issues, which reprinted old stories and cost a quarter). Reading my diary of the late 60s, though, I am reminded that I actually did get comics quite often, about once a week. As a matter of fact I kept them all to this day and collected them again in the 90s so let's just say I have a *lot*.

An interesting entry in my diary from 4/27/69 exhibits outrage over their cost going up to 15 cents: "I got a comic book. From 12 cents they raised it to 15 cents! A few years ago it was 10 cents!"

Now my literary pursuits went beyond comics. I truly liked to read the Encyclopedia. Ours was Funk and Wagnalls (a repeated line from *Laugh-In*, a show of the late 60s and early 70s: "Look *that* up in your Funk and Wagnalls!"), each volume bought at the supermarket every week for $2.99, Volume 1 only 99 cents. The supermarket sold other encyclopedias from time to time, and I'd always get volume 1, since they were 99 cents, so I had a lot of single volumes of encyclopedias, each covering about the first half of articles starting with the letter "A". I know a lot about Aardvarks, Abalone, Peter Abelard, and places like Alabama, Afghanistan and Africa, all pre-1970.

I read anything I could get my hands on, including the novels my brother had to read in High School. My love was Science Fiction, though, so new books I bought were always of that genre. I couldn't buy many new books, so I went to the library, where again I concentrated on Science Fiction. There, I made an amazing discovery in the late 60s—some of Science Fiction was dirty! That made it all the more exciting.

This is by no means an exhaustive summary of what we did inside. Of course, we did other things as well. My brother and I had plenty of time to get on each other's nerves and fight. And I always had time to tease my little sister.

CHRISTMAS

Christmas was such a delight for me, and my parents made sure it was as pleasant as could be. My father in particular made Christmas Eve great. He would send us kids downstairs to his parents' apartment when he "heard" Santa was about to appear. We would wait very impatiently downstairs for Santa, which of course was my parents bringing our presents to the bottom of the Christmas tree (real, of course). Under our tree was a Lionel train set with a track layout that my father had attached to a flat board, which was in actuality a mattress board. I loved that train. When it was time for us to come up, my father had the train running full speed and the record player at full volume, playing Christmas music, usually the Guy Lombardo Christmas Album. It was noisy but awesome. We couldn't open the presents until my slow grandparents made their way upstairs, but it was always worth the wait. The things we really wanted we got; some items were cheaper substitutes. These are the happiest moments of my life. At the time for some reason I held onto my nuts as I waited to open the presents; perhaps I was afraid they would fall off from all my excited jumping.

My father was very meticulous (anal) with all Christmas decorations and the train setup. There would be a lot of shouting by him. But it all came out great in the end. I particularly liked the "bubble lights" on the tree, the bubbling occurring from the heating of a toxic (of course) colored liquid by the hot incandescent light bulb on the bottom. One bit of dangerous fun I would have would be to throw the tree "icicles" (made out of aluminum then) on the electric train tracks, which made them spark. Well, kids will be kids…

WE NEED A FEW GOOD "MEN"

OK, this one is pretty particular to me (and my brother), but "The Queens Nautical Cadets" was like a nautical Boy Scouts, though not quite the same. On Friday evenings we would meet at a nearby public school and use its facilities to pretend we were in the Navy, learning drills, rank structure, how to make knots (which is "not" easy), and doing all sorts of Navy-like things. We wore Navy uniforms, and could move up in rank. The officers were adults that were former Navy, all the way up to Captain. It wasn't all learning drills, though—we played sports too.

My brother belonged to this organization in the mid-60s and of course I wanted to do everything my brother did. I was too young at age 7, though to be a "recruit." They made a special exception for me, and finally I joined.

It was a disaster. The first evening I was trained in how to make a "right-face," "left-face," and "about-face" by an adult "officer" in the stairwell, as there wasn't anywhere else to do this. The instructor was black, a new experience for me; it wasn't a good one, as he was very impatient with me. I just wasn't learning fast enough how to do these things correctly, and he was quite stern about it, like in the real Navy. At one point he just said, "No, you're doing it all wrong…," which made me feel bad. But, hey, this *was* the Navy (sort of).

I was just too young for Naval discipline and being constantly told that I was "a man now" (what had happened to the rest of my childhood, after age 7?). The discipline was like my parochial school education on steroids. When I exhibited weakness or indecision, they would bark at me to be a man. One example was when they had pizza at the gym and asked if I wanted any. I said, "I don't know." Instead of them saying "Come on, have some pizza…" one of them barked, "You're a man now, can't you decide if you want pizza?" I quickly replied, "No, sir!" so I could get away.

They took the whole Navy thing very seriously. If I passed an officer without saluting, he would stop me and chastise me for not saluting. This place just made me nervous.

It also made me want to laugh at times, but that was forbidden. I remember when a fellow recruit did something out of line and to punish him (using shame, of course), they had him wear his hat inside out. I thought this was so funny, but I knew if I laughed one bit I'd be in big trouble. It took a lot of concentration not to laugh.

They loved rough sports. The meanest, roughest sport you can do inside is play dodge ball. And that we did, together with the older kids. They threw that basketball with a vengeance. It scared the hell out of me. I would never go on the offensive, and would just avoid the ball, even standing behind pillars. Unfortunately, that left me at the end as one of the few left standing and then it got really scary.

As a recruit for some weeks, I went to this thing in civvies, but then came the day for me to get my uniform. By then I was disillusioned with the whole thing, and my parents warned me how expensive the uniform was, that they wouldn't get it unless I stayed with the organization, but I said I wanted it anyway. We took a trip to an Army and Navy Surplus store in Manhattan and got my uniform.

The uniform was cool, I admit, but I had a tough time with it while using a urinal. You were only given what seemed liked seconds for a pee break, and the damned pants didn't have a zipper—instead it had 13 buttons. Sometimes I just didn't pee.

There was a ceremony wherein I graduated from seaman recruit to seaman apprentice. All the gym was occupied with us kids and the parents were there too. The whole thing made me very nervous. I would have to walk, with the right turns and junk, to the Captain to accept a certificate and I didn't think I could do that, with everyone watching. As it came close to my name being called, I threw up, in front of the crowd. The Captain handled this with his usual Naval aplomb: "He's sick! Get him out of here!"

I was rejoined with my parents, who of course were concerned and gentle to me about it. That was my last time there, uniform and all. I told my parents that I didn't like it, and I was sorry about the uniform. They were OK with it all.

My brother made it to seaman third class, but he quit not long after as well. He didn't like the part where we had to beg people for donations (which I did as well and it sucked) and he didn't like how he was pushed into liking the Navy and that he should sign up as soon as he was old enough, just a few years away for him. They took him and others to a real ship to entice them how cool the Navy was, but what "impressed" him the most was the tight bunks he saw, with the highest bunk so close to the ceiling that it was directly under the steam pipes. And thus ended his service as well…

WHAT WE ATE

Well, eating is something you do in any decade, but even this has changed a lot for me personally and I'm sure for everyone else.

"Special" in my childhood culinary experience but certainly not unique was eating stuff that my parents were accustomed to from living in farms in Europe. Thus, I ate (and liked most of this stuff), things like pig's feet (in a jelly made from boiling them and letting it harden in the refrigerator), pig stomach stuffed with cubes of meat and potato (actually one of my favorites), chicken feet (after being used to make soup), beef tongue, chicken hearts and gizzards, and a variety of *wurst* (best English equivalent is "sausage"), sometimes made at home from casings made of real intestines and happily cranked by me in a mechanical wurst-making device that you fed the casings and meat and other stuff you wanted in the wurst.

By the way, those chicken feet were fresh—we used to go to a nearby chicken butcher that had live chickens, pigeons, and other animals (I never understood who ate pigeons, though). You'd pick out the live bird and they would butcher it, including taking out the feathers. They would ask if we wanted the head, to which I always said yes—I would play with it at home (sick little monkey I was). Let me tell you, the soup made from those feet was marvelous!

Some of you may find this stuff disgusting and indeed most of it I wouldn't touch anymore, but it was what I was accustomed to growing up and seemed perfectly acceptable. My father would eat stuff that I wouldn't eat, like calves' brains and blood wurst. We ate regular "American" stuff, too, like steak, hamburgers, hot dogs, *liver*, spaghetti and meatballs ("American" as you can get) and the rest. One thing very different from my experience now and my kids' experience is that we almost never ate out or used takeout. In the late 60s we started to have pizza delivered, but that was it. Restaurants were expensive, and were only used on very special occasions, like graduations, First Communions and Mother's Day. Of course, with my Germanic heritage, they were usually German restaurants.

One thing missing from today was fast food chains. I think the first McDonald's in my neighborhood arrived there in 1969 or 1970. For years after that it was the only fast food chain we had. So where did we get "fast" food?

The answer in part is small luncheonettes. These places sold hamburger, hotdogs, sandwiches and little else. To say they were "small" is almost an understatement. They consisted of a long counter and a few booths. They cooked behind the counters. And some had no bathrooms.

Nevertheless, these luncheonettes served, at least what appeared at the time, great food. The hot dogs were good, and the hamburgers superb. I think it was actually the grease they used that made hamburgers taste so good, but it didn't matter. And they toasted the buns in the grease. Mmmm…as for the fries, they were scrumptious as well.

For a while, when my mom had a job and my brother and I were in the same grammar school, which would put the years to about 1963-65, my brother and I would eat at luncheonettes every day for lunch. I suppose my mom gave us about a buck for both of us as hot dogs were only 15 cents then, as were sodas. A slice of pizza as well was 15 cents. So, two slices each and a soda each totaled 90 cents.

My brother and I used to shun pizza, which only my mom ate in the early 60s, until she gave us some pizza crust. From then on, we were fans. My dad turned on to pizza too, as us good Catholics couldn't eat meat on Fridays and thus sometimes ordered pizza.

There was also a larger luncheonette that actually called itself a restaurant—the Blue Restaurant. There you could get takeout turkey dinners that we really liked because the turkey was sliced paper thin and the fries were wonderful. We only got this treat when my mom didn't have time to cook because we went somewhere and came home late.

Another treat was Chicken Delight. This was actually an early fast food chain, though it was delivery only—there was no "restaurant" to go to. Their motto, said in their commercials, was, "Don't cook tonight, call Chicken Delight." When my mom wasn't sure what to cook, my brother and I would hum this motto. My mom would complain it was expensive, but my dad would usually give in (my mother was the sensible one with money, while my dad, though not foolish with it, would spend extra to keep us happy). The Chicken Delight chicken was very good, and their fries were excellent.

We didn't have any Subway franchises for subs, wedges, hoagies, heros, or grinders (depending on what part of the country you are from) but we did have the lunch counter at S. S. Kresge, which, like Woolworth's, was a small department store. Kresge's offered the "submarine" sandwich, the longest sandwiches I ever saw at the time, later to be known as "subs." Alas, Kresge's closed in the latter half of the 60s and thus went away our subs, though you could get something like them at Woolworth's. Kresge Corporation would become Kmart ("Kresge" mart) in 1977.

So, though we were devoid of many fast food chains, we had our options for quickly prepared foods.

9 SURVIVING PAROCHIAL SCHOOL

A lot has been said about parochial school, i.e., private school for Catholics. George Carlin, one of my favorite comedians of all time, has related in his comedy routines and the epic record *Class Clown* many hysterical stories about parochial school, and just about everything he has said has hit home for me. It was quite an experience going to parochial school in the 60s and being taught mostly by nuns.

The beginning was rough, of course. There was no pre-school or day care in those days, so you didn't get separated from your mom until the ripe age of five, for Kindergarten. I would ask my brother what Kindergarten was like, but I just didn't understand. I thought it was literally a "garden."

Well, it wasn't. My first day of school was a horrifying experience in which I mostly cried for my mother. I couldn't believe she abandoned me in a strange place with a bunch of kids that I didn't know and with a strange teacher dressed like a penguin—who wasn't very nice. She was known as "Sister," but I didn't have one yet and she didn't look like anyone's sister, she was much too old for that.

The kids weren't great, either. They played with toys and didn't invite me to join them. When I did try to join them in play, they chastised me. I took that very seriously and personally. The teacher would demand that I play with them, but I constantly got rebuffed. I was stuck between a rock and a hard place. This showed up in my "grades." In my very first report card I got a "U" (Unsatisfactory) in "Getting Along With Others."

A kid named Charlie, whom I would become friends with years later, had the same problem. He would stand there like me, with his hands in his pockets, looking half-asleep out of boredom. His mom told him to play with the others at all costs. So, one day he did. He got rebuffed as usual, but forced his way into the playing field. The teacher called him a bully and told his mother that Charlie should just sink back into his old ways.

The nun clearly didn't like me. She seemed to single me out for punishment of things I never did. In one case, she accused me of peeing in my seat when clearly it was dry; the dude in front of me had peed in his seat. My punishment was being locked in the "cloak room," a long closet where we hung our coats and kept our galoshes. The light was turned off. I was terrified. [In fact, I blame life-long claustrophobia on that one incident.] Eventually I was released, but scarred for life.

My mother wasn't too happy about the cloak room punishment and other undeserved punishments. When she asked the nun about it in an Open School Night (antiquated term for "Parent-Teacher Conference") the nun clearly explained why she always punished me:

"I just don't like his face."

This is not to say I didn't have some bathroom issues in school, but that was because they made you afraid to ask to go to the bathroom (officially, then called "lavatory") at "unscheduled" times (which was twice a day, once in the morning and once in the afternoon). During "scheduled" times the boys would regimentally stand on line to use the boys' room (with one student assigned as the paper towel dispenser, or "monitor," as he was called). There was actually good reason for this. Some meatheads would get their jollies by backing up the toilets with paper towels (that's why we needed monitors of that precious paper), which would not only gob up the works but would initiate hilarious announcements over the "low-fi" classroom PA speaker from the Principal that such heathens would be punished severely.

One time I had a stomach ache and pooped in my pants. [Again, I was afraid to ask to go to the bathroom—especially while were reciting the Pledge of Allegiance and afternoon prayers.] The announcement was made in the classroom to the front office via the PA and summarily from the front office to my brother's classroom. They were very careful as to how they referred to normal bodily functions those days, so they referred to my predicament as an "accident." My brother immediately went to the front office, worrying about me, thinking I was hit by a car or something. He had walked me to school as usual, but somehow I had gotten into an *accident*! I don't know if he was more embarrassed or relieved to hear that I had just crapped in my trousers.

My brother found the incident additionally embarrassing. At that time money was short in my family and my mother actually had to work in addition to my father, a fact of incredible embarrassment to my father. So, he had told us never, ever, ever to admit that my mom worked (God forbid to admit that in old-fashioned families like mine in the early sixties!). The office had tried to call my mom at home to pick me up but no-one answered. They asked my brother where she could be, and he knew she was working somewhere, but he couldn't tell them. He felt like an idiot. Finally, they let him take me home, and my grandparents took care of my "cleanup."

Speaking of the bathroom (a favorite subject of mine, I guess), as the years went on in parochial school the battle of keeping kids from going there to commit mischief continued. In December 68, they really put their foot down, after some kids put paper clips in the bathroom sink; the Principal demanded that no-one could go to the bathroom at unscheduled times without a note from a parent. I never understood this. If I had an unplanned diarrhea attack (and I don't know of any *planned* ones, except maybe now in preparation for a colonoscopy) how could I get a note from my parents to go to the bathroom? If I went home and got one, wouldn't I go to the bathroom there? This still remains a mystery to me.

[If I may jump ahead to High School and the early seventies, they didn't like us going to the bathroom during class time, either, for fear of probably doing more than just stuffing up toilets, though I'm sure that still was a concern. To keep toilets from being stuffed up with toilet paper, and I assume to cut down costs of that precious luxury, they used heavy lead dispensers with "no waste" written on them that broke off the paper after unrolling maybe two sheets. It wasn't very hygienic perhaps, but it sure cut down on toilet paper usage. As for messing around in the boys' room, they simply removed the stall doors. That worked for me; I was much too timid to spend much time on a crapper while people could watch me.]

OK, let's get away from toilets and "accidents."

Things were definitely tough for me in my early parochial school days. When we moved from playing to learning, I found out that I was actually stupid. The teacher would show flash cards to the class and I would have difficulty reading the words on them while others had no problem.

One day at school they administered eye exams to all. They found out that I couldn't read smallish letters from a distance. I was nearsighted! My parents took me to an optometrist. I was a little apprehensive over this. I had seen some people with glasses, but it was a relatively rare thing to see back then (no pun intended). In fact, when I was very young I used to think glasses were attached to people.

But the optometrist set me up with glasses and a whole new world opened for me. I could see the flash cards and in no time at all I could read the words on them as well as everybody else, and soon I exceeded the abilities of most. [And at home I didn't have to sit right in front of the TV anymore!]

So, glasses made me switch from feeling inferior to feeling superior. But there was a cost. Glasses weren't fashionable back then at all; they were of horrible designs and lenses (made of ordinary glass) were heavy and thick. Few kids wore glasses, for fear of being spotted as different and being ostracized. In fact, my mother went for many years without glasses because in the thirties only one girl in her class wore glasses and she was so taunted about it my mother decided it was better to have inferior vision. Things weren't much better in the sixties, and I had to put up with kids pointing out that I was different, calling me "four-eyes," and telling me my eyes were bad because I must read too much (indeed, I read a lot, but there is never "too much" reading). But it was worth it. Except for a period much later in my life wherein I wore contacts, while I was out prowling for women, I have always worn glasses. No la-ser surgery for me.

As one would expect, things were pretty strict in parochial grammar school. It definitely was of a military nature. In the schoolyard before morning classes and before afternoon classes, when the first bell rang you were supposed to freeze in your spot, like the end of an old TV show. At the next bell, you were to stand at attention. At the third bell you had to quickly *but quietly* assemble in line with the rest of your class, in last name alphabetical order. Each class had its predetermined turn to go into the school building. Each class was essentially a "troop."

Talking in line was a major offense. This would mostly likely lead to a *class punishment*. The philosophy of punishment in parochial school was that if someone broke the rules the whole class had to suffer. I think the logic was, like the military, that if someone broke the rules the rest of the troop/class would be angry with that person and pressure them to behave. But there was a major fault in this philosophy; the ones who broke the rules were often the bullies, and you wouldn't mess with them. So, many times innocent me had to write "I will not talk in line" one hundred times, or something like that. My father saw what I was doing once and when I explained he just shook his head and said that was unfair, I shouldn't do it. I had to plead with him to do it, or I would get "into trouble." So I did many "Bart Simpson's" in my day—but on paper, not a blackboard. On Sunday, October 5, 1969 I reported in my diary, "I finally finished my homework punishment, which is altogether 2,550 words, 13 pages, 24-1/2 sides of loose leaf." On Tuesday, December 16, 1969 I recorded:

> I did not go to school because I did not feel good and I couldn't finish my Science punishment, which was writing "I must get a complete signature on my tests" 200 times. But I went to school in the afternoon…

Notice I specified a "complete" signature (I assume from my parents). Did I get an *incomplete* one? Rather harsh, eh?

My diary records many attempts to combat bad conduct, all of which failed. One was having us move our seats constantly, many times in 6th and 7th grade. But I don't think they did it right. From my diary, December 2, 1968: "The teacher moved the kids who had bad in Conduct to the *back* [emphasis mine, in current time] of the class."

Another punishment was to take away our "library period," which we essentially enjoyed because it got us away from our class and having to listen to a teacher; they would replace this "free time" with something like an extra period of Social Studies, like I recorded in my diary on March 5, 1969. I recorded the same exact punishment on March 23. Only *some* kids were allowed to go to the school library on May 21, "because of conduct reasons. I couldn't go, but later [the teacher] said she made a mistake and that I should of [sic] went down to the library." I recorded on May 28 that we were then split into two groups: "the good group and the bad group; there's none in-between them. The first group to go down was the good group of course (I was in it). The bad group, which consists of almost all of the two last rows, went after us." In 7th grade they instituted shop for the boys and sewing for the girls every other week, with library only every other week from that. Here I got into trouble (October 23, 1969):

> I wasn't allowed to take out a book because last Thursday, while I went to shop, I forgot to give my book to someone so they could bring it down for me. My punishment was: I can't take a book out of [the] library for one month.

And then, the following on December 18, 1969:

> We had a Shop test for the first time, but I couldn't finish it because I had to go to the library because the teacher wanted me there because I forgot my library book. Now I'm not supposed to go to shop for 2 months.

I don't want to use the old saying, but it seems so appropriate: You can't make this stuff up!

One really crummy punishment to all, *including our parents*, was to make us stay late at school, which of course worried our parents (they were not notified in advance). I recorded in my diary that they tried this on May 18, 1969. They also tried it on May 23, but: "Only some kids could go home at regular time because of conduct reasons. Only three boys could go home. I was one of them [another, my best friend]."

Sometimes, if the bullies did something really bad (I have no idea what), they would be sent to a Father (Priest) who was notorious for straightening out bad kids. The mere mention of his name would send chills down our spines. I remember once a really bad bully went calmly to that Father—and minutes later that bully was reduced to a blubbering blob of jelly. I always wondered what that Father did to him…

Corporeal punishment was practiced, though not often in those days. Parochial schools were steering away from that, thank God (though the cloak room incident was bad enough for me). My parents had horror stories of their experiences in parochial schools in the thirties that I can't match. My mother had her ear almost taken off by a teacher and my father told me that Priests used to inspect kids' feet and if they found them dirty they would clean them with a brick (not of soap). They would also have to hold out their fingers and let the teacher whack their fingertips with a heavy wooden ruler.

We did have a teacher that was oddly kinky in her corporeal punishments, though I only saw her do it once, and it was a lay teacher, not a nun. She had a boy take down his trousers and spank him, behind her desk. That scared the heck out of me.

My brother was left-handed, and this of course was considered evil. Every time he was spotted writing with his left hand, he would be hit on that hand with a ruler and be forced to write with his right hand. It worked. He remains a left-handed person who nonetheless writes with his right hand.

[A little interesting aside about my brother. When my parents attended his first open school night they were told that he was just not that smart and would probably not even be accepted one day into a Catholic High School. My parents were devastated. Eight years later he was accepted into a Catholic High School. Four years after that he was accepted into College. Four years after that he graduated *magna cum laude* and earned a fellowship to attend Cornell University for graduate school. He eventually got his Master's there and then his Ph. D. Dr. Mandeli is doing just fine, using his Ph. D. in Statistics for medical research at a major Manhattan hospital.]

Parochial school was quite old-fashioned, and in some ways for no apparent good reason. They were certainly old-fashioned in writing instruments. Nobody under fifth grade could use a pen, I guess because they were considered dangerous. In a way they were (give me a minute) but when they finally let us use them they made us use the most "unsafe" kinds. The ubiquitous Bic pen was already around and well, ubiquitous, so that would have been the most logical choice of an ink-based writing implement. But for some reason it was "banned." We were forced to use pens with ink cartridges or even fountain pens. Both were "dangerous" (see, I promised) because they were potentially messy. The fountain pen was the messiest writing tool of all. We literally had bottles of ink on our desks, which were not built to accommodate them (earlier desks, which I actually saw later in High School, had holes to accommodate them) and those bottles were always precariously perched so that they could slide down the smooth, slanted desks and stain our trousers (which were fortunately navy blue) and skirts.

The pens themselves were messy—the ink flow was not consistent. In fact, we used "blotters"—cards of soft, absorbent paper—to dab our pen points onto, to suck out excess ink that got on that point. Of course, the blotter was also a tool for combating boredom, for the process of "blotting" ink was kind of interesting, and you could make cool patterns from collections of blots.

What behooves me is that they gave us a weapon that really could make a mess of things. The fountain pens had a lever on them that you pulled on to suck ink into the pens when inserted into the ink wells. You could also use that lever to squirt ink on people—and though we had navy blue pants we also had white shirts. Also, if you were vicious enough, you could stab someone with a fountain pen. They had hard metal on the ends, which were sharp.

I have no idea why we couldn't use Bic pens. One theory though is that you could easily take one apart and use it as a spitball shooter. Or maybe they were just too wary of any kind of modern technology.

Now that I have alluded to parochial school fashion, I must expand on that. The boys didn't look bad, in their navy-blue pants, white shirts, and navy-blue ties. Of course, nobody wanted to tie a tie in the morning, so many of us used clip-ons. Unfortunately a funny gag was always to pull on someone's tie and watch it come off. Unfortunately, that would often break the plastic clip.

We also had to wear Buster Brown "regulation" shoes, which were pretty ugly. They actually had to be the Buster Brown brand, and a certain "model." That model was relatively expensive, which ticked my parents off to no end. I wonder if the school got a kickback. But at the end of every summer they had to buy them at the Buster Brown shoe store, and that's when you would first see some of your classmates for the new school year.

You might think that you could get away with not wearing that exact shoe, but there were shoe police. One day, for some reason, I couldn't wear my regulation shoes. I wore my cool "roach killers" (so-called because they were pointy, so you could theoretically squash roaches with them, even if they got into a corner). I really thought they were the coolest, and both my brother and I had them, no doubt inspired by the *Beatles*. But I was nabbed quickly and told *never* to wear those to school again.

The girls wore the same ugly plaid skirts and tops that can still be seen today (I have also noticed they are standard fare in the Caribbean). Long green knee socks helped cover most of the leg. The outfits were definitely not attractive, and that of course was the point. They didn't want us boys to covet our female classmates. [Interestingly enough, one year they allowed the nuns to wear shorter outfits, which showed a lot of leg—that brought about many impure thoughts, and about *nuns*.]

This brings up sex education in parochial school. Basically, it was "handled" in one day. We had two "assemblies" that day, divided between the boys and the girls. The boys were told to stay away from the girls. Some had been noted following girls home, which was not acceptable. Sex itself wasn't mentioned, but Hell sure was.

We tried to find out what the girls were told, but apparently they were too embarrassed to relate this. I still wonder.

This was the sixties, and, of course, school included air raid drills. I don't remember a "duck and cover" exercise like they had in the 50s, but we did have drills that when the alarm sounded we had to go into the hallway and face the walls, placing our hands behind our necks. Somehow this would make for a safer nuclear holocaust. I think all it would have resulted in were radioactive shadows on the walls, of kids standing with their hands behind their necks.

All things being equal, I rather enjoyed parochial school in the sixties. It was an innocent adventure, and actually quite funny at times. It was the stupidest things that were funny. For example, we used to have "audio-visual" presentations—a kind of ancient multimedia event. The way we pulled this off was by playing a record with the audio and showing slides on the wall with a slide projector. To keep the two in sync, the audio provided a beep when someone was supposed to switch the projector to the next slide. That little beep—an insubstantial sound—was the funniest sound in the world. *Beep!*

10 LIFE IN THE NAKED CITY

I was born and grew up in New York City, otherwise known as the Big Apple, though nobody really called it the "Big Apple" in the 60s; that was a name that had been coined in the early part of the century and had fallen into disuse. It was rejuvenated in advertising campaigns in the 70s (to revitalize a decaying city with tourism) and the name has retained popularity. One thing NYC was called in the 60s was "The Naked City." This was coined by NY Photojournalist "Weegee" (Arthur Fellig, 1899-1968) as the title of a 1945 book that was a collection of his stark black-and-white photos of NYC. In 1948 a movie about a police investigation in NYC, filmed on the streets of NY, was given the same title and a TV show that played 1958-59 and 1960-63 was given that title as well, and filmed in NYC as well.

As a kid I didn't call NYC by any coined names. My family and I referred to Manhattan, what most consider NYC, simply as "the City." We lived in Queens, which was a county of NYC, but our address was Long Island City, NY. That was the section of Queens we lived in, also known as Astoria (we actually lived in Astoria, but the Post Office was Long Island City, or LIC; the area actually known as LIC was towards the west, by the East River). In a way we felt separate from NYC and lived differently than most people in Manhattan. In fact, we were more suburban than urban, but not quite suburban either. Think of brick buildings mostly of two apartments each, two stories in all, though we had six apartments in our building, three stories in all, intermixed with plenty of trees and other flora and what seemed to be good air.

It was a healthy environment to grow up in, I would say. Though we were of a limited mix of nationalities, which did not prepare us well for the future, everyone pretty much got along. I can honestly say, even though being a bit of a nerd, I was never beaten up by a bully, though I was bullied from time to time to some degree. Certainly the streets seemed safe, and I had no major problems. I was pretty happy where I was.

My brother and I would complain to my father, who owned the six-family apartment building we lived in, that we wanted to live in the suburbs, specifically on Long Island. My father didn't seem to have a good concept of the suburbs, as he compared them to "farms." There is certainly some truth to that, as the burbs on Long Island were certainly much less developed than now, and indeed as one crossed into Suffolk County there was in the 60s a lot of potato farms and the like. Our forays into Suffolk in the 60s pretty much bore this out. Though many neighborhoods were not "farms" per se they were very rustic. Indeed, I secretly wondered if I would be comfortable in such an environment. I would certainly miss not being able to walk to everything. My mother would miss that even more.

My father took pride in us owning a six-family apartment building, as did I. But in all honesty we made very little money from rentals. The expenses of maintaining our building, which was built in the 20s, usually exceeded our rental income, even with my father acting as Super as well as Landlord. Many years we claimed our house as a loss. My parents were nice people and very kind to their tenants, which was their downfall. They just weren't good business people. They hated to raise rents. There was one woman who had lived in the building well before we did (we moved in when I was 6 weeks old, from the Bronx) and in fact her husband had been the Super. But her husband died when I was very young and for the rest of her life she was a widow. Until her death in the 70s she paid about $65 a month for her five-room apartment.

My parents had made a good real estate investment in the apartment building, back in 1957, when they bought it for $27,000. It was a solid building, which we found out when we finally had an in-wall air conditioner installed and discovered three layers of brick on the front of the house. When my parents divorced in the 1990s they thought they got a bargain by selling it for $300,000. However, now its value is approximately $5 million. And at over 90 years old it is in great shape.

My father's parents helped buy the house, though I am not sure how much. The entire block of these attached six-family apartment buildings had been owned by Joseph Genovese, who owned many drug stores under his name. Those drug stores were later sold to JC Penny, and after time became known as Eckerd, and then Rite Aid. Reportedly, this Genovese had no connection to the Genovese crime family, one of the "Five Families" of the city's Mafia.

To save money, my parents, brother and I lived with my father's parents in the same first-floor apartment. This didn't work out well, and in 1960 we moved to a second-floor apartment of our own. My grandparents lived directly downstairs from us until they died in the 1970s. In the home office I am typing in right now, my grandfather's ancient radio with a wind-up mechanical clock on top of it still stands.

We were lower middle-class. As already stated, we didn't make much, if anything, from the apartment building we owned and my father was a blue-collar worker. He was very talented at what he did, being a machinist, but that line of work just never paid that much. In the early 60s he made not much more than $100 a week, even with overtime, and in the later 60s passed the $200 a week mark. I know he was very good at what he did, as when his shop was bought out by a Pennsylvania company, only he, his boss, and the most senior worker there were enticed to follow the company's new location in Pennsylvania in 1969. My father refused to move, despite many offered perks.

My mom was the thrifty one. We always ate well, but she always bought the cheapest brand of beer, soft drinks, ice cream and snacks. She knew how to stretch a dollar, and like many women of her era, religiously collected trading stamps. These stamps, collected at a supermarket checkout, the amount based on what was spent in that transaction, would be carefully mounted in books. When you had collected a certain number of books full of stamps, you could trade them in at a trading stamp company store for various items, like toys, furniture and appliances. The only thing I remember that my mom got was a metal bookcase for us kids—nothing for her.

As previously stated, my mom also worked part-time, as a house cleaner and High School lunch counter worker, which made my father feel immensely inadequate. So, times were evidently tough—but us kids never knew about it.

One thing my mom did to save money that I hated was to tell the subway token clerk I was under five years old when I was actually 6 or 7, to avoid the 15-cent token fee for me. This ended when the token clerk finally said there was no way I was under five. Instead of embarrassed, I was happy the "scam" was over and I could be my real age.

THE WORLD'S FAIR

Part of the fun of the World's Fair
Is the Subway Special that takes you there.
There's a good time feelin' in the air
On the Subway Special to the World's Fair.
Trains are easy to catch anywhere.
Anytime, night or day.
Just pay 15 cents—hop aboard!—and you're on your way.
Yes, part of the fun of the World's Fair
is the Subway Special that takes you there.

The above little ditty teased us in commercials in 64 with pictures of incredibly happy passengers on a subway car heading to the NY World's Fair of 1964-65, complete with footage of the Fair which looked empty except for the ecstatic couples that had just been delivered there. After the song, an announcer proudly stated that "Your Transit Authority has 430 spanking new picture window cars for the elevated ride to the World's Fair." (see YouTube). It certainly had been a long time since NYC saw "spanking new" subway cars, as the ones in service generally went back to the 20s and looked it. I never considered a subway car to have "picture windows," but I guess that is how they saw it, as the "official" subway line of the Fair was the No. 7 train, which was actually on an elevated track that passed over Grand Central Parkway, and not in the dark depths of subway tunnels. As for calling it a "Subway Special," the price wasn't special—back then 15 cents could take you anywhere in the NYC subway system.

"World Fair's" are expositions that travel around the world, and have been since 1851. They have presented technological innovations (such as the Eiffel Tower, left as a permanent structure after acting as the entranceway to the 1889 Paris World's Fair) and exhibitions of world culture. They are sanctioned by the *Bureau International des Expositions* (BIE) in Paris—except for the 64-65 NY World's Fair (more on that later). Previously NYC had had two, one way back in 1853 and another in 1939-40. The 64-65 NY World's Fair was on the same site as the 39-40 one, in Flushing Meadows Park, Queens, which had been built on top of the Corona Ash Dumps (the "valley of ashes" referred to in *The Great Gatsby*), filled with ashes from coal-burning furnaces, horse manure and garbage.

The World Fairs continue to this day, one being presented in Kazakhstan in 2017 and one planned in Dubai in 2020.

I was at a pretty good age for the NY Fair, which ran for two six-month seasons, April 22 – October 18, 1964, and April 21 – October 17, 1965. So I was a bit short of 7 when it opened and 8 when it closed—years where such an attraction would be totally amazing and impressionable to me, and indeed memories of it are ingrained in my brain.

My parents had to shell out only a buck for me, as was the admission for kids under 13. My brother was at the edge of that limit (12-13), but knowing my parents they probably never paid more than a buck for him either. My parents had to spend 2 bucks each for themselves the first year and $2.50 apiece for the second. Even in those days, 6-7 bucks for a family of four to see a spectacular attraction like the World's Fair was certainly worth it—and if you took the subway, as was suggested, it was only 60 cents for carfare for 4 each way. Driving there would incur a parking fee of $1.50.

The World's Fair was like a local Disney World. In fact, it is more reasonable to state that Disney World is like the NY World's Fair, as part of it was designed by Walt Disney and his Disney Imagineers. The attractions they designed were prototypes of attractions planned for Disney World, which at that time was indeed in its planning stages readying for its opening in 1971. Robert Moses (1888-1981), the "Master Builder" of NYC and its environs in the 20th century, as head of the World's Fair Corporation (WFC), tapped Disney and his Imagineers to develop concepts and rides for major corporations that wanted to exhibit at the Fair, an idea which was very copacetic with Walt Disney, who offered corporations to do this for them and allow his name to be used for one million dollars. In all, Disney and his team designed four attractions for corporations.

For Ford, which wanted to introduce its new model, the Mustang, Disney created a ride in a convertible Mustang that was conveyed quietly on a track using "WEDway" technology ("WED" for Walter E. Disney; it was later used in the WEDway People Mover in Disney World). The ride conveyed its occupants through a creepy prehistoric world of *animated* dinosaurs, utilizing another new Disney invention, "animatronics." [The ride also moved on to the future, to show a wondrous "Space City."] The dinosaur animatronics were later used in Walt Disney World (specifically, Epcot), in its Universe of Energy. For General Electric, Disney designed the animatronic-rich Carousel of Progress, which provided a rotating stage show of three different decades past and the present/near-future. This attraction was literally moved after the World's Fair to Disneyland, and then in 1975 to Walt Disney World's Magic Kingdom Tomorrowland, where it still operates, albeit with some updates. Disney also provided the Fair its animatronic Abraham Lincoln, which was meant for the U.S. Pavilion but rejected for that and instead made part of the Illinois Pavilion. The animatronic Lincoln still performs in Walt Disney's World's (Epcot) Hall of Presidents, now along with his presidential brethren. For Pepsi, in a ride sponsored by UNICEF, Disney provided the "It's a Small World" ride, which perhaps has the most mercilessly repetitious theme of all time. Walt Disney World's Magic Kingdom hosts a version of the ride to this day, theme and all, though not physically being the same ride at the Fair.

But there was much more to the Fair than Disney creations. Pavilions were built by 23 States, about 40 foreign nations (including municipalities like West Berlin and city-states like the Vatican) and 28 corporations. The corporations were the real concentration of the Fair—including those that Disney had a hand in as well as IBM, Travellers, RCA (to exhibit color TV), US Royal Tires, Eastman Kodak, Westinghouse, The Bell telephone system (to exhibit videophone mock-ups), and DuPont.

We went to the Fair a number of times, though I can't recall exactly how many. We went as a family on weekends, though once we went during the week with just my mom, taking that famed "Subway Special." One thing I remember well on that visit without my dad was a machine that manufactured, on demand for a Quarter, fairly large dinosaur figures. You put the Quarter in, and the machine manufactured in a mold (like *Creepy Crawlers*) a green Brontosaurus, which when delivered out of the dispenser was very hot, exhibiting a gross lack of concern by the machine manufacturer for safety. We had to hold it with paper napkins after initially burning ourselves a bit. But I thought it was the "coolest" thing anyway.

With my dad and mom on the weekends we visited a lot of pavilions. We, of course, insisted on going to the Ford pavilion as described above because it involved sitting in new cars (though the importance of it being a new model, the Mustang, pretty much escaped me) that moved by themselves. I think it was the first time I sat in a convertible as well. There was a problem, though— only one of us could sit behind the wheel (admittedly disabled anyway). My brother and I fought over who would sit behind the wheel. My father got fed up and just put me there after my brother had already sat there (the littler kid always wins). In the process of switching seats my brother hit his head hard against the rear-view mirror, which really made him mad. But, hey, I got what I wanted!

As they say, watch out for what you want, you may get it! When the ride passed through the dark and scary dinosaur diorama (and they were moving!) I wasn't so crazy about the driver's seat, being a bit closer to the realistic animated dinosaurs who, though I knew they weren't real, I thought would jump at me.

Actually one of the most disturbing things I saw at the Fair was a group of DuPont scientists, dressed in lab coats and all (which reminded me of "scary" doctors) performing demonstrations of freezing objects with liquid nitrogen. They bounced a rubber ball to show it was real, poured liquid nitrogen on it, and dropped it down a long plastic tube, where it broke into tiny pieces like glass. I never saw anything like this before, and instead of fascinating me it frightened me. Then they asked for help from the audience, and for some reason I thought they would grab me to do something evil and diabolical, which I thought they were. I owe this fear to being in the hospital just two years earlier for my ear infection—they really looked like doctors.

On the other side of the coin, some of the Fair was rather sedate and boring. My father insisted that we go to the IBM pavilion even though it had a tremendous line. But my father promised that IBM would have the best attraction of all, and I understand his thinking. IBM was cutting edge technology, who knew what they would show? As we waited and waited on line my father kept promising it would be worth it. When we finally got to the attraction we were seated in a circular open-air theatre. The excitement was very palpable. Then, the theatre seats rose up into the air in unison, as the crowd ooh'ed and ahh'ed. My father looked at us with a smile, as if "See, I told you!" When the motion stopped we saw that we had risen to the level of a large movie screen. The movie screen displayed basically a commercial for IBM, albeit with a mosaic of images, and how it was going to improve our lives. When the movie ended, our seats descended like our expectations. That was it. There was no more. My father was dumbfounded as to how IBM would provide such a boring attraction.

But if you think that's boring, wait until I tell you about the Austria pavilion. It was basically a small room with a travel guide or two telling you about why you should go to Austria and what you could see there (it could have been more—but see below). My parents were planning an Austria trip (already discussed earlier, in 1965) and my Uncle and his family were with us that time, and he and his wife, as well as my mom, had grown up Austria. Anyways, it was a lot of blah, blah, blah, and I decided to leave the pavilion and walk outside. Very quickly I got lost—at the NY World's Fair! It was frightening, but eventually my parents and brother noticed I was gone and I learned to stay with them at the World's Fair from then on.

It is interesting to note that a little girl of about 4 also got lost at the Fair, by its Belgian Village. The Village was an attraction introduced late in the first year of the Fair, and introduced the Belgian Waffle to America. The girl's family was very interested in trying this new treat, but she was not, and wandered off, getting lost. They got her back of course in short time and about 30 years later she would marry me. Yes, my wife and I were both lost kids at the NY 64-65 World's Fair. What we didn't know at the time is that if we had stayed lost a bit longer 250 color TVs in the Fair would have shown our faces!

Of course there was other neat stuff going on at the Fair. At the Bell exhibit we were introduced to videophones, which appeared to work but at the time were impossible to bring into fruition, as the POTS (remember—Plain Old Telephone System) could not support them. We had to wait decades for things like Skype and FaceTime to finally give us video telephonics.

RCA showed us live TV of ourselves, as we rode on a conveyor. This was a first for us. Then, later down the conveyor, we saw ourselves as videotaped earlier, but this time on color TV. This may have been the first time I saw color TV, but at the very least it was the first time I saw myself on color TV.

And, of course, we saw "It's a Small World" for the first time, which I admit was really cool then. It was very representative of the Fair's theme of "Peace Through Understanding," dedicated to "Man's [I know, sexist] Achievement on a Shrinking Globe in an Expanding Universe." I think it very appropriate that in the county that the World's Fair was held, we have the most successful diverse place in the world. I find it sad that after all these years there is still much hatred between diverse groups in the world.

My parents were very excited at night when Guy Lombardo and His Royal Canadians appeared. This was a big band that ushered the New Year in for decades at NY's Waldorf-Astoria, before *Dick Clark's New Year's Rockin' Eve*. They were also fans in general of Mr. Lombardo, and it was his Christmas record that we played and played at Christmastime. My parents were so tickled pink to be able to dance to his band live.

My parents would have Robert Moses to thank for Guy Lombardo, as he was a fan as well and friends with him. Guy lived not in NYC, but in the seaside suburban town of Freeport, not very far from me now on Long Island—and in fact, Guy Lombardo Avenue was named after him. But even at the Fair in 64-65 he was an oldie and my brother and I were terribly bored as our parents danced. It is interesting to note that Robert Moses could have had a much more "hip" act at the Fair—the Beatles.

A week after the Beatles had appeared on *Ed Sullivan*, a fan suggested in a letter to Moses that the Beatles would be a great addition to the Fair. He responded, "absolutely nothing doing." Just five months later, he changed his mind, but by then the Beatles were too big for the Fair. However, they did pass through the Fair on their way to appear at Shea Stadium on August 15, 1965; their helicopter from Manhattan landed on the Port Authority heliport in the Fair. They waved to about 200 local Queens kids and from there went in a Wells Fargo armored truck to Shea.

The Shea Stadium concert was extremely successful, with a record attendance of 55,600, but the sound of the crowd was so deafening that none of the Beatles (or anyone else) could hear what they were playing.

[By the way, in that same Port Authority building, fairgoers would first see models of the World Trade Center.]

To me, the Fair in general was awesome. I loved the futurist aspect of it, and looked forward to an exciting 21st century. Aside from going to the attractions, it was a great place to walk around and see new things. At night it glowed with the colors of the rainbow. To this day when I pass the fairgrounds I still look over at what remains—the Unisphere (a 35-ton metal globe), the observation towers of the NY Pavilion (which, in *Men in Black*, were interplanetary vehicles), the main part of the NY Pavilion (which you can see in *The Wiz*), and the Queens Museum of Art, known during the Fair as the New York City Pavilion, a holdover from the 39-40 Fair. There are other remnants, but these are the most obvious.

The 64-65 NY World's Fair was certainly a lot of fun for the fairgoers, but not always fun for the planners and NYC. As already noted, the BIE refused to sanction it. One of their bylaws was that a country could not host a World's Fair more than once a decade, and the U.S. had already had a sanctioned Fair in Seattle in 1962. [See the Elvis Presley movie *It Happened at the World's Fair* (1963) to see what it was like.] The BIE also did not usually sanction Fairs that lasted more than a year, though it had made an exception for the previous 39-40 NY World's Fair. Robert Moses challenged the BIE's authority, though he knew it meant the countries that belonged to the BIE could boycott the Fair and therefore not build pavilions there. Moses was more into making the Fair profitable, and knew that corporations could supplant missing pavilions from countries. Moses wanted a minimal bureaucracy and a gift to New York to remain after the Fair, Flushing Meadows Park, instead of expensive permanent structures (he was Parks Commissioner during the 39-40 Fair). [He also proposed to Disney 8 acres of playground area for him to develop, but Disney rejected that proposal.] The BIE did indeed boycott the Fair.

But despite the boycott, some countries (such as Spain and Ireland) that were part of the BIE still had national pavilions built there anyway, and foreign *corporations* were invited to build, not representing their country. As such, "unofficial" pavilions from private countries or industrial organizations came from Austria (as little as it was), Denmark, France, Greece, Hong Kong, Morocco, Polynesia, Sweden, Switzerland, and West Berlin, the only city (not including Vatican City, which is a country) besides NYC to have a pavilion.

Surprisingly, the Fair was a financial disaster. Investors only earned 62 cents on the dollar and NYC recovered only $1.5 million on its loan of $24 million to the WFC (and not until 1972). The turnout was much lower than expected. The WFC expected 40 million people in the first year and 30 million in the second. In the first year it only had 27 million paying customers. Moses sought to improve the Fair for the second year to entice more visitors, promising a "brighter, gayer place," but failed to get any new pavilions built. One thing he did succeed in getting for the second year was a visit to the Fair from Pope Paul VI, who stopped by during a NYC visit after attending the UN and offering Masses at St. Patrick's cathedral and Yankee Stadium. But it was too little too late. Despite raising prices for adults the second year from $2.00 to $2.50, the Fair did much worse the second year, with only 17 million paying customers. Most blamed Robert Moses for mismanagement.

At the end of the Fair we heard that the next to return to New York would be in the early 1990s. Not only did this not happen, but is highly unlikely to ever happen. In 2001, the US withdrew its membership in the BIE. Also in 2001, the US government enacted Title 22 Section 2452b, which prohibits the Department of State from spending any money on USA Pavilions at World Expos. The last World's Fair in the US was back in 1984, in New Orleans. A young event planner is trying to raise $16 billion to create a "World's Fair USA." Even if he were to pull off this achievement, it is unlikely NYC will be able to host this 1000+ acre project.

SPORTS ACHIEVEMENTS

The 60s were a great decade for NYC for sports.

After losing two MLB teams in 1957, the Brooklyn Dodgers to LA and the NY Giants to San Francisco, leaving us with one MLB team, the Yankees, the NY Mets were founded in 1962. While their stadium, Shea Stadium, was being built in Queens (near the World's Fair), the Mets played their home games at the Polo Grounds stadium, just north of Central Park in Manhattan. I remember the construction of Shea, as young as I was, eagerly anticipating its completion even though I wasn't much of a sports fan; being a budding engineer I was fascinated by the progression of its construction each time we passed it on the highway. Shea would be completed in 1964, and the Mets would play there until 2008, when Shea was demolished to make way for Citi Field Stadium, where of course they play to this day.

Meanwhile, in football, a new team called the Titans of New York was founded in 1959, becoming the second football team in NY, the first being the well-established NY Giants football team (known as the "football" Giants during the concurrent Giants baseball team). Like the Mets, they played at the Polo Grounds, waiting for construction of the same stadium, Shea, to play their home games in. In 1963 the Titans were renamed the Jets, and, like the Mets, they moved to Shea Stadium in 1964. The Jets played there until they moved to the Meadowlands Sports Complex in New Jersey in 1984.

The Yankees had great seasons in the first half of the 60s, winning American League Pennants in the contiguous years of 1960-64. They won the World Series in 1961 and 1962.

The Giants got to play against the Green Bay Packers in the 1961 NFL Championship Game but were zipped by them, 0 points to the Packers' 37.

They played the Packers again in the 1962 NFL Championship Game, but lost to them again, 16-7. In the 1963 National Football League Championship Game the Giants were matched with the Chicago Bears, whom they also lost to, 10-14. The Giants would not get into the playoffs again until 1981.

The big surprises came from NY's new teams, the Mets and the Jets, in 1969. First, the fledgling Jets won the 1968 AFL championship game against the Oakland Raiders 12-2 at the Jet home in Shea on December 29. Two weeks later, on January 12, 1969, the Jets defeated the NFL champions, the Baltimore Colts, 16-7, in the third AFL-NFL Championship Game in professional American football, and the first to be known as the "Super Bowl," hence Super Bowl III. This game has been called one of the greatest upsets in American Sports history, and the first AFL win of the new cross league contest, the Super Bowl, itself a creation of the 60s (1967). Joe Namath (1943-   ), affectionately known in NY as "Broadway Joe," controlled the game, by completing 17 out of 28 passes for 206 yards, becoming MVP, but without throwing a single touchdown pass in the game or any passes at all in the fourth quarter. The Jets were the only team in Super Bowl history to win with just one touchdown until the New England Patriots did the same exactly 50 years later in Super Bowl LIII. The Colts will never get a chance to battle the Jets again in a Super Bowl as they are now in the same football conference—the only case of an impossible rematch in the Super Bowl.

The Mets won the World Series in 1969, in the 8th year of their existence, the first expansion team to win a division title, pennant or World Series. Like the Jets, they played against Baltimore—the Orioles—and won, also accomplishing one of the greatest upsets in Series history. Prior to the 69 season, the Mets had always finished last or next-to-last. The Mets won when they shut out the Orioles in Game 5 of the series, on October 16, 1969. Even in parochial school, the single TV in the school was wheeled around the classrooms of the upper grades for all of us to see. Of course, NY had a parade, on Monday, October 20. In my diary I recorded that I should have been off from school:

> I had school today despite it's Mets day today. Mets day is not a holiday, but the Mets…had a parade today in New York City because they won the World Series.

In basketball, the New York Knicks eliminated the *Baltimore* Bullets from the 1969 NBA Playoffs. However, they lost to Boston in the Division finals.

Well, that was the good stuff that happened in NYC in the 60s. There is bad stuff worth commenting on as well…

CRIME AND CORRUPTION

The crime rate in NYC steadily increased during the 60s, to unprecedented levels. What stood out, though, to its inhabitants were the frightening stories that they read in the papers.

On August 28, 1963 two young women were brutally stabbed to death in their Manhattan apartment. Each was stabbed over sixty times, and it appeared one was raped as well. This became known as the "Career Girl" murders, as they represented the thousands of young women who had come to NYC to seek a career. After hundreds of detectives failed to find the perpetuator for months, two detectives arrested a 19-year-old black man in April 1964, whom they coerced a confession out of through beatings. On December 1, 1965 another man, drug addict/burglar Richard Robles, a white man, was convicted of the murders and sentenced to life in prison. The original suspect had been wrongly incarcerated for 1,216 days. This incident was used by the Supreme Court, among other examples, in its decision to require Miranda rights to be read ("you have the right to remain silent") upon arrest. The two detectives who coerced the false confession were never formally charged.

On May 22, 1965 a woman in a Queens subway station was fatally stabbed by 12-year-old girl. That same night a truck was asked by a group of young people to be snuck into the World's Fair for five cents each, but they jumped off early and when one of the driver's friends demanded the five cents from one of the young people and didn't get it, he killed him with a hunting knife.

Perhaps the most infamous murder case of the 60s in NYC was the murder of Kitty Genovese on March 13, 1964, only one of 636 murders in the city that year. Catherine (Kitty) Genovese, 28, was stabbed eight times in the chest and abdomen and four times in the back in an alley near her apartment in Kew Gardens, Queens. She was returning home from a bar where she worked as a barmaid and co-manager, which she had left at approx. 3 AM. Unknown to Ms. Genovese, she had been stalked by Winston Moseley (1935-2016) since she had stopped at a red light, where Moseley was parked, his intention that night being "to kill a woman." After he followed her closely in his car, he stopped when she parked, exited the car, and ran after her, stabbing her twice in the back when he caught up to her. Ms. Genovese screamed "Oh my God, he stabbed me! Help me!" Several neighbors heard her cry, but only one opened his window and shouted at Moseley. Moseley ran away and Ms. Genovese made it to the rear entrance of her building, entering its hallway but unable to unlock the door to get further in and to her apartment. Moseley came back ten minutes later, looking for Genovese and eventually finding her. When he did, he stabbed her more and raped her as she lay dying. After he fled, Kitty was still alive, lying in the arms of a brave 70-year-old neighbor who did not even know if her attacker had left. Police were called, responded quickly, and Kitty was still alive when put into an ambulance, but died before getting to a hospital.

As bad as the above was, it did not receive much immediate media attention, as senseless killings were becoming more common in NYC. But *The New*

York Times did an investigative piece published two weeks after the murder titled "37 Who Saw Murder Didn't Call the Police." The article explained that people didn't want to get involved because they were afraid—though not clearly of what. The article stated, "For more than half an hour 38 [sic; don't know why the article doesn't match the number in the title] respectable, law-abiding citizens in Queens watched a killer stalk and stab a woman in three [sic; there were two] separate attacks in Kew Gardens." It quoted the assistant chief inspector, in charge of all Queens detectives, a 25-year veteran of homicide investigations, to be still shocked two weeks after the murder, and that "if we had been called when he first attacked, the woman might not be dead now." The article stated that when the police were called only two women were in the street to wait for them. The man who had made the call reportedly said, "I didn't want to get involved." One "witness" was reported to have said he was "tired" and "went [back] to bed." One woman said she thought it was just a "lover's quarrel."

This incident thus became the shame of New York, and in particular Queens (one Brooklyn friend of mine used to bug me that this would never happen in Brooklyn). The 2004 *Times* article, "Kitty, 40 years later", reported that "Newspapers spread the story across the nation and as far away as Istanbul and Moscow. Clergymen and politicians decried the events, while psychologists scrambled to comprehend them." The apparent callousness of the "witnesses" was explained by psychologists as a new social psychological phenomenon—the "bystander effect" or "bystander apathy," informally known as "Genovese syndrome," which states that the greater the number of bystanders, the less likely it is that any one of them will help.

The 2004 *Times* article admitted that "there were fewer than 38 witnesses and that many of them could not have seen much of the killing." According to the article, Joseph De May Jr., a maritime lawyer, spent hundreds of hours analyzing the murder. DeMay: "Yeah, there was a murder…Yeah, people heard something. You can question how a few people behaved. But this wasn't 38 people watching a woman be slaughtered for 35 minutes and saying, 'Oh, I don't want to be involved.'" In fact DeMay made two claims in the article: "that the great majority of the 38 so-called witnesses did not see any part of the actual killing; and that what most of them did see, or hear, was fleeting and vague." DeMay also corrected the *Times* original claim that there were three attacks instead of two; the *Times* blamed the error on "confused police accounts," though this would remain uncorrected for years. Charles Skoller, the former assistant district attorney, supports part of Mr. DeMay's conclusion: "I don't think 38 people witnessed it…I don't know where that came from, the 38. I didn't count 38. We only found half a dozen that saw what was going on, that we could use."

In a 2016 *Times* article about the death of the killer, Winston Moseley, in prison for almost 52 years the *Times* finally admitted, "While there was no question that the attack occurred, and that some neighbors ignored cries for help, the portrayal of 38 witnesses as fully aware and unresponsive was erroneous. The article grossly exaggerated the number of witnesses and what they had perceived. None saw the attack in its entirety. Only a few had glimpsed parts of it, or recognized the cries for help. Many thought they had heard lovers or drunks quarreling. There were two attacks, not three. And afterward, two people did call the police. A 70-year-old woman ventured out and cradled the dying victim in her arms until they arrived."

The increase of the homicide rate in NYC in the 60s was shocking. In 1960 there were 482 murders in NYC, a city of nearly 8 million. 1961 retained a similar figure, 481, which corresponded to 4.7 killed per 100,000 of the population. In 1962 the number rose dramatically to 631 total, but then decreased to 548 in 1963, in part probably because of Mayor Wagner's increase of Transit Police in the subways, a growing place of crime. However, in the period 1964-66 the yearly totals of murders stayed in the 600s. In 1966 the rate was 7.6 per 100,000. Then, every year the number of homicides increased greatly—746 in 1967, 986 in 1968, and 1,043 in 1969. The numbers would rise in the early 70s, with 1,691 murders in 1972 and similar numbers in the later 70s. In 1971 the rate rose to 12.6 in 100,000, and would not fall to single digits again in the 20th century. To put things in perspective, the most murders in NYC from when such things were counted (1928) to the present, was 2,245 in 1990; the lowest number of murders was 290 total, in 2017—the latest statistic. This is about 200 less than the best year in the 60s—1960.

Crime got so bad for Manhattan taxi cab drivers that in 1967 bulletproof partitions began to be ordered to separate the front seats from the back. As already noted earlier, closed telephone booths were used for nefarious purposes and would be replaced with open ones in the 70s.

Why did the crime rate increase so much in the 60s? Surely part of the blame belongs to the increasing use of narcotics. Crack was a driving force of crime increase in the 80s. There were certainly not enough police, especially in the subways where crime increased greatly; in fact, as noted above, when Transit Police numbers were increased the crime rate went down. According to VillageVoice.com, in a 1968 crime conference, the Manhattan Borough President, the Bronx Borough President, and the Brooklyn District Attorney declared that police corruption helped spark the rising crime rate. "It is senseless to believe youngsters do not see this or to expect that it will create in them a respect for the law," said Manhattan Borough President Percy Sutton.

Another theory is that crime was caused by leaded gas, which can lower intelligence and increase aggression levels. Lead in gasoline did not begin to be phased out by the EPA until 1974 and lead in gas was not actually banned in the US until 1996, about the time crime fell in NY and other cities. Before 1974, leaded gas emissions grew and grew unencumbered as the number of automobiles grew. According to cumulative data by the Federal Highway Administration (FHWA) the number of motor vehicles increased steadily from

1960 to 2006, increasing by an estimated 3.69 million each year since 1960.

By the way, we have Thomas Midgley Jr. (1889-1944) to thank for leaded gasoline, used as an antiknock agent. He also added CFCs (such as Freon), which caused ozone depletion. In fact, it is said "he had more impact on the atmosphere than any other single organism in Earth's history."

Besides the elimination of leaded gas, why did the crime rate *decrease* so much after the 90s? There are a number of theories, and please don't shoot the messenger. One is that abortion was not legalized until 1973, and many would-be neglected children and criminals were simply not born. A less controversial theory was proposed by Malcolm Gladwell in his book *The Tipping Point*; he argues that crime was an "epidemic" in the 60s (ending in the 90s) and a small reduction of crime due to the police was enough to "tip" the balance (there were also an increase in the number of police later in the 20th century). In the 1990s, we also saw the end of the crack epidemic. The 90s also saw the use of improved police tactics, including using computerized tools provided by CompStat, and adopting the "broken windows" theory. That theory purports that visible signs of crime, anti-social behavior and civil disorder create an urban environment that encourages further crime and disorder, including serious crimes. Thus, it suggests that policing methods that target minor crimes such as vandalism, public drinking and fare evasion help to create an atmosphere of order and lawfulness, thereby preventing more serious crimes.

There was indeed rampant police corruption in NYC in the 60s. This was exposed by Officer Frank Serpico (1936-   ). In 1967 he reported credible evidence of widespread systematic police corruption. But nothing was done. He met another officer who helped him and Serpico contributed to a *New York Times* article in 1970 that exposed the corruption. The extent of police corruption included allegations that "several policemen invited a New Jersey gambler to set up shop in the Bronx when a bookmaker in that borough went broke and the policemen lost their source of graft." What was revealed was a pattern of extorting money from criminals, other payoffs, and other corruption.

During a period of less than four months in the summer and fall of 1969, eight bombings rocked major institutions in New York City, including banks, federal buildings, courts and corporate offices. While no one was killed, the bombings caused several injuries, jolted the city, damaged property and became symbols of the radical movements that were challenging the foundations of American society. They were set by the "Weather Underground" or "the Weathermen," an American militant radical left-wing communist revolutionary group founded on the Ann Arbor campus of the University of Michigan. Their objective was to overthrow the US government, with revolutionary positions characterized by Black Power and opposition to the Vietnam War. What they did was introduce domestic terrorism to NYC. Some disagree it was "terrorism," but then what else was it?

Despite all the above, none of my immediate family were victims of crimes in NYC in the 60s. However, I reported in my diary on July 6, 1969 that one of our tenant's apartments was broken into and ransacked. They had been away for some time. "The police came and said that the robbery probably happened two weeks ago and that they found a knife on the roof."

RIOTS

1964 saw race riots in Harlem in Manhattan and Bedford-Stuyvesant in Brooklyn, linked to a single incident in Harlem. These riots are said to be precipitating events to further riots in Philadelphia, Rochester, Chicago and Jersey City, among others.

Patrick Lynch, the superintendent of three apartment houses in a predominately working-class white area in Manhattan's upper east side, hosed down some black students from his stoops, shouting racial epithets. The angry wet black students started to pick up bottles and garbage-can lids and threw them at the superintendent. One of a group of three kids from the Bronx that witnessed this, 9th grader James Powell, ran after the superintendent into his building. Within two minutes Powell exited the building. Having witnessed all this, off-duty police officer Tom Gilligan shot Powell three times, the first missing him, Gilligan claiming it was a warning shot. He also claimed Powell had a knife, which other witnesses said did not exist, though one was found in a gutter eight feet from the scene. In either event, young Powell died.

Rioting commenced immediately and lasted six days. On the 5th day, Harlem had quieted, but the riot started anew after a UN demonstration to protest terrorism and genocide committed against Black Americans.

In total, 4,000 New Yorkers participated in the riots which led to attacks on the New York City Police Department, vandalism, and looting in stores. At the end of the conflict, reports counted one dead rioter, 118 injured, and 465 arrested.

The Stonewall riots (AKA the Stonewall uprising or the Stonewall rebellion) were a series of spontaneous, violent demonstrations by members of the gay community against a police raid that took place in the early morning of June 28, 1969, at the Stonewall Inn, located in the Greenwich Village neighborhood of Manhattan.

The Stonewall Inn had been at the time the only bar for gay men in NYC where dancing was allowed. An illegal dive with no running water behind its bar, it had been converted from a heterosexual nightclub/restaurant in 1966 owned by the Genovese crime family, by three members of the Mafia into a gay bar. With no liquor license, a corrupt cop would collect a payoff ever week. Drug sales and other transactions regularly took place. The Inn would regularly be raided by the police, but with warning.

On June 28, 1969 four plainclothes policemen raided the Inn, without warning. As patrons were forcefully pushed out of the bar, a crowd of 100-150 gathered outside. A particularly aggressive female patron got hit by a police baton and rallied the crowd to "do something." When she was heaved into the back of the police wagon, the crowd became a mob and went "berserk." They tried to push over the paddy wagon. They threw rocks, bricks, garbage cans and garbage through the Stonewall windows. They uprooted a parking meter and used it as a battering ram on the doors of the Stonewall. They lit garbage on fire and stuffed it through the broken windows of the Stonewall.

Police entered the Stonewall and were trapped. The Tactical Patrol Force (TPF) arrived to free them. The TPF formed a phalanx and attempted to clear the streets by marching slowly and pushing the crowd back. It took a long time to do that. In the meantime, the interior of the Stonewall was demolished.

The next day thousands of people had gathered in front of the Stonewall, which had opened again The throng surrounded buses and cars, harassing the occupants unless they either admitted they were gay or indicated their support for the demonstrators. One person climbed a lamppost and dropped a heavy bag onto the hood of a police car, shattering the windshield. As on the previous evening, fires were started in garbage cans throughout the neighborhood. More than a hundred police were present but after 2:00 A.M. the TPF arrived again. Police chases continued, but when police captured demonstrators, the crowd surged to recapture them. Street battling ensued again until 4:00 A.M.

The Stonewall Riots received a surprising amount of support from the heterosexual public. It started a movement that LGBTs would now fight for their rights. It is now considered the birth of gay pride.

CRIPPLING STRIKES

The United Federation of Teachers (UFT), founded on March 16, 1960 as the labor union that represented most teachers in NYC public schools, organized a major strike less than eight months after its founding, on November 7. This one-day strike saw an estimated 15,000 teachers refusing to report to work. 4,600 teachers were formally suspended, as the strike was considered illegal, but later the suspensions were cancelled. Some progress was made for teachers, though their low salaries were not raised. On April 11, 1962, as contract talks between NYC and the UFT broke down, a walkout of 20,000 teachers occurred, completely shutting 26 buildings and seriously disrupting classes at virtually all locations. Again, this only lasted a day, but resulted in the NYC Mayor and NY Governor providing an additional $13 million for NYC schools, allowing increased funding of teacher salaries. The following year another strike was averted, within one day of a walkout scheduled for September 9, 1963. A raise was successfully negotiated for teachers.

However, in 1968 the UFT did go on strike again, with disastrous consequences. The strike dragged on from May to November 1968, shutting down public schools for a total of 36 days, leaving more than 1 million students unable to go to school throughout that period.

The strike resulted from a confrontation between the UFT and the new community-controlled school board in the largely black Ocean Hill and Brownsville neighborhoods of Brooklyn. That school board abruptly dismissed a set of teachers and administrators, almost all white and Jewish. The newly created school district was an experiment in community control over schools. Fewer grades were issued, and one school abolished grade levels completely. The schools expanded the role of Black and African history and culture in the curriculum. Some schools began to teach Swahili and African counting. One school with a large number of Puerto Rican students became completely bilingual.

Though many visitors, students, and parents supported the schools' shift to student-focused education, teachers were taken aback by the level of control exercised by the school board, and many objected to the board's new policies concerning personnel and curriculum. The UFT denounced the Ocean Hill–Brownsville curriculum, saying that awareness of one's racial heritage would not be helpful in the job market.

The strike ended on November 17, 1968, when the New York State Education Commissioner asserted state control over the Ocean Hill–Brownsville district. The dismissed teachers were reinstated and three of the new principals were transferred. The Ocean Hill–Brownsville district lost direct control over its schools; other districts never gained control over their schools.

The events surrounding the strike were a factor in the decision by Rabbi Meir Kahane (1932-1990, assassinated) to form the vigilante organization Jewish Defense League (JDL) which later morphed into a terrorist organization with the stated goal to "protect Jews from anti-Semitism by whatever means necessary."

Being in a private (parochial) school, "unfortunately" I was not affected by any of these strikes. But the public-school kids, losing so much time in school in the 68-69 school year, had to later make up for some days on holidays, including during a major snow storm in 69 (see ACTS OF NATURE below).

The 1962–63 NYC Newspaper Strike ran from December 8, 1962, until March 31, 1963, lasting for a total of 114 days. It started when workers from the New York Typographical Union walked out from four major newspapers and five other papers suspended operations on a voluntary basis. The issue was over automation by computers and wages, in which the unions were looking for an increase of $38.82 per week over two years compared to $8 over the same period offered by the Newspapers.

Before the internet, Newspapers were of vital importance. Though there was TV, many preferred the written word over that, and there were some things you got in a newspaper that you didn't get on TV—the local sales, employment ads, personal ads, and, most important to me, the *comics*. Fortunately for me and other kids and adults alike, Chuck McCann provided us with the comics on local TV, as told in Chapter 4. But my father always read the paper when he got home, in his case the *New York Daily Mirror*, and I'm sure he was hurting for the written page of news.

The newspaper strike was finally resolved by NYC's Mayor Wagner with the aid of a negotiator, and the unions settled for an increase of $12.63 per week, $4.63 more per week than was originally offered. An analysis performed by *The New York Times* showed that the nine affected newspapers lost a total of more than $100 million in advertising and circulation revenues and that the industry's more than 19 thousand employees lost $50 million in wages and benefits. A couple of papers raised their price from 5 to 10 cents. One paper, my father's beloved *New York Daily Mirror*, went out of business because of the strike, shutting down on October 15, 1963. It sold its name and "goodwill" to the *New York Daily News*, and thus that became my father's paper of choice and that is the paper I remember always being in our house in the 60s. It is also the paper that my father's obituary would appear in one day.

A newspaper strike over automation again and other issues began on September 16, 1965. The Newspaper Guild struck *The New York Times*, and the Publishers Association, minus the *New York Post*, closed down the rest of the city's papers. The Guild wanted it written into their contract that the company would find new spots within the organization for all present Guild employees who were automated out of a job, with company-provided retraining if needed. This strike, with a lockout of 17,000 news industry employees, lasted until October 10, 1965.

The Social Services Employees Union (SSEU) closed NYC's welfare offices of 8,000 workers for 28 days, from January 2 to February 1, 1965. This victory, celebrated to this day, resulted in a caseload cap, 100% paid health insurance and a 9% pay increase, as well as a clothing grant for welfare *recipients*. However, it put an end to "midnight raids" on welfare recipients. These raids were made to identify welfare fraud, specifically whether there was a man in a house occupied by a family that received welfare grants as a fatherless group. NYC's welfare recipients grew to 1.2 million in 1975 and the city's welfare agency accounted for more than one-quarter of the city's budget.

A NYC Transit Strike was called by the Transport Workers Union (TWU) and Amalgamated Transit Union (ATU) after the expiration of their contract with the NYC Transit Authority (TA) at the end of 1965. From January 1, 1966 to January 13, all service on the subway and buses in the city ceased. This earned the unions a package worth over $60 million, including wage increases from $3.18 to $4.14 an hour, an additional paid holiday, increased pension benefits, and other gains. Gains averaged nine percent for the next eight years. In fact, the settlement provided $52 million in two years, a settlement so successful that it inspired other union leaders. Meanwhile, the strike cost NYC $1.5

billion in lost wages. It increased the cost of a commuter token for a bus or subway ride to 20 cents on July 5—up from the 15-cent charge that had lasted since 1953.

Taxi cab drivers and mechanics went on strike over a contract dispute on March 24, 1965, leaving up to 95% of NYC's 12,000 cabs immobile. This strike spread to Chicago. In NYC, the concern was about visitors for the World's Fair having difficulty getting around.

The "foulest" NYC strike was the 1968 garbage strike, which left the city without garbage pickup for nine days, starting on February 2. On February 5, the *Times* already had reported that the city looked like "a vast slum as mounds of refuse grow higher and strong winds whirl the filth through the streets." At that point there were about 30,000 tons of trash on the streets. It was reported on the lower East Side that "Garbage was piled chest-high. Egg shells, coffee grounds, milk cartons, orange rinds, and empty beer cans littered the sidewalk." Mayor Lindsay threatened to call in the National Guard to order truckers to remove the trash, but NY Governor Nelson Rockefeller did not agree, and instead had his counsel try to come up with a way for the state to take over the sanitation department, an effort which put his counsel in the hospital for exhaustion. Lindsay thus continued union negotiations, which he failed at, taking too hard a line with them. Rockefeller forced an end to the madness and smell by using the premise of a health emergency to seize state control of the Sanitation Department. He offered a $425 yearly wage increase (previously only $400 was offered) and future arbitration, which the union accepted. Despite the fact that 100,000 tons of garbage had accumulated by then, New Yorkers were outraged that Rockefeller had caved in, but Lindsay was also blamed for letting the situation escalate.

Living in a neighborhood with six-apartment attached buildings, I personally was happy to see the putrid mess cleaned up. Thank goodness it wasn't summer.

THE BLACKOUT

On November 9, 1965 a single human error made days before in setting a safety relay at too low a voltage to be tripped placed 30 million people in eight Northeastern states and Ontario, Canada in total darkness for up to 13 hours.

The most I remember that night was being worried about my mom, who had been out supermarket shopping that evening when power was lost. I stood at the window anxiously awaiting her return. There wasn't any reason to wait away from the window, anyway, as moonlight from a bright full moon in a cloudless sky and passing cars provided light, while inside our apartment all I had was my dad and brother walking around with not-so-powerful flashlights.

My mother finally got home, of course, with stories of the blackout outside. We had never experienced anything like this, and though fearful I was also a bit intrigued. I was still safe at my home, with my family finally reunited. We broke out the candles and made the best of it. Fortunately the temperature was comfortable.

The loss of power seemed sudden to me, though it had to have taken a bit of time to go from full power to nothing. It is said that famous disk jockey Dan Ingram (1934-2018), whom I remember would play his jingle "Dan Ingram, Ingram, Ingram" often, was playing Jonathan King's "Everyone's Gone to the Moon," and he noted that the record sounded slow, as well as the commercial jingles after it. He reported that electricity itself was slowing down and measured at lower frequency. His lights dimmed and went out.

The phones were working, as they were powered by a different source, from the phone company, but trying to make calls mostly failed as the phone lines became extremely busy.

NYC was dark by 5:27 PM, though some areas were spared a blackout at all. I don't know when we got power back, but the entire city had power restored by 7 AM the next day.

Measures were taken to prevent the cascade event that put so many people into darkness, but they obviously were not good enough, for NYC had a second blackout in 1977.

Though people stuck in elevators and subways certainly did not have a good time, NYC was safe during the 65 blackout. During the blackout period NYC experienced the lowest amount of crime on any night in the city's history since records were first kept. Only five reports of looting were made. I remember the streets were quiet.

By comparison, the blackout that occurred in NYC on July 13–14, 1977, though it affected a smaller area, confined mostly to NYC, was anything but quiet and safe. Caused by lightning strikes and what then-mayor Abe Beame called "gross negligence" by power company Con Ed, the 77 blackout was characterized by "violence, vandalism, theft and discomfort" in Beame's own words. He added, "The Blackout has threatened our safety and has seriously impacted our economy. We've been needlessly subjected to a night of terror in many communities that have been wantonly looted and burned. The costs when finally tallied will be enormous." There were 1,616 stores damaged in looting and rioting. A total of 1,037 fires were responded to, including 14 multiple-alarm fires. In the largest mass arrest in NYC history, 3,776 people were arrested. In addition, 550 police officers were injured. The "discomfort" Beame referred to was the oppressive heat wave that occurred during that time, with no air conditioners or fans to provide comfort. As for the impact on NYC economy, which was already in a downturn, a congressional study estimated that the cost of damages amounted to a little over $300 million.

I found the blackout of 77 personally uncomfortable and frightening. Even though it was night, it was *hot*. The streets were not quiet, the sounds of sirens and large masses of people keeping me from falling asleep, already difficult to do in the heat. I lay awake for hours, and when I finally slept and awoke the next morning power was still out. It would not come back until late in that day.

There was another blackout in the Northeast, this one in a wider area than even 1965, in fact one of the widest power outages in history, affecting 50 million people, on August 24, 2003. This was initially frightening as it occurred less than two years after 9/11, and everyone I knew suspected terrorism—there had been speculation then that terrorists would hit our power grid one day as the beginning of a new massive wave of strikes. Fortunately, the actual cause was "old power lines, summer heat, overgrown trees, outdated equipment, and human error." Unlike in 77, NYC didn't descend into crime and looting. In fact, police reported less crime during the 2003 blackout than during the same period in 2002. I think we all were just happy that it wasn't terrorism.

ACTS OF NATURE

Not all problems are created by humanity, and NYC experienced some problems from nature in the 60s.

On September 12, 1960, Hurricane Donna swept through NYC, after causing massive destruction along its path in the Caribbean, Florida, and the East Coast. Donna was at the time the 7th costliest Atlantic hurricane; the total cost of damage was estimated at $900 million (1960 USD), or about $32 billion today. The cost in lives was great, estimated at 164-364 total. Because of the loss of life and destruction, there never will be another hurricane "Donna"; the name was retired.

It is amazing to me that I actually have memories of Donna, for I was only three years old when it passed NYC. I remember looking outside our picture windows and seeing wind and rain like I had never seen before. I also saw a large branch fall on my father's 1956 Chevy Bel-Air's front hood, and my father running outside to take it off his car. I was worried for his safety, and very happy when he came back inside. The huge branch (possibly a small tree) barely dented the heavy car, but left behind scratches that would later rust. That rust-mark would remind us for years of Hurricane Donna.

There was a drought in NYC from about 1963-66, which I remember calling "the water shortage." The drought in the Northeast actually lasted during the entire decade, according to the US Geological Survey. According to climatologist W.C. Palmer, the Northeast drought was "such a rare event that we should ordinarily expect it to occur in this region only about once in a couple of centuries."

A water conservation campaign occurred in NYC from November 11, 1963 to May 1, 1964. An "intense" campaign started on April 1, 1965. 1965 was the driest year on record since the late 19th century, and was most severe in northeastern PA and Southeastern NY—where NYC lie. For New Yorkers, this meant measures like banning skyscrapers from using air conditioners, city fountains not running, laws against watering lawns and washing cars, and constant reminders to not waste water in the home. On some days in the summer, the water pressure was so low that water barely flowed out of taps (NOTE: Bottled water did not exist yet). What did come out often looked undrinkable, not very clear.

In February 1969 NYC was hit by a severe winter storm (a "nor'easter," as we call them) that dropped 20 inches of snow and more [sources vary on the amount] throughout NYC. At least 94 people in the US lost their lives in the storm. In NYC, 42 people were killed, half of them in Queens. Thousands were stranded on roads and airports, and schools were closed for several days. As was the norm, Manhattan was cleared out first (though paralyzed for three days) but boroughs like Queens were considered secondary and had streets uncleared for over a week after the storm. Living in Queens, this affected my family greatly. From my diary, Monday, February 10, 1969:

> Today there was no school because of the snow. New York City had 13 inches of snow yesterday. Today, in some places, without exaggerating, the snow was almost as high as daddy. Daddy did not go to work today.

I recorded in fact in my diary that my father wasn't able to drive to work for the rest of that week. On Friday, though the streets were still not ploughed to get his car out yet, the subways were running to his job and he could get to them. My brother regularly used a city bus to get to school, and they were not running until Friday as well. As for me, I would walk to school, it being only 6 short blocks away; but my school did not re-open until Thursday. I remember climbing "mountains" of snow that had been ploughed from the avenue to get to school, which I actually considered fun. Wednesday, February 12 was Lincoln's Birthday (not combined with Washington's to create Presidents' Day yet) so my brother and I did not have school anyway, but the public schools kids had to go because they had lost so many days from the 68 teacher's strike.

The lack of proper cleanup was blamed on Mayor Lindsay, who was already unpopular for other issues. The snowstorm became to be known by his name, and when he visited Queens after it, he was booed and insulted, as his four-wheel-drive truck tried to clumsily make its way through the snow-bound streets. During a walk through Fresh Meadows, Queens, one woman actually said he was a wonderful man, to which the beleaguered mayor responded, "And you're a wonderful woman, not like those fat Jewish broads up there," pointing to women in a nearby building who had criticized him. Though recorded, the *New York Times*, Associated Press and WNEW radio declined to run with that quote.

PORNOGRAPHY

When my mother would take me into the vicinity of Times Square in the 60s, we would cross streets and avoid entire blocks that were filled with porn shops, X-rated movie theatres, strip clubs, bath-houses, peep shows (pornographic shows viewed through small wall openings) and "massage parlors" (venues of prostitution). Their advertising was very blatantly displayed, and men would stand at the doorways of these places telling passersby "This is the place, this is the one, come inside."

This was an embarrassment to Mayor Wagner, who cracked down on "obscene" magazines early in the 60s. He was particularly motivated to clean up the city before millions of visitors would arrive for the World's Fair in 1964. From April to August 1963 police made 166 obscenity-related arrests, all but 36 of them in or around Times Square.

On Sunday, May 5, 1963 an irate monsignor Joseph McCaffrey referred to Time Square as a "disgrace" that he wanted cleaned up "now," reminding everyone of the many tourists that would arrive for the World's Fair in a year. Within two months Wagner announced that he was ratcheting up his anti-obscenity campaign, with an anti-pornography police unit and even a special court to deal with obscenity cases.

Five months later a Reverend by the name of Hill went on a hunger strike, and promised to continue until Wagner made good his promises. He said the mayor had done nothing. The mayor put his deputy mayor in charge of anti-obscenity efforts. This was enough to satisfy Hill, who stopped his hunger strike. People were arrested for selling "dirty" books and some were sentenced jail time, including erotic publisher Ralph Ginzburg (1929-2006), who received a 5-year sentence in a federal court in a case in which he was indicted by US Attorney General Robert Kennedy, the President's brother; he only served 8 months. In November 1963 Wagner began shutting downtown cinemas that screened underground movies.

The battle against pornography by mayor Wagner and later mayor Lindsay (who used it as part of his campaign) would turn out to be fruitless. This was because the US Supreme Court (called the "Warren Court" from 1953-69, after its Chief Justice) made many pro-pornography decisions in the US in the 60s. From "The Morality Of First Amendment Jurisprudence" by Phyllis Schlafly (A.M., Harvard University, author of 20 books), "Since a series of Warren Court decisions in the 1960s, perhaps no single side of any issue has won in the Supreme Court as often as pornography." She adds:

> In the short space of thirteen months, May 1967 to June 1968, the Warren Court handed down a series of twenty-six decisions that changed dramatically the law of obscenity. These decisions elevated pornography and other assaults on decency

to the level of a First Amendment right. The Supreme Court reversed dozens of judges, juries, and appellate courts in sixteen states, made laws against obscenity unenforceable, and lowered drastically the standards of decency in communities throughout America.

This avalanche of pro-pornography decisions started on May 8, 1967, with *Redrup v. New York*. The case involved the sale of books published by William Hamling, a wealthy publisher of lewd magazines, who financed the defendant's case. The most shocking aspect of this case is that Hamling had been [Supreme Court] Justice Fortas's client before he joined the Court. Despite this connection, Justice Fortas did not recuse himself, but instead voted to reverse Robert Redrup's conviction for selling pornographic books published by Hamling.

Following the *Redrup* decision, from June 1967 to June 1968, the Supreme Court handed down nineteen more pro-pornography decisions that simply cited *Redrup* as the reason for reversing lower court decisions. The majority of these decisions consisted of only one or two sentences [of text], a pattern Justice John Harlan referred to as the "Redrup treatment." For example, in *Mazes v. Ohio*, the Court reversed the judgments of the Ohio Supreme Court, the Ohio Court of Appeals, the trial judge, and the jury, in a single sentence: "The petition…is granted and the judgment of the Supreme Court of Ohio is reversed. *Redrup v. New York, 386 U.S. 767.*"

So, pornography in NYC remained in NYC and grew. In 1967 massage parlors proliferated in Times Square and other parts of the City following the City Council's removal of licensing requirements. In October 1968 Al Goldstein started publishing *Screw* Magazine in NYC; in September 1969 Bob Guccione started selling Penthouse in America, after founding it in the UK in 1965.

See any episode of HBO's *The Deuce* to see how bad it all got by the 70s.

Pornography never saw an end in NYC, or anywhere, but happily Times Square was cleaned up. Perhaps too much to counter its tawdry past, Times Square is more like Disney World now.

THE LOOMING FINANCIAL CRISIS

The total labor force, the number of workers in manufacturing, and the number of factories all declined during the 1960s and 1970s. NYC's manufacturing base and its skilled laborers had been emigrating to the suburbs and to other states since World War II. With the departure of much of the middle class, the city's tax base shrank). During the 60s, a gradual economic and social decay set in. By 1966 the City was already $5 billion in debt.

Immigration was up, and there was an influx into the City of poor people. The Immigration and Nationality Act of 1965 lifted restrictions of immigration from Africa and Asia, and the preference given to northern and western Europeans over southern and eastern Europeans. Though well-intentioned (in my opinion it saved my neighborhood as it resulted in a great influx of Greeks which revitalized it, and overall Queens was revitalized by the influx of Asians, now a quarter of its population), at first these additional people were a drain on the economy.

There were economic problems in the US that of course affected NYC. President Lyndon Johnson was committed to alleviating the suffering of America's poor. As President, therefore, he proposed an expansive domestic agenda aimed at reducing poverty, expanding educational opportunities, increasing the safety net of public services for the poor and unemployed, and tending to the health and financial needs of the elderly. This became to be known as "The Great Society." These measures were supported by Congress. For example, with close to one-half of the elderly living without health care, and roughly one-third living below the poverty line, often due to high medical expenses, Johnson's call for a federal program of medical insurance for the elderly—Medicare—found ready support. With more than half of America's adults lacking a high school diploma, Congress also passed a bundle of programs designed to increase aid to schools and provide training for those without the skills or education needed to advance in the work force.

Financing "The Great Society" turned out to be a problem. A lot of money was being spent to finance the War in Vietnam. By 1968, the United States was spending $22 billion a year on that war, a full 12% of the total federal budget. When created in 1966, Medicare cost $3 billion, and its costs rose rapidly. Tax hikes would have provided relief, but Johnson feared that increasing taxes to finance the war or pay for his Great Society would undermine support for both. He thus insisted on proceeding on both fronts without raising taxes.

NY Mayor Lindsay, on the other hand, had no qualms about raising taxes. In 1966 the settlement terms of the transit strike, combined with increased welfare costs and general economic decline, caused Lindsay to lobby the New York State legislature for a new municipal income tax and higher water rates for city residents, plus a new commuter tax for people who worked in the city but resided elsewhere. He got what he wanted. The City Tax has remained with us, with current tax rates from 2.9% to 3.6%. Lindsay also imposed hiring freezes and across-the-board budget cuts; 13,000 municipal employees would be slashed from the payroll.

Even with tax increases and other measures, NYC would fall further into debt. The city neared bankruptcy under its next mayor, Abe Beame, in the 70s but avoided that step with the aid of a $2.3 billion federal loan. However, President Ford rejected a requested bailout. Everyone who lived in NYC on October 29, 1975 remembers the headline of that day in the *Daily News*: "FORD TO CITY: DROP DEAD."

11 OUR VIEW OF THE FUTURE

Our view of the future was bright, at least for me. This optimistic outlook was fueled by TV shows like *Star Trek*, movies like *2001: A Space Odyssey*, and the utopian vistas experienced at the World's Fair. But upon closer inspection, as an adult now, I realize those utopian prognostications were flawed.

One of the reasons I loved *Star Trek* so much was its portrayal of a gentle, beautiful future. In this future Earth was a virtual paradise (and even stated as much in a later TV incarnation, *Deep Space 9*) where people were healthy, long-lived, happy, didn't need money, and there was no crime or wars— every problem in the 60s had been solved. But as sci-fi author Robert Silverberg once quipped, "Utopias are boring. Dystopias on the other hand, are interesting." So *Star Trek* became less utopian as its episodes proceeded. People were at odds with each other. In one episode, Kirk admitted he was bullied at "Starfleet Academy." War did not exist on Earth, but had spread to the stars. Ordinary diseases were replaced by new exotic alien ones. Crime did indeed happen, as in one episode, "Conscience of the King," where people were murdered because they had witnessed another crime—a Eugenics-inspired mass murder of thousands of people on an Earth colony. Speaking of Eugenics, *Star Trek* referred to "Eugenics Wars" in two episodes, one that would happen in the 1990s and the other in the early 21st century. There was a World War III referenced that killed millions around that time. And in one of *Star Trek*'s worst episodes, "The Way to Eden," there were even hippies, people who dropped out of normal life.

Star Trek's creator and producer, Gene Roddenberry, wanted to portray a utopia, but realized that would result in boring TV. Great ideas like the "Prime Directive," which stated that his characters could not interfere with the development of other, less advanced civilizations, was put on the wayside many times, as it "interfered" with good stories being told. To quote Captain James T. Kirk in one episode, wherein he assumes the dialect of a planet patterned after 20s Chicago gangsters, "Who's interferin'? We're just takin' over."

In the episode "Assignment: Earth," the crew uses the sun's gravity assist to go to the past to see how the Earth survived the year 1968. At the time it was a plot device for the crew to interact with the present (while also serving as a pilot for a new series), but in reality 1968 was indeed one of the most tumultuous years of our past—the Vietnam War was raging, students were protesting, both Martin Luther King and Robert Kennedy were assassinated (in fact, Mr. Spock states, "there will be an important assassination today"), and it seemed like the country was falling apart at the seams, with nuclear annihilation looming in the background. In the episode, the crew meet upon the mysterious Gary Seven, whose ancestors are from Earth but had been transported to another planet where they were trained for centuries to have their descendants come back to Earth to keep humanity on the right path to become a healthy civilization (hence the pilot, which never sold). In his current mission Mr. Seven was to prevent the launch of a "nuclear orbiting platform," by the US in response to other powers doing so (we can't be the first because we're the good guys).

Space-based weapons as above were actually an old idea that was abandoned years ago. From "The dozen space weapons myths" by James Oberg:

> Stationing weapons in space for use against ground targets has long ago been recognized as far more expensive and less flexible than basing them on Earth, say, in a submarine. Even planning a space-to-space attack can take hours or days or longer for the moving attacker and target to line up in a proper position. This goes double for nuclear weapons: putting them into space on a permanent basis was last taken seriously in the Sunday comics in the late 1950's. So these accusations [of the US planning to deploy them] seem to confuse proposed projects (usually already rejected—that's why the proponents go public with their ideas) or even Hollywood science fiction for actual hardware.

The 1967 Outer Space Treaty expressly forbade the use of orbital nuclear weapons, though the Soviet Union deployed one anyway.

The beauty of *2001*'s space scenes was certainly awe-inspiring. My favorite scene is when a man-ape from the "dawn of man" throws a bone into the air and a smash-cut of thousands of years is made to the 21st century in space, the bone replaced by a sleek satellite orbiting the Earth. From there commenced other satellites and a spacecraft making its way to a beautiful two-tiered rotating space station, all to the music of Strauss' "Blue Danube."

What I didn't know when I first saw the above was that the "satellites" shown were *Orbiting Nuclear Warheads*. The very first shown is a US one, and the next a Chinese one. In fact, in the novelization of *2001*, Arthur C. Clarke has at the end of the novel the star-child detonating them all, to save humanity from its foolishness. Stanley Kubrick was going to do this in the film, but decided against it because he did not want people to associate this movie with his previous one that ended in nuclear disaster, *Dr. Strangelove*. In addition to the orbiting nuclear warheads, *2001* portrayed a future of continued mistrust between the US and a still-extant Soviet Union, to the point of keeping secret from the Soviets the monumental discovery by the US of an ancient alien artifact on the Moon.

In *2001*, all was not especially pretty. The Space Station and in particular the spaceship *Discovery* were very antiseptic-looking. The space station was very white inside, the whiteness of the floors and ceilings in stark contrast to orange-colored chairs that stood out so much from the bleak white landscape I remember the audience guffawing at the sight. Indeed, I always found the scene of astronaut Frank Poole exercising in the very white *Discovery* carousel (accompanied by the melancholic strains of the "Gayne Ballet Suite") to be very depressing. Speaking of white, the final scene of Bowman in the futuristic hotel suite is very bright, each floor panel emitting bright light.

The characters are cardboard-like in *2001*, perhaps intentionally to display their stripped humanity. They are soft-spoken and a lot of what they say is not important; in fact, in the Moon scenes there is just a lot of "sucking up to the boss," Heywood Floyd. The two "zombies" on the *Discovery*, Bowman and Poole, blithely go about their business, ignoring each other, Poole not even showing interest when getting birthday greetings from his parents. It has been said that the dialog of *2001*, minimal as it is, is amongst the most boring in cinematic history. It is also said that the most "human" character in the movie is HAL, the computer. Even as I marveled at this movie as a child, its lack of humanity struck me. I wondered if that part of it would happen too.

There were wondrous projections in the 60s of "manned" space exploration and colonization, fueled in part by films like *2001*. We just assumed that the "Space Age" we were in would continue in its ferocity. Having a colony on the Moon in 2001 certainly seemed plausible, at the rate we were going. I remember that a popular date bandied about for the first Mars mission was 1984, and indeed in the *2001* novelization there were already colonies there too. When we made it to the Moon in 1969 we thought we could do anything; a popular phrase used to be "If they could put a man on the Moon why can't they _____?" But putting people on the moon proved very costly, more costly than expected. The entire cost of the Apollo program as reported to Congress in 1973 was $25.4 billion (the preliminary estimate had been $7 billion); In 2009, NASA held a symposium on project costs which presented an estimate of the Apollo program costs in 2005 dollars as roughly $170 billion. That was all to put 12 (and tried to put 14, with Apollo 13 included) white men on the Moon, and return them home safely with a total of 842 pounds of lunar rocks and soil, leaving some scientific packages behind to continue their analyses. The Apollo program wasn't a great Return On Investment (ROI), when you just look at these cold figures and disregard the prestige and history that went along with it. Also, many technologies developed for these missions were applicable for use on Earth, but this was not immediately seen. Three more planned Apollo missions—18, 19 and 20—were cancelled. And, as we know, no-one has stepped on the moon since the last mission—Apollo 17, when the last humans to leave Earth orbit to this day landed on the moon on December 11, 1972, and left on December 14th. For nearly 50 years now the Moon has been undisturbed by us. At the time of this writing, only 4 of the 12 who walked there are still alive.

Mars of course was never visited as we had predicted, but is coming closer into our grasp, with a mission possible in the 2030s. China has joined the "space race," as well as commercial endeavors which will get us on the Moon again and elsewhere. Our predictions in the 60s were off; God willing, they all will happen in this century.

In the 60s we also predicted great advances in travel. Cars would be faster in the 21st century and might even fly. Well, they aren't faster, and some speed limits remain low from the oil crisis of 73 though most have been raised again. They also don't fly, though there is always seemingly someone working on that. Even in 1985, in *Back to the Future*, it is established that just 30 years from that time (perhaps tongue-in-cheek) cars would fly. Obviously 2015 passed by without this achievement. The fact that cars would be *smart* in the future, so smart in fact that some are driving themselves in field tests, wasn't usually on the prediction list.

Jet travel was expected to be fast, very fast, in fact supersonic. That seemed a reasonable prediction, and in fact supersonic transports (SSTs) were indeed being developed in the 60s. In the US, on January 1, 1967, Boeing won the government-funded contract to build an SST, which it called the Boeing 2707. The wide-bodied 2707 was promised to seat 250 to 300 passengers and convey them at cruise speeds of approximately Mach 3—three times the speed of sound, or very roughly 2,000 MPH at cruising altitude.

The contract called for the first aircraft on September 30, 1970 and the second on December 31, 1970, when flight testing would start on the first. Airline deliveries "could" have begun in mid-1974. Environmentalists objected to the SST, however. Specifically, they were concerned about sonic booms. In tests sonic booms caused building damage. They were also concerned about the boom effects on people, and effects on the Ozone. Rising costs, unpopularity and the lack of a clear market led to the US SST program's cancellation in 1971 before the two prototypes had been completed.

Meanwhile, in November 1962, a joint venture between England and France known as the Concorde project was announced, to develop an SST. Its maximum speed was Mach 2 and seated 92 to 128 passengers. It entered service in 1976 and stayed in service for 27 years. The Russians developed their own SST, though it was in service a shorter time.

On March 11, 1976, NYC's Port Authority banned any SST flights there, right before they were to begin in NYC. I remember this as a long battle.

The SSTs were always very expensive for passengers, who shelled out over a $1000 a ticket for a shorter but more cramped (basically coach-style) flight on the Concorde. Economically, they were never very feasible. "Slow" aircraft got larger and offered relatively luxurious accommodations for the same price—with coach much cheaper. There are no commercial SSTs today anywhere in use in the world.

So, flight travel takes as long as in the 60s, a half-century ago (assuming you travelled in a jet then; prop aircraft were still widely used in the 60s, and were much slower). In fact, it's a bit slower, as aircraft have slowed down to increase economy. But, if you have the money, you can fly in style like never before—in fact, eat a gourmet meal and sleep in a fully reclining chair or even in your own compartment. And the majority of aircraft provide entertainment on a small flat TV on the back of the seat in front of you—as seen back in 68 in *2001*!

The future presented at the World's Fair, with dioramas of futuristic planned communities and wonderful, though predictable, gadgets like video phones was quite convincing to me as a child, and I just couldn't wait until I was an adult living in that future. The fact that it was unrealistic didn't occur to me then; I thought things would just happen as shown, on schedule.

The problem with planned communities, of course, is what you do with the haphazardly designed communities of the present. You can't just wipe them out or abandon them and start all over. As mentioned earlier, thinking about having video phones is all fine and good, and relatively easy to mock up but impossible to bring into fruition with the POTS system we had for telephonic communication. A new infrastructure to replace POTS and support video communication did indeed get built, but many years after the World's Fair I attended.

A video surfaced in 2012 on YouTube which had been originally presented by "Philco-Ford" Corporation in celebration of their 75th anniversary in 1967. This video, which stars future game show host Wink Martindale (1933-) and actress Marj Dusay (1936-), who had played a beautiful alien in the *Star Trek* episode "Spock's Brain," makes some amazingly accurate depictions of 1999 (or just a bit premature for that year). It is of course utopian in nature and goes too far, but it is the most accurate film in the 60s of the "future" that I have seen.

In the above the man and woman follow standard 60s gender roles, something which prognostication then usually displayed. But interesting is that the woman performs what appears to be online shopping, on a flat screen monitor, thicker than we have now but definitely of a technology beyond CRTs. What is displayed on her monitor is not web pages, but what looks like items that are scanned by a camera. She selects an item of her choice to buy.

Later, the man sits before the same consoles and pays for what his wife has bought after viewing her bill on a screen (shaking his head disapprovingly, I might add). He pays for it electronically, and the amount gets debited from his bank's computer. The man then makes a printout from a sleek console of his financial data and the narrator points out that all household documents are on a computer and can be printed any time. He then walks over to another sleek device, which the narrator refers to as "an electronic correspondence machine" or "home post office, which allows for instant written communication between individuals anywhere in the world."

The e-commerce and e-mail prediction alone from this 1967 film is staggering. It shows that a lot of thought went behind what we would want when the technology could provide it. There are also wall TVs that actually take up most of a wall. Fast international transportation is implied. It also depicts us as slaves to our machines, as the people can only consume how many calories they are allowed by the computer, and are instructed on their exercise regimen they have to perform daily. The child is home schooled, by—a computer.

At the end of the film there is a party, in which a visitor asks for the copy of a video. "I guess you want it in 3-D," the homeowner asks. "Yeah, we finally made the switch," the visitor responds. He adds, though, "What's next?" The homeowner says with a smile, "Well, you never really know." The narrator concludes the film by saying, "What's next? The things you have seen are technically possible. It remains only to apply what we now know to fulfill these dreams of tomorrow."

The legendary Walter Cronkite, perhaps the most likable and trusted man in TV News of all time, walked through the same computer set as in the above movie in the same year, 1967, as part of the CBS show *The 21st Century*. This too is available on YouTube. But he called it the "home office":

> Now this is where a man [sorry, women out there] would spend most of his time in the home of the 21st century. This equipment here will allow him to carry on normal business activities without ever going to an office away from home. This console provides a summary of news relayed by satellite from all over the world…I might check the latest weather…This same screen may give me the latest report on the stocks that I might own. With equipment like this *in the home of the future we may not have to go to work—the work* [guffaw] *would come to us.*

Thus, telecommuting (the word itself not coined until 1973) and the modern internet were predicted over 50 years ago, in 1967. 2012 estimates indicate that about 40% of the US workforce could telecommute at least part of the time.

The words "in the home of the future we may not have to go to work—the work would come to us" send a chill down my spine. Now, no matter what weather conditions, or other factors that prevent our commute to work, we *still have to work*. There is no respite. It…comes…to…us. So does the stress. About one-third of workers report high levels of stress.

This is in stark contrast to the promise made in the 60s that we would have more leisure time now. I remember being promised 35-hour work weeks in the 21st century. Economist John Keynes (1883-1946) predicted that technology would reduce the work week to 15 hours by 2030. Others predicted a 22-hour work week, six-month work year or a standard retirement age of 38.

Instead, the average American works about 46.7 hours a week, about 8 hours less than in 1920. The number of mandatory vacation days in the US is—ready for it?—0. We are the only advanced economy with no national vacation policy. By comparison, the UK mandates 28 days and France 30 days. Even fast-paced Japan requires 10 days.

American salaried (or "exempt," as it's called, being exempt from most labor laws) employees are expected to work all hours, usually with just two or three weeks of vacation, and to bring their work home, which some spend very late hours doing. We have become an overworked, overstressed society due in part to our own technology. Technology has not decreased work for us as Keynes predicted, but has increased it and intruded into our leisure time by following us home.

WITH APOLOGIES TO MR. WOLFE…

…I did go home again.

A couple of years ago I visited the home I grew up in and took pictures of it outside. The apartment buildings looked great, just like in the 60s, a half-century earlier; there was no evidence of aging. What stood out to me as different were the cars parked in the street, very futuristic looking compared to 50 years earlier—though perhaps not as much as we would have expected them to be. There were more in-wall air conditioners in the apartment buildings, and the windows were modernized. There were gates in front of every house, true of the later 60s but not the early 60s. I also noticed our small garden in the front had been paved over.

I actually went in the vestibule and was happy to see the same beautifully polished classic brass mail boxes that my mom used to keep shining. Instead of a simple buzzer that we had in the 60s to unlock the door, there was a speaker and camera.

I would have loved to have somebody let me in and allow me to look at our old apartment. But that seemed a foolish endeavor, and I just went outside again. I imagined myself as a kid in the 60s transported 50 years in the future, seeing some new things but basically feeling like being in my home time—which might have disappointed me then.

A BRIEF SUMMARY

The 60s were a decade of intense change that ripples through to today. Much has changed in our society since then, much of the change in that decade alone. Society has so radically changed that a liberal of the 60s might find comfort as a conservative now. What is considered liberal now might be surprising (but perhaps acceptable) to a liberal then.

In writing this book I learned how just a few major things affected the entire decade and beyond. The Beatles for example changed so much in music and style, and were constantly emulated, leaving a huge imprint on society. In the movies, the James Bond franchise received so much adulation and was emulated as well, constantly in TV programming. Of course, the Vietnam War helped define the decade—not the war itself but its effect at home. People who usually had "gone with the flow" became outspoken protestors and agitators, as the drafting of young men into that conflict to die in a jungle so far from home for dubious reasons was totally intolerable. I think protesting the war opened the floodgates for other protests of social injustice, though these had a life of their own as well. Everyone wanted to be treated as human beings, with dignity, including African-Americans, women and gays. People had had enough.

Some protests were made by striking. Just in NYC there were major, crippling strikes to get better pay and benefits, and these of course were not limited to NYC; they were just generally bigger news in NYC because of its size and population. Some strikes were very successful, while others gained little for union workers.

For me, personally, with all its faults and chaos, at least with the eyes of a boy, the 60s were a great decade to grow up in, pleasant for the most part and certainly never boring. I would not prefer any other decade for my childhood.

NOTES

CHAPTER 1: History, Culture and Counter-Culture

1. Information about the Civil Rights Act of 1964 was taken from a transcript at https://www.ourdocuments.gov/doc.php?flash=true&doc=97&page=transcript
2. Information about The Voting Rights Act of 1965 was obtained from http://nvrmi.com/?page_id=41
3. The charter of NOW was taken from http://coursesa.matrix.msu.edu/~hst306/documents/nowstate.html
4. The official story from the State Department about the Cuban Missile Crisis was taken from a State Department site itself, https://history.state.gov/milestones/1961-1968/cuban-missile-crisis
5. The "real" story of the above crisis was taken from https://www.theatlantic.com/magazine/archive/2013/01/the-real-cuban-missile-crisis/309190/
6. The Vietnam War stats are taken from the article "Vietnam War Facts, Stats and Myths" from https://www.uswings.com/about-us-wings/vietnam-war-facts/
7. Some material about the Vietnam War was taken from Britannica.com.
8. "Happyland" is described in http://tuoitrenews.vn/business/20779/multibilliondollar-property-project-in-southern-vn-urged-to-speed-up)
9. The fact that one general claimed that for every man drafted, three or four more were scared into volunteering was taken from the 1958 House Committee on Appropriations Hearings.
10. The argument that "up to 60 percent of those who served throughout the Vietnam War did so directly or indirectly because of the draft" is made in

Conscription, Protest and Social Conflict: The Life and Death of a Draft Resistance Movement by M. Useem, New York: Wiley (1973).
11. The defense recruiting reports statistics are from "The Draft Lottery and Voluntary Enlistment in the Vietnam Era" in the Journal of the American Statistical Association, by J. Angrist (1991).
12. The statement "The draft itself encompassed almost one-third of all eligible men during the period of 1965–69" was made in *The Draft, 1940–1973* by G. Flynn, Lawrence, KS: University of Kansas Press (2000).
13. The Gerald Ford amnesty is described in learning.blogs.nytimes.com.
14. Lottery statistics can be found in sss.gov.
15. Facts about war protests were taken from *wiki* and history.com.
16. The speech JFK presented to Congress on May 25, 1961 can be found at http://www.space.com/11772-president-kennedy-historic-speech-moon-space.html
17. The speech JFK presented at Rice University on September 12, 1962 can be found at https://er.jsc.nasa.gov/seh/ricetalk.htm
18. Information about the Moon shots was taken from nasa.gov.
19. The nasa.gov page that addresses the Apollo 9 splashdown is https://www.nasa.gov/mission_pages/apollo/missions/apollo9.html
20. The nasa.gov page that addresses Apollo 10 is https://www.nasa.gov/mission_pages/apollo/missions/apollo10.html
21. The nasa.gov page that addresses Apollo 12 is https://www.nasa.gov/mission_pages/apollo/missions/apollo12.html

CHAPTER 3: Classic TV Before It Was Classic

1. Information about the "incident" wherein Petula Clark touched Harry Belafonte's arm can be found in the *wiki* article about Harry Belafonte.
2. Chuck McCann's reading of comic strips on TV during the 62-63 NYC newspaper strike is documented in http://www.vanityfair.com/culture/2012/11/1963-newspaper-strike-bertram-powers and http://www.chuckmccann.net/earlytv.htm)

CHAPTER 4: Music and Style

1. Information about Jim Morrison's death, according to Marianne Faithful, can be found at http://www.dailymail.co.uk/tvshowbiz/article-2718742/My-ex-boyfriend-killed-Jim-Morrison-Marianne-Faithfull-says-The-Doors-rocker-died-drug-dealer-ex-gave-smack-strong.html
2. An article about the "27 Club" can be found on *wiki*.
3. The *Time* magazine article about bikinis can be found on Slate.com.
4. Inside info on Woodstock provided by Christopher Duignan, who had attended.

CHAPTER 5: Dealing With Ancient Technology

1. Information about "Digi-Comp 1" can be found at http://www.retrothing.com/2009/10/build_your_own_.html
2. The "Friends of Digicomp" Yahoo group is at https://groups.yahoo.com/neo/groups/friendsofdigicomp/info
3. Information about "Zeroids" can be found at http://www.zeroidz.com/Zeroids.html
4. Information about the Hasbro Amazamatic car can be found at http://www.samstoybox.com/toys/AmazeAMatics.html

CHAPTER 6: Ancient Medicine

1. Statistics for the "Hong Kong" influenza pandemic can be found at http://www.immunize.org/timeline/
2. Material about deinstitutionalization of mentally ill patients and anti-psychotics is sourced from *The Body Keeps the Score: Brain, Mind, and Body in the Healing of Trauma* by Bessel Van der Kolk, M.D. (Random House, 2014).
3. Some material about mental health is sourced from "A Brief History of Mental Illness and the U.S. Mental Health Care System", which can be found at http://www.uniteforsight.org/mental-health/module2
4. Information about ECT can be found in http://www.psych.med.umich.edu/ect/history.asp
5. The quotes from "Mental Health in New York State 1945-1998," by Bonita Weddle are taken from http://www.archives.nysed.gov/common/archives/files/res_topics_health_mh_hist.pdf
6. Some material about Willowbrook was taken from http://www.library.csi.cuny.edu/archives/WillowbrookRG.htm

CHAPTER 7: Safety

1. The 1968 Buckle Up for Safety campaign can be found at http://www.michigan.gov/documents/msp/Seat_belt_timeline_03_web_386202_7.pdf)
2. The Department of Labor website can be found at dol.gov.

CHAPTER 10: Life in the Naked City

1. Some information about the 64-65 World's Fair was taken from http://butkus.org/information/worlds_fair_1964/world_fair_1964-1.pdf
2. Some information about the 64-65 World's Fair, especially from the financial point of view, was taken from *Tomorrow-Land: The 1964-65 World's Fair and the Transformation of America* by Joseph Tirella (Globe Pequot Press,

2014).

3. Information about bringing the World's Fair back to the U.S. can be found at https://www.bloomberg.com/news/articles/2015-12-17/bringing-the-world-s-fair-back-to-the-u-s
4. The 1964 *NY Daily News* article about the Kitty Genovese murder can be found at http://www.nydailynews.com/new-york/nyc-crime/kitty-genovese-stabbed-death-kew-gardens-1964-article-1.2143881
5. *The New York Times* 1964 investigative piece about the Genovese murder can be found at http://www.nytimes.com/1964/03/27/37-who-saw-murder-didnt-call-the-police.html?_r=0
6. The 2004 *Times* article on Genovese can be found at http://www.nytimes.com/2004/02/08/nyregion/kitty-40-years-later.html
7. The 2016 *Times* article about Moseley and the Genovese murder case can be found at https://www.nytimes.com/2016/04/05/nyregion/winston-moseley-81-killer-of-kitty-genovese-dies-in-prison.html
8. Information about the 1969 bombings in NYC was taken from the *Times* article that can be found at https://cityroom.blogs.nytimes.com/2009/08/27/1969-a-year-of-bombings/?_r=0).
9. Information about the 1960 UFT strike was taken from the *wiki* article on Charles Cogan. Information about the 1968 strike was taken from the *wiki* article "NYC teachers' strike of 1968."
10. Some facts about the 1965 newspaper strike were obtained from http://www.villagevoice.com/news/susan-brownmiller-ponders-the-1965-newspaper-strike-6712489 and https://www.researchgate.net/publication/232901664_The_news_about_the_newsworkers_press_coverage_of_the_1965_American_newspaper_guild_strike_against_the_New_York_Times
11. Some facts about the SSEU union strike were taken from http://www.afscme.org/blog/50-years-after-historic-strike-the-struggle-continues
12. Facts about the 1965 taxi strike were taken from https://news.google.com/newspapers?id=k0pQAAAAIBAJ&sjid=BFcDAAAAIBAJ&pg=4583,4787410&dq=taxicabs&hl=en 4000
13. Facts about the 1968 garbage strike were taken from http://untappedcities.com/2015/02/11/today-in-nyc-history-the-great-garbage-strike-of-1968
14. Information about the 2003 Blackout was taken from http://www.huffingtonpost.com/2013/08/14/new-york-city-blackout-2003-photos-power-outage-10-years_n_3755067.html and http://www.npr.org/2013/08/11/210700217/how-a-massive-power-outage-sent-people-dancing-in-the-street,
15. Information about the water shortage can be found from (http://www.nyc.gov/html/dep/html/ways_to_save_water/water-supply-

shortage-management.shtml
16. The climate change that created the water shortage is described in http://www.newenglandhistoricalsociety.com/1965-drought-new-englands-worst-ever/)
17. The 1969 nor'easter is described in https://cityroom.blogs.nytimes.com/2009/02/10/remembering-a-snowstorm-that-paralyzed-the-city/?_r=0
18. Mayor Lindsay's inappropriate quote is reported in https://cityroom.blogs.nytimes.com/2009/02/10/remembering-a-snowstorm-that-paralyzed-the-city/?_r=0
19. Information about the clean-up of NYC from pornographic businesses before the World's Fair is taken from *Tomorrow-Land: The 1964-65 World's Fair and the Transformation of America*, already cited.
20. The quote from Phyllis Schlafly about pornography is taken from http://www.law.harvard.edu/students/orgs/jlpp/Vol31_No1_Schlaflyonline.pdf
21. Some material about NYC's financial crisis is taken from (http://www.city-data.com/states/New-York-Economy.html
22. Material about the nation's economy in the 60s was taken from http://www.shmoop.com/1960s/economy.html
23. The imposition of the City Tax in NYC by Lindsay is documented in http://www.nydailynews.com/archives/news/winds-change-john-lindsay-new-york-spring-1966-chapter-343-part-1of-2-article-1.899176

CHAPTER 11: Our View of the Future

1. Space-based weapons are described in (http://www.thespacereview.com/article/826/1
2. Information about SSTs can be found in https://www.flightglobal.com/pdfarchive/view/1967/1967%20-%202245.html
3. The banning of SST flights over NYC is described in http://www.nytimes.com/1976/03/12/archives/port-authority-bans-sst-flight-was-due-next-week-port-authority.html?_r=0
4. The promises of shorter work weeks is described in http://www.cnn.com/2015/01/12/opinions/schulte-leisure-productivity/index.html

Special thanks to Denise Tortorelli for review and copywriting.

ABOUT THE AUTHOR

Steven Mandeli, shown on the back cover as he appeared in the early 1960s, is a software engineer and educator by trade, as well as an actor, comic, and avid writer who has penned books, essays, and screenplays on a variety of topics. He was known as the "little engineer" from an early age, as he was always building something. He grew up in Astoria, Queens, NY, where he attended St. Joseph's Parochial School. Having an interest in engineering, he attended Brooklyn Technical High School, where he switched gears a little to study electrical engineering instead of architecture. He holds a Bachelor of Science degree in electrical engineering from Polytech University, a master's degree in computer information systems from the University of Phoenix, and a patent. He worked as an electrical engineer in places like Northrup-Grumman for 15 years, and then switched to software engineering, which he continues doing, in one form or another, to this day. For over 13 years, while also working as an engineer, he taught courses in writing, critical thinking, and information technology.

His brain cluttered with useless trivia, he loves to talk and write about "back in the day." His affinity for puns drives his co-workers crazy, but at least that is better than his singing. He ventured a few decades ago from Queens to Long Island. There he lives with his wife of more than a quarter century, his younger daughter, two dogs and a parrot. His other daughter ran away to Texas and visits sometimes, with her hubby and Steve's beautiful granddaughter. His life isn't bad, but he yearns to sell a boatload of books and screenplays or be "discovered."

Contact Steve at kmandeli@optonline.net.

Printed in Germany
by Amazon Distribution
GmbH, Leipzig